I KNOW WHAT I'M DOING—

and Other Lies I Tell Myself

DISPATCHES FROM A LIFE UNDER CONSTRUCTION

JEN KIRKMAN

Simon & Schuster

New York London Toronto Sydney New Delhi

Simon & Schuster
1230 Avenue of the Americas
New York, NY 10020

Copyright © 2016 by Block of Cheese, Inc.

Note to readers: Some names and identifying details of people portrayed in this book have been changed.

First Simon & Schuster hardcover edition April 2016

SIMON & SCHUSTER and colophon are registered trademarks of Simon & Schuster, Inc.

For information about special discounts for bulk purchases, please contact Simon & Schuster Special Sales at 1-866-506-1949 or business@simonandschuster.com.

The Simon & Schuster Speakers Bureau can bring authors to your live event. For more information or to book an event contact the Simon & Schuster Speakers Bureau at 1-866-248-3049 or visit our website at www.simonspeakers.com.

Interior design by Lewelin Polanco

Manufactured in the United States of America

10 9 8 7 6 5 4 3 2 1

Library of Congress Cataloging-in-Publication Data is available.

ISBN 978-1-4767-7027-7
ISBN 978-1-4767-7029-1 (ebook)

This book is dedicated to my friends, both men and women. I don't need to name names. As Ice-T said in his song "M.V.P.S.": "Too many to name. Y'all right here in the studio, so why I'ma name ya? Y'all know I ain't even got to tell y'all, y'all are players."

You've all kept me sane when at times it felt like things would never get better. You have the best senses of humor—once you've comforted me—you'll make fun of me. I trust you all implicitly. Our love is unconditional.

This book is dedicated to my family as well. Mom and Dad, please don't read this one. Just know that yes I got paid for it and that is all that matters. And if I was paying attention correctly at church as a kid, Jesus hung out with prostitutes, so really, nothing in this book can't be forgiven. But just in case. Maybe just rewatch those videos of my preteen dance numbers instead of reading this book.

And lastly, this book is dedicated to anyone who is misunderstood because romantic relationships elude them. Being "normal" seems not meant for you in this lifetime. People who crave intimacy but settle for less. People who fall hard. People who want love but are afraid of being loved back. I. Hear. Ya.

CONTENTS

I KNOW WHAT I'M DOING—

and Other Lies I Tell Myself

INTRODUCTION

Ugh, my parents are going to read this.

I know that I'm forty years old (and even older by the time this book is in your hands), and I shouldn't care. Just be a grown-up and don't be afraid to speak your truth, Jen! And you know, funny person Bob Odenkirk once said that people should make their art, whatever it is, "as though their parents were dead." Why am I starting this book with sentiments about dead parents? Look, you know what I mean (or he means). My parents will have to handle the information in this book in their own way, whether it's calling to yell at me or just bursting into tears at the sight of me next Thanksgiving. They created another human being and that human being went on to live her own life, make her own mistakes, have her own sex, and oh, God. It's not just my parents. YOU'RE going to read this.

For a stand-up comedian who talks about her life onstage, I'm weirdly, fiercely private. (By the way, I've also tried to respect the privacy of some people I've written about in this book by giving them aliases, including my sister Gail, who insisted that I call her Violet—not because she has anything to hide but she always wished that was her name.) I'm so afraid of being judged. And yet, I won't even know if you're judging me because you're reading this and I'm not there. I can't see your looks of disapproval.

Here's the thing: I've never talked publicly about my secret on-again, off-again Friend With Benefits of twenty years. My ex-husband has no idea that while we were still married, I almost embarked on an affair with a new man I felt emotionally bonded to. (A different guy from Mr. Friends With Benefits.) It's new to me to reveal that, yeah, I get really lonely sometimes and I think of myself as the surrogate girlfriend for my male friends who date twenty-six-year-olds but come to me for conversation. Oh, God, please don't pity me. It's worse than judgment.

I really want you to know how much I've learned from my less than perfect experiences. I hope I don't make it seem like this short-lived boyfriend I had was just some idiot with abs—he also had a really great design aesthetic! And I promise, I really, really do *not* have hep C. (You'll read about that . . .) My editor said I don't need to include a picture of the lab paperwork. And if you know anyone in Dublin, please, again, apologize that I called their city a "bunch of cunts"—and I can't believe that I just wrote "cunt" in my intro, to a *book*. *This thing could be in a library someday.*

So why did I write all of this down, then? Because Simon & Schuster paid me to? Partly. But I begged them to. I wanted to write this book. I think that people, not just women, will relate. I know I'm not Ernest Hemingway, although I do agree with him that my only regret in life is probably going to be that I did not "drink more wine." (I'm not totally positive that Hemingway actually said that but according to some drink coasters I purchased at a museum gift shop he did. The quote is printed right on them.) My job isn't to win Pulitzer Prizes and stuff like that, but to provide a voice in your head, other than your own, that sounds like you. My voice is here to say, "Hey, I have those same thoughts and do those same stupid things and am generally awesome despite what people might think about my lifestyle choices." And I'm also here for your voyeuristic pleasure. I'm happy to show you what it's like for a single-and-not-so-good-at-the-mingle woman of forty.

The thing is, the other stories that make up who I am—devoted friend and family member—just aren't that funny. This is supposed to be a funny book written by a funny person. I'm not going to tell the story of how I stayed home one Friday night to do laundry and return e-mails. There's no funny story about how much I love my best girlfriends and how many times we got misty-eyed over a bottle of a blended wine and Trader Joe's Camembert Cheese and Cranberry Sauce Fillo Bites about how lucky we are to have one another. Or my male friends who are like the brothers I never had. The kind of guys I can text late at night and they listen to me instead of sending me pictures of their dicks.

There's nothing funny about the fact that about seven months after my divorce, I met Jake. I was afraid that getting involved so quickly after a marriage ended wasn't smart. I felt that I should play it safe, keep my options open, see other people. I wouldn't commit. Eventually, because I decided to stay open to every other possibility but a committed future with him, after two years he told me that he had to end our "friendship." I spent a year of my life not speaking with him. Luckily, I had this book to write.

Since then we've both had relationships, careers ups and downs, and lots of therapy. We put our past resentments to rest and now— we have an actual, normal, *friend*-ship, not some ambiguous, co-dependent bowl of crap. Things always change if we let them. We don't have to be freaked out by change, says the woman who is freaked out by all kinds of change—including pennies. Seriously, Congress, ban them.

There's nothing funny about the fact that I mention "Fish N Chips" and cheese often in this book, but over the two years it took to finish, I renounced my pescatarian ways and went back to being a full vegan. I just couldn't ignore the fact that red meat was *easy to give up*—I never liked it. But the dairy and fish industries are just as bad for the environment. See? I can see you not laughing. I can *feel you* not laughing at my plant-based existence.

There's nothing funny about the time that my dad hit his head, his brain swelled up, and he could have died but for the quick decisions of my family members who still live near him and surgeons who saved his life. I flew to Boston to be by his side before the operation and after. He couldn't speak and there was nothing behind his eyes except a childlike fear. We used to go to Disney World every year together so I bought him a Mickey Mouse stuffed animal at the airport. He loves Mickey. But see, that isn't funny. It's sad. I guess the one funny part was when his mean, lazy nurse was loudly placing a phone order to Dunkin' Donuts instead of changing his bedpan and I went over to her, in what I call my Mark Wahlberg moment, and whispered in a thick

Boston accent, "Yah gettin' some cahffee fah yahself? That's nice. My fathah needs his fahckin' bedpan changed. *Now*."

My mother was mortified that the daughter she had been bragging about, the one from television, just put on a fake Boston accent and then called the nurse an asshole. That's a little funny, I guess.

But this book also isn't about me being a hero or a shero. This book is about what a confused jackass I can be, have been, and will continue to be—though hopefully the ways in which I am a jackass will keep changing—just to keep things interesting. For example, did you know this is not my first book? It's not. That one was a *New York Times* Best Seller called *I Can Barely Take Care of Myself: Tales From a Happy Life Without Kids.*

While I was writing *I Can Barely Take Care of Myself* (and do you mind if I call it *ICBTCOM*? Thanks. It's a lot to type.), my life was going crazy. I was going through a divorce—one that my husband and I mutually wanted but still, it was sticky and legal-y and cost-y. I had promised I wouldn't write any details about it in my book such as, "I was crawling out of my skin being married," and would instead focus on the crazy, uninformed things that people say to childfree people like me. As it turns out, that really is enough material for a book of its own.

This book is about what happened next in life. Which was just more . . . *life.* Finally getting divorced (it's been a couple of years and I think it's okay to admit that I really *was* crawling out of my skin being married), living alone again, having boyfriends, continuing to avoid children, having breakups, traveling alone, turning forty, and getting some gray pubic hair.

My divorce blew up life as I knew it, and I saw all of the pieces of me fall back to Earth and spent two years putting them back into place. I mean "blew up" in a positive way, not like an asteroid that came to Earth and took out my family farm that wasn't insured. This blowup was more like a fuse box exploding. I was left in the dark for a while. Had to rely on others to help me figure out where I could find the light again. And I had to finally buy my very own toolbox—even if it was a pink one called "Just For Her."

People tilt their head with concern when I tell them that at age thirty I met someone, dated him for four years, was engaged for another year, and married for almost two years, but that at age thirty-seven, it ended in divorce. Which is just a legal term for "No one has farted in my bed in two years." There's no need to pity me.

Having been married and now having married friends, I'm familiar with the sentiment, usually worn as a badge of honor by spouses, that: "Marriage is hard. We work at it. After our fight last night we decided we need to start communicating better." And those of us who aren't married nod in support. Sometimes I feel like there is no badge of honor for the divorced or the single. That if we admit to being lonely, or feeling like a failure sometimes, or wanting someone there while we take our morning vitamins in case we choke, we'll be bombarded with, "See? You should pair up with someone. You can't go through life like this!"

Yeah, guess what? Life is work. I'm majorly under construction right now. I hate admitting to that. I feel like I'm a chewed-up area of road and everyone is staring at the yellow caution tape that surrounds me wondering, *Why is she taking so long to fix?*

Newly divorced and happy, my friendships came back to life and my relationship with my family improved. As my mother said, "I don't know what it is, Jennifah, but you look younger this year than you did last year. You seem to have less baggage." (Mom, are you calling my ex-husband "baggage"?)

I spent most of my life trying to fit in—whether it was lying to the rich girls at school that my parents' house had three bathrooms when in fact we had only one tiny bathroom adjacent to our kitchen, or lying to my friends when they all got their first menstrual periods within a few months of each other and I told them I'd had it since age twelve. I didn't even want to fit in to make myself comfortable—I wanted to fit in to make everyone *else* comfortable. *Don't worry*, my little co-dependent brain thought, *you can still talk to me. I'm just like you!* I even wore a tampon before I started getting my period just to trick myself that I hadn't totally lied to my friends.

Growing up, I always felt like I was looking over my classmates' shoulders—not to cheat, but just to make sure I was getting the answers right. Whatever *it* was, I wanted to be doing *it* just like everyone else. I got so concerned with doing my life "right" that I assumed my own instincts sucked and learned not to give in to them. And I think that's what most adults do too, except that instead of looking at their neighbor's math test, they are looking at their neighbor's house, and spouse, and kids, and car, and thinking, *Oh shit, I'm not doing it right!*

The first time I went to therapy was over ten years ago; I said to my shrink, "I don't relate to anyone my age. All they do is wonder when they're going to settle down. Who cares?" Then I proceeded to pay her every week to talk about how I was beginning to worry about when I was going to get my life together. *I* started to care—based on what *other* people wanted.

The thing is, I don't relate to most people my age. I'm not some forty-year-old married woman spending my nights drinking chardonnay and pretending to like Rihanna music. I'm not a cougar hanging out at dive bars, doing shots, and hoping to attract the attention of some twenty-five-year-old ukulele player/artisanal cheese store clerk. (Although I have made out with two twentysomething men in the last few years. I'm done now. I promise. I'm not going to end up like Madonna, where people wonder if the boys in my Instagram photos are my backup dancers/lovers or adopted sons.)

I'm not a woman who stopped at forty and realized that she never pursued her dreams. I've always pursued my dreams and my career is where I want it, although I'm also happy to admit when I want more. I'm single but I'm in love with me. It sounds defensive and corny, and I know that most people already know that they're supposed to love themselves, but I don't think I always really got what that meant. I grew up in the suburbs of Boston. There was no talk of loving oneself. If you did, someone would get in your face and say, "What? You think yah so fahkin' great or somethin'?" Yeah. I guess I finally do think I'm so fahkin' great . . . or something.

I have pecked and poked away at writing this book on airplanes, in hotel rooms, and in coffee shops heading to, away from, and in the following cities: Atlanta, Austin, Boston, Buffalo, Chapel Hill, Charlotte, Chicago, Cleveland, Dallas, Denver, Dublin, Eugene, Grand Rapids, Halifax, Indianapolis, Kansas City, Las Vegas, Los Angeles, Lund, Madison, Melbourne, Miami, Minneapolis, Nashville, New

Orleans, Oklahoma City, Omaha, Palm Springs, Philadelphia, Phoenix, San Francisco, St. Louis, St. Paul, Stockholm, Tacoma, Toronto, Tuscon, Vancouver, Washington, DC, West Palm Beach, and Winnipeg, and I've been putting the finishing touches on it in every coffee shop in New York City. I abandoned sunshine and swimming pools in Los Angeles to go live in New York for a few months of winter. Why? On one silly level because I lived in Brooklyn for four years back in 1998 to 2002 and I found it poetic that twelve years later I was back writing my second book and not having to temp for a crazy stockbroker who used to throw his phone at me—his *landline. Ouch.*

It had been a long time since I'd asked myself, *Where would I like to be right now?* and not *Where do I have to be right now?* It's been over a decade for me on the West Coast and there's something about never having to check the weather before you walk outside that makes you soft. I don't feel like comedians should get too comfortable. The other day on the subway there was an empty seat at rush hour. There was some water pooling right under the seat—probably the result of some melted slush from someone's snow boots before me. I sat down, my boots just centimeters from the unknown moisture. An expressionless older man sat across from me. He pointed at the water. He looked at me and said, "Honey, that some urine right there." It made me laugh. When I was just twenty-four that would have undone me. Urine? How dare urine be on the subway? How dare anything not be perfect, including that guy's grammar? My life already isn't perfect and now I have to contend with reality? Other people's bodily fluids? But now—even though I quickly changed seats—I pondered, *Who am I to not see some urine once in a while?*

Also, Bill told me that I should go to New York City. Oh, Bill is a palm reader in New Orleans. He's about seventy-five years old; his white skin clashes with his oil-black, not-very-secure toupee. Bill is also mostly deaf and very effeminate—very stereotypically gay with dashes of Southern gentleman and RuPaul.

I was vintage dress shopping on Chartres Street in the French Quarter when the woman selling me the dress told me that she thought I seemed like I had some questions. I said, "No. I don't. It fits perfectly and I'm ready to buy it." She leaned in. "No. Not questions about the dress. Bigger questions." She told me that her friend Bill could help. I looked around the store thinking that maybe Bill was hiding behind a shoe rack. She walked me outside and pointed me to the place next door, a shop that sold incense, candles, tarot cards, palm readings, and hope—false and otherwise.

I'm not naive. I know that Bill and Dress Shop Woman probably have a little mutual agreement. She sends him women who seem to be seeking more than a dress and his readings probably end with, "I don't know if I see a husband in your future but I see a beautiful pair of vintage earrings, honey."

I walked into the voodoo shop and asked for Bill. The woman behind the counter shouted his name multiple times as Bill and his bad ear continued to peer out the window. Finally, Bill turned around and fanned himself with his hand. "My goodness, I *thought* I sensed someone there." I followed Bill to a back room. (Yes, of course there were hanging beads that I had to push aside.)

Bill held my hand and gave me the full report in his Creole-esque drawl. He gasped. "Oh, honey, your life line? It don't stop, girl. This thing goes into your wrist. Your life is lonnnnng." He seemed burdened by this. He perked up. "Long is good. If you like it long. Some people can't handle it when it's too long." I wasn't sure if we were still talking about life.

He stopped examining the lines in my hand and instead just held on tight. He pressed a button on an old-fashioned tape recorder, as though he were going to interrogate me at the county jail in 1984. He said, "With your permission, we will make a recording of this. You can play this back when you need a reminder of what we talked about." I haven't played the tape since, and not just because I can't get my hands on a tape recorder (though oddly I still have a pair of underwear from 1990).

He held my hand and said, "You can do anything. You're free. Now, do you like where you live?" I told Bill—even though I didn't think I should be the one talking during my palm reading—that I was experiencing a little bit of a Los Angeles malaise. "So go somewhere," he said. Very reasonable. Then he gave an obligatory glance at my palm and said, "I see you living in London." I told Bill that I missed New

York. He said, "Okay, so go to New York. Honey, we don't always have to do what our palms say. We have free will. New York City isn't for everybody but if it's for you, go. My God, some people need that fast pace. And some people like it given to them nice and slow." I still wasn't sure if he was still talking about life.

Okay, so Bill probably isn't psychic, but he was *really good* at repeating back to me what I already said. But what I'm saying here is, I learned a lot of lessons these past few years. I'll hold in my heart that even though I have no answers, life is imperfect and funny and sometimes you think something is just water but then you find out *that some urine right there*. But that's okay. We can step over the urine. We have free will.

1

THERAPIST, MAY I?

Women marry men hoping they will change. Men marry women hoping they will not. So each is inevitably disappointed.

—ALBERT EINSTEIN

In the spring of 2011, Matt, my husband of less than two years, and I were sitting in an overpriced-and-not-covered-by-insurance couples therapist's office in Beverly Hills. Even deciding who to choose as a psychologist had been the subject of a few bickering sessions as we each wanted to make sure that we were going to get absolutely fair treatment.

"We can't go to the therapist that your therapist recommended, Jen, because your therapist told you that she's also writing a script in her spare time. Does she say things like, 'You'll have to make changes to your Act Three of life'? Her judgment can't be trusted!"

"Well, *your* therapist took you on a walk to CVS one day so that he could *run errands* during your session! Are we going to end up at a marriage counselor who specializes in picking up dry cleaning?"

So, we mutually decided to go out of network and pay out of pocket. Three hundred and fifty dollars per hour (technically per "fifty minutes") to sit in a room with a woman we knew nothing about—except that she had a PhD and possibly an eating disorder. She had six Venti cups of Starbucks on her desk and even her skin seemed too thin. We sought her expertise in relationships but deep down we were looking for permission from someone other than ourselves to end our marriage.

During the planning of a wedding there are more than enough people willing to hover around or crawl up your ass to give unsolicited advice or ask endless questions. Mothers-in-law call with requests like, "Is it okay if I invite my best friends Charles and Linda from my college days? I know they don't know either you or Matt and I'm actually not sure if they're still alive, I'll have to check. But if they are alive, they'll be really proud." Friends call to ask you where you're registered because they lost the wedding invitation. Other married friends e-mail you links upon links to places that they honeymooned that you'll absolutely love. "Don't forget to get up early for the pineapple pancakes and you have to go on the whale watch even though the waters are so choppy you'll leave a blazing trail of fruit chunks over the side of the boat."

But when you're the first of your group to get a divorce, nobody with any experience is around to offer any guidance.

After listening to us describe a typical week together as a married couple, Dr. Boney-Venti concluded that Matt and I were more like roommates than husband and wife. This made sense. What was so maddening about feeling like I had fallen out of love was that I hadn't fallen out of every *kind* of love. I didn't hate Matt. When I walked in the door and saw him on the couch I was always so comforted and happy. He was my best friend. We talked to each other all day long. I ran everything by him. He ran everything by me. He was so easy to be around. I truly loved him. He was family. But that was the problem. He felt like my brother. And the one time I didn't feel like having my "family" around was when I was in bed at night. It felt so strange and schizophrenic to care for and love a man so much but not exactly want to share a mattress anymore. I started going to bed earlier and earlier just to read—which sounds relaxing but that shouldn't be the life of a thirty-seven-year-old woman living in Los Angeles. I know people who are dead who don't even retire to their rooms at eight thirty to read.

Matt revealed to Skeletor, PhD, that sometimes he felt like I didn't even like him as a person. He felt picked on. The way I made comments about his ill-fitting pants or why can't he walk more quietly to the bathroom in the middle of the night? He was right. I did nitpick, but I never thought it hurt him. I never thought about it at all and *that* made me feel shitty. How much had I not thought about him? And for how long?

Dr. Ann O. Rexia turned her attention to me. What did I want from Matt that I wasn't getting? I said that we don't have fun together. Sometimes I think he just tolerates me, but doesn't truly get me.

HOLD ME CLOSER . . . *FAN* DANCER

Matt and I spent Fourth of July 2008 away from the loud, overcrowded fireworks display at Venice Beach or any parties that could involve errant bottle rockets and subsequent missing fingers. We opted for a quiet outdoor dinner at the home of our friends Margaret and Andrew. Six couples sat around emptying six bottles of wine. It was unusually humid and Andrew brought out an industrial-size fan. We tried to eat corn on the cob while all of our hair blew in our faces. We looked like the *Saturday Night Live* spoof version of a Victoria's Secret Angels push-up bra photo shoot. That's when I got an idea and shouted out, "We should fan dance!"

I had just remembered an acting teacher I had in college who encouraged us to runway walk in class to help make us less self-conscious. One time she said, "You girls can't break through in an acting scene if you can't love yourselves!" She plugged in a boom box and shouted with love, "Now walk! Walk sexy! Walk funny! Just walk to the music!" She hit play and the sounds of Salt-N-Pepa's "Shoop" filled the room. Even though I have suffered actual real chemical depression fixed only by lots of therapy and Prozac, when I need a pick-me-up, fake modeling in my room to pop hits of the 1990s is a good quick fix.

I stumbled to my purse to find my iPod and scrolled to Madonna's "Express Yourself." Even my guy friends—who didn't get the full effect of long hair whipping around their confident shoulders—got into the spirit and let their shirts billow in the breeze as they did their best to fan dance.

What you need is a big strong hand to lift you to your higher ground
Make you feel like a queen on a throne

Matt sat at the table making origami with his napkin. I grabbed his arm. "Come on, Matt! Fan dancing!"

"That's okay. You dance. I'll watch."

That was our thing. Matt sat out what I enjoyed and just watched. We did our own thing. In fact, we really had no-thing that we did together, except arrive and leave in the same car and . . . be engaged. But I didn't know then that if you're going to have a husband—it's best to find one who wants to fan dance with you.

I jumped in with everyone else taking turns pretending to model, striking poses until it was too much for us—it turns out that drunk people plus high winds and long hair near fan blades is just as dumb as drunk people setting off fireworks. As Margaret and I cleared the dishes, she said to me, "It's great that you are so comfortable with who you are that you don't need your husband to join in and fan dance. He really seems to admire and appreciate who you are and accept you."

I knew so little then about what makes marriage work that I accepted what Margaret said without pushing myself to think, *I don't want to be accepted; like I'm a cancer diagnosis or the fact that 1 percent of the population has all of the world's wealth. I want to be joined.*

You shouldn't get married just because you don't want to die alone. You should get married because you don't want to go through *life* alone. I work for a living onstage. I don't want a passive audience in real life. I want someone up there with me. I want someone to push me out of the way and say, "This is *my* fan dance, bee-yotch!" I mean, I guess I could always marry a gay man. But that wouldn't be fair to him.

Anyway, back in our psychologist's office, Dr. Bones told me that lots of couples feel this way. Many couples don't have everything in common but they find things that they like to do together. The way I see it, this is not a solution. This is the problem. Married people who want you to stay in their cult or therapists who want your money next week will always encourage people on the brink of divorce to stay together. They say things like, "All marriages are like this. It takes work." But some couples don't just not have the same hobbies; they don't have the same values, goals, and, ultimately, respect for who the other person is. Most people don't look that closely under their own hoods.

They wait until the engine feels like it's falling apart and all the amateur mechanics in their lives just assure them that all they need is an oil change. The unhappily married people know that that's the wrong diagnosis. They know that their muffler is about to fall out and cause a hugely embarrassing incident in the driveway. They don't need an oil change. Or a hobby. They need a divorce.

The only person who looked me in the eye and told me the truth back then was an elderly Armenian jeweler who runs a shop on Ventura Boulevard in Studio City, California. I don't remember his name or the name of his store. But I remember how his pupils bore through my soul—or maybe it was just that weird big magnifying glass he had over his left eye.

I'd gone to him because for months the finger I wore my wedding ring on was insanely itchy. I'd tried everything: topical Benadryl, cleaning my rings nightly, and scratching my finger like a meth addict. The skin was raw and constantly peeling. I knew that Matt didn't cheap out and he thought he bought me a real solid white-gold ring but I wondered if maybe the person who sold it to him was some kind of scam artist who only claimed it was real gold.

I didn't want to hurt Matt so I didn't mention that I was having doubts about the realness of the ring, but one Saturday morning I snuck off to What's-His-Name's Jewelry Shop. I asked the old man to please test the rings and let me know if they were authentic. I left them for the week, telling Matt that I was having them professionally shined. In those seven days, my finger cleared up and my skin no longer looked like shredded cheese. That's all the proof I needed that something was indeed wrong with the wedding band. I went back to Can't-Remember-His-Name's Shop and showed him my finger. "Look! All better! So, what did you find with the ring? At least we have the receipt and we can go back to this shady ring salesman and tell him the con is up!"

The elderly man handed me back the ring. He said, "It is a hundred percent real. There is nothing that should cause allergy in that ring." I stood quietly, probably looking confused because he continued, "Miss Jen, it is not my business but I am very much into how our emotions cause our wellness and our sickness. And if I may be so frank, I don't think the ring is the problem. I think it's you. You don't want to wear that ring anymore. Anyway. No charge."

That Armenian jeweler was absolutely right. I didn't want to wear that ring or what it symbolized anymore. This jeweler had more insight into me after five minutes in his shop than any therapist could with five years on their couch. The old man would probably make a terrible therapist because his greatest joy seemed to be dispensing advice without charging—that, and he could never tell clients that their time was up because every clock in his shop was broken.

2

IT'S A FAMILY AFFAIR
(BUT WHY DOES IT HAVE TO BE?)

Happiness is having a large, loving, caring, close-knit family in another city.

—GEORGE BURNS

Let's talk about this preexisting condition called Family. We're not working on farms anymore—there's no need to stick around your old hometown and have your family as your "best friends." I would totally get married again if someone really needed me to, but I would never want to go through another wedding—a wedding that involves, literally, everyone and their brother attending. What's romantic about making out with someone in front of your uncles? I think the sexiest man in the world is the guy who could approach me at a bar and say, "Hi, I'm an orphan."

I was always very uncomfortable with the concept of having a mother-in-law. No woman ever says to herself, *Well, I've met the man I want to spend the rest of my life with. But you know what else I need? I'm going to need a sixty-five-year-old woman to come along as sort of a package deal. I want her to insist on going to Target with me and getting oddly competitive during adult yoga class at her local YMCA during the Christmas Eve day class.*

If the mother-in-law isn't a total judgmental nightmare, then she's the overenthusiastic type. It's a way of controlling her destiny as she feels that the cycle of life is continuing and her son doesn't need her anymore. Wanting to bond over pinot grigio brands (but just one glass!) is a mother-in-law's way of saying, "He may enter your vagina but he EXITED MINE and without ME there would be no HIM and whether you like it or not that very fact makes me ever present in this threesome you never asked for. Cheers!"

My mother-in-law loved me from the moment she met me. It didn't feel right. It felt like she was just in love with the concept of having a daughter-in-law. She didn't really know me. I was convinced if she really knew me she would hate me.

I know I sound so ungrateful by complaining that my mother-in-law liked me too much. My friend Shannon would say, "You're lucky. My mother-in-law never knew that her own son was an atheist because he was afraid to tell her. And now that we're getting married by a justice of the peace she thinks I turned her son against God. Like I have that kind of power! Or I'm some Antichrist. If I had any power, I would turn him against her but SO FAR MY SPELLS HAVE NOT WORKED."

I'm like a cat—except that I have no desire to drag my tongue across fur of any kind or eat wet food that smells like a rotting ocean floor without a spoon. The way in which I'm like a cat is in its early and final years. I'm either very skittish and run from people who want to get on a snuggling-and-patting level with me the moment they lay eyes on me for the first time—or I'm like a cat who has weeks left to live . . . when I feel overwhelmed I want to hide under a porch and hiss at anyone who tries to get close to me. My mother-in-law would call me more often than my own mother did to tell me that she missed me. I always wanted to say, *Miss me? You didn't even know that I existed for the first fifty-nine years of your life!*

Whenever I gave in to a request to hang out with her or talk to her, it seemed to keep her satisfied for a while—until she got bored of holding the ball in her mouth and would nudge me to start playing catch again. Her inner dog was too overwhelming for my inner cat. I finally had to acquiesce to allowing her to Skype with me once in a while so that I didn't seem like a total bitch. I always thought during our Skype sessions (which consisted of a four-minute delay as two women who barely knew each other just said "Hi" and waved), *Someone is going to have to whip a boob out for this to get interesting.*

But of course my mother-in-law is not to blame for anything going wrong in my marriage. I'm the last person to tell you what *to* do when getting married, having a ceremony, or combining families, but I can tell you what NOT to do.

SOME ADMITTEDLY FUCKED-UP BUT HONEST ADVICE FOR COUPLES BEFORE, DURING, AND AFTER THEIR WEDDING

1. When registering for gifts don't become an asshole. Don't monitor the Crate & Barrel website and get mad at your friend Susan because she only bought ten out of the twelve nut bowls. "But there are twelve kinds of nuts and they need their own bowl!" Let it go. This is about love, not nuts. What a couple does with their nuts in their own home is not Susan's problem.

2. When you are picking out items to put on your registry—just remind yourself that it's okay to take part in this ritual but don't think you have to become someone you're not. I registered for a gravy boat. I'm a vegetarian. But I thought, *A home needs a gravy boat.* Why? Who said that? You don't need fine china if you know you'll never use it—except once, ironically, when you and your spouse order pizza.

3. If it's your wedding day and you have explosive diarrhea but you haven't eaten anything, find your friend who is the most in love with her husband. Take her into the bathroom. Apologize for the smell. And ask her, "Did *you* have explosive diarrhea on *your* wedding day?" If she says no, please consider that these aren't the good kind of nerves but rather your body trying to tell you that you don't want to get married.

4. If you ignored the explosive diarrhea and are now walking down the aisle and you're crying but you think it might be because you're scared and upset, consider turning around and taking a moment outside to collect your thoughts or maybe take up smoking.

5. If you make it all the way to the altar and during your mother's reading of some poem that you picked out for her to read you just start thinking, *Oh my God. I'll never kiss another man again*, ask yourself if you're just freaking yourself out or if that really bothers you. If it bothers you—run.

6. If you are at the altar thinking, *I can't run. That is rude*, don't worry about manners. It's harder to get divorced than it is to run away down the aisle. And you're giving everyone in that room a story to tell for the rest of their lives.

7. If you're at the altar thinking, *I can't run. What will my family say?* ask yourself, *When I'm home deciding whether or not to buy a new couch, or whether to get Chinese or Thai takeout do I call up my cousin Sheila and ask what she thinks?*

8. If you are the disc jockey at your own wedding because you found the idea of making a mix "fun"—maybe you should just throw a cocktail party sometime instead of legally binding yourself to another person.

9. If you are happy that you decided to go through with your wedding, have sex with your spouse that night. In fact, go in a broom closet and hike up that dress, or pull down those pants, and go for it. Do not fall into the trap that modern couples fall into, telling themselves, "We've had sex before. It's not like we're losing our virginity tonight." No. Have sex that night. You will always look back on it and think it's weird that you decided to drink together until five a.m. instead. Your friends thought it was weird too.

10. Lastly, be grateful that your friends and family came to your wedding and bought you presents but don't be afraid of your basic instinct to say, "FUCK BRUNCH." Family will pressure you to attend a "morning after" brunch as a way to—I don't even know what. Keep the party going? Get closure on the events of the day before? Make a married couple spend time with their families and some mini-quiche first thing in the morning? And sober to boot? Go tie some cans on your car, write "Just Married" on the windows, and get going on your honeymoon. And as for your friends and family, as Marie Antoinette said, "Let *them* eat brunch."

3

WHOMP! THERE IT IS.

Guilt: the gift that keeps on giving.

—ERMA BOMBECK

The thing is—before seeing a marriage counselor or a ring doctor in the spring of 2011, I had completely lost my sex drive after the first year of my marriage. Up until then, every relationship I had ever been in started with can't-live-without-his-scent, animal attraction, sex. It was an instinct I felt with all of my ex-boyfriends. Underneath the love, friendship, and trust was this constant feeling of *I want to climb up on you.*

Matt was the first boyfriend who didn't elicit this instinct from me. He was also the first boyfriend who caused me absolutely no anxiety. I had convinced myself that this non-spark we had was a sign of our maturity. He balanced me out. I should marry this balancing act. Then I learned later, with lots of therapy, that only people who feel unstable feel that they need balancing out, and that should never be a lover or boyfriend or husband's job—because to put it in heady psychology terms, that just ain't sexy.

I blamed myself for my lack of sex drive that year. I thought that I was on the wrong birth control pill. Maybe my natural hormones weren't reacting well to the synthetic hormones—like ex-wives who don't want to see their kids' hot new stepmoms at the soccer game. I got off of the Pill. Doing so immediately caused such lousy cystic acne that I had to wear turtlenecks in the summertime and act like I was just really into French film. I thought that maybe I was depressed. I saw my doctor and got on Wellbutrin, which at least had the added effect of not making me want to smoke a cigarette. (I had taken to smoking cigarettes whenever I started to feel stressed about not being horny.) The Wellbutrin made my heart race so fast that even if I did end up having sex it would have thrown me into cardiac arrest. I got off of the Wellbutrin. I had all kinds of things tested, like my thyroid. I even hoped there was some kind of flashlight that a gynecologist could shine up into my vagina and see if there were any cobwebs up in that thing making it impossible to feel alive.

The one thing I didn't think about doing was talking to my husband about it. I was too ashamed. I wasn't that great at marriage. We *talked* a lot. But we didn't *communicate* well. I was so closed off from my feelings. I was also apprehensive about starting that conversation and possibly hearing my husband say that maybe he just wasn't that slayed by me anymore. Some people say that women are more sexually active in their late thirties, while others say that's just a myth. All I knew is that I didn't feel like me. I didn't even have a crush on Robert Downey Jr. anymore. He was always the man of my dreams during his pre–heroin arrest years and new sobriety years. I took a few years off from crushing on RDJ when things started looking bleak for him. I didn't think I could be with someone who doesn't come home at night because he's so high he walked into a stranger's house and passed out in the spare bedroom. And I hated the haircut he had in prison. I would not have stood by him through that. I need something to run my fingers through during a conjugal visit.

But what I'm saying is, it freaked me out—like a generator kicking on after the main power goes out—when I met Kevin in January 2011, about a year and a half into my marriage. I was in New York City to tape an episode of a stand-up TV show for Comedy Central. A bunch of comedians from Los Angeles were flown to NYC for the taping. Matt didn't come with me. I loved New York and he was never that big on it. My sister Violet took a train in from Boston to see the taping and (mostly) to crash in my fancy hotel room. She has insomnia, but for some reason hotel beds lull her into a womblike slumber.

My comedian friend Brian brought his friend, native New Yorker Kevin, to the taping. We all had drinks after. More comedians filled

the bar. My sister talked to people and this Kevin stranger and I
ended up talking just to each other. He said to me, "You seem like
someone I would want to know. I'm glad you ended up sitting next to
me." *Whomp!* Something happened in my stomach that reverberated
into my heart. This was clearly the first sign of a rare cardiac disease
that had thus far gone undetected. It all started to make sense now.
I had to come to New York City from my home in Los Angeles to
tape a quick spot on a stand-up comedy show for Comedy Central.
But, I started to fantasize, the *real* reason I was in New York was so
that when my heart condition made itself known I could be within
walking distance of some of the finest hospitals and research centers.
With my sense of humor and no fear of public speaking, I imagined
I would become the spokeswoman for this unknown Whomping Disease and talk to auditoriums full of people about the importance of
early detection and reassure them that while there's no cure for a case
of the Whomps and the way they tititlate a heart—there is a way to
live with hope.

It's a story I predicted I would tell for years. "It seems so silly but
coming to New York City in January of 2011 to be on television didn't
save my career but it saved my life!" I would have to give up stand-up
comedy, something I'm sure I would find unfulfilling anyway once I
began my role as health ambassador. I would need to give up a life of
telling jokes to drunks in order to be taken seriously enough to appeal
to Congress often, imploring them to spend less money on senseless
wars and more money finding a cure for us afflicted with the Whomps.

Whomp! Whomp! Whomp! It happened again. I grabbed my heart.
Kevin grabbed my shoulder. "Are you okay?" When his hand touched
my shoulder there was a ricochet effect. I realized that this wasn't
some incurable disease—it was worse. I was maybe attracted to Kevin.

It's not that Kevin was even my type or that I consciously felt like
pawing him but his energy—something about him—made me feel . . .
all of those things I hadn't felt in years. Or maybe my hormones just
kicked back in after all of the acupuncture treatments and Kevin just
happened to be there.

He asked me for my number because he figured we could "kick
around" the next day in New York City with our mutual friend. I love

kicking around! Whatever that was! I wasn't going to be in town the next day. My flight left at eight in the morning. But hey, why ruin a fun night with a new friend with the truth? I instinctively gave him my e-mail address instead of my phone number. He never made a move on me. My sister made a move on me as she hip-checked me, sliding into the booth. She said to Kevin, "I had to get my little sister. Sometimes she needs to be told to go to bed!"

As we put on our flannel pajamas and hopped onto the king-size hotel room mattress—as though it were night one of living our Grey Gardens lifestyle—my sister said, "Were you flirting with that guy?"

I tried to explain to my older sister, who lives on a farm and raises horses, that in the big city of New York and in the cosmopolitan world of comedy, men and women stay out at all hours of the night together because they are *artists*—not because they are *flirting*.

I laid my head on the goose down pillows that I'm normally allergic to except when I'm drunk. I prepared myself mentally for the worse-than-news-of-a-dead-relative feeling I was going to receive via a phone call in three hours—the wake-up call from the front desk. Once the lights were out and all was quiet on the bedroom front, my sister, lying on her side with her back to me, got in the last word. "Besides. He's not your type."

What did my sister know about my type? I stewed while sitting on a Virgin America plane back to Los Angeles listening to the soft sounds of their oddly soothing club music and appreciating the soft purple lights that didn't challenge my dehydrated, hungover eyeballs. I watched out the window as the baggage handlers loaded suitcases into the bottom of the plane. I actually spotted my suitcase. For a childfree person like myself, it almost evokes in me a maternal feeling. "Be gentle with her, she has breakables inside, and a wobbly wheel!"

I immediately regretted having checked a bag, knowing that waiting for it to come down the chute at baggage claim in L.A. could add as much as an extra twenty minutes to my travel experience. Twenty minutes I could spend nursing my hangover in my bed. I mean *our* bed. *The* bed that I shared with my *husband*. I glanced at my wedding and engagement rings. I talked in my head to my sister. *Yeah. I know I'm married. I love my husband and I'm looking forward to our*

Sunday-night dinner at home tonight. I will even tell him about the new friend I met.

I reflected that even though I was not interested in Kevin, he actually *was* exactly one of my former types: a skinny, messy-haired guy who wears all black. He was the 2.0 version of the type of guy I had hankerings for in high school and maybe he'd graduated from flushing algebra books down the toilet in the boys' room and now just wanders around parties in leather pants, full of life and wanting to make friends for a night. My husband's job required him to work and travel long hours. He had to dress comfortably. I couldn't ask someone who sits in front of a computer straining his back and eyes to sit there like David Bowie in vinyl pants and some kind of androgynous frilly blouse.

But hey, opposites attract, right? I'm sure I wasn't Matt's perfect type either. If Matt was just a friend and I had to hook him up with the perfect woman, I'd have picked a tall, lanky girl with long dyed red hair, tattoos, seriously needed but ironically horn-rimmed prescription eyeglasses, and hands that can't stay manicured because she's a bass player or the type who sews and glues a lot of cool art-type things to sell on Etsy. I'm more like the young version of the older women I want to grow into—sort of a Joan Rivers/Iris Apfel-type mixed in with a little bit of a Led Zeppelin groupie meets aging-disco-queen thing. Matt often seemed to distance himself from me when we walked down the street and I was in one of my sequined jackets. In theory, he supported my fashion choices. He said he found it hilarious that since he'd met me when I was only thirty, I was already embracing a midlife flair with many faux fur coats.

As we taxied to our runway, I couldn't stop thinking about how I no longer cared about "types," to the point where I realized, *Oh shit. Kevin is my type. I still have a type. I'm a married woman who went against type.* The plane took off, revving up to speeds that still weren't as fast as the thoughts in my head. It must be okay to be with another type than the one I married. People do this all the time, right? Short women with straight black hair and small lips play the "Free Pass" game and say things like "My husband's free pass is Julia Roberts."

Besides, I was just turning Kevin over in my thoughts on an airplane. I wasn't fantasizing about him. I couldn't even fantasize if I wanted to. I couldn't remember the details of Kevin's face. I didn't know what his nose looked like. See? Maybe he wasn't even my type after all. He could have had some weird Michael Jackson nose that's easy to pull off like a Band-Aid. As the plane leveled out, I did too. I had done nothing wrong. I spent some time with a new friend. I didn't put my wedding ring in my pocket and twirl Kevin's long curly hair in my fingers. *Ah! There's something. I don't like long curly hair. Kevin has long curly hair. This will never work.*

The flight attendant announced that the use of electronic devices was now permitted. I decided to check Facebook—the greatest place to find out who someone really is by stalking their pictures. I found Kevin's Facebook page and was able to browse his photos without asking for a friend request. This activity is still perfectly within a married woman's rights. I can't look at pictures of my new friend? What is this—the 1950s? I might as well quit my job and bake cakes in high heels! I clicked through Kevin's life. He's a homeowner. That's impressive. But his home is in the country part of New York. Not my style. I only like pine trees during the Christmas season. I couldn't stand the smell emitting from trees year-round that makes me feel like I have to hit the mall and buy everybody gifts. He has lots of women friends. That's always a good sign that he's evolved, possibly a feminist. Blech. What was this picture? He hosted a ukulele party? That's annoying. I don't see myself dating someone who pulls out a tiny instrument during cocktails and starts plucking away. Well, this session was productive. I felt nothing as I looked at pictures of Kevin. He would really be just another type that eventually I would get annoyed with, right? "Kevin, pick up your ukulele and that sweatshirt you wear in every picture off of the floor! Pick up those pine needles off of the carpet! Why does it smell like pinecones in here? I'm losing my mind in the woods! Why can't they build a Starbucks that's more than forty-five miles a-fucking-way?"

I clicked off Facebook, never requesting his friendship, and went to write an e-mail to my husband to let him know I would be grounded soon and ready to spend some time together. That's when Kevin's e-mail popped up. The subject heading: "Hello Unique Lady!" The body of the e-mail said, "Just wanted to see if you would be willing

to let a dork like me tag along with you as you spend the day traips-
ing around New York City spreading smiles to everyone by just being
you—and doing whatever silly and fun Jen things that you do!"

Fun? I hadn't been fun in a long time. I hadn't joined my husband
to go see bands. (Too loud.) I had skipped parties that started after
nine p.m. (Why go anywhere when we have an array of snack bowls
from Crate & Barrel and our very own wine decanter?) Kevin didn't
know the REAL me. I must have fooled him by having a night of temporary fun-sanity.

I looked at my ring. And then I started to cry. I didn't have a tissue
or a napkin so I wiped my eyes with the stiff barf bag. I felt that's all
the comfort I deserved for having these thoughts. I didn't even go to
Catholic school—I had no idea where this guilt was coming from. I
immediately spilled my feelings about everything in an e-mail. That I
was having doubts about the marriage, that I hadn't even wanted to
have sex with Robert Downey Jr. recently, and that I didn't think this
was some kind of pre–seven year itch, or something to work through.
I really think that I, we, made a mistake and that we shouldn't be
married anymore.

Instead of sending this e-mail to my husband, I sent it to Kevin.

Somewhere over the Midwest Kevin e-mailed me back and said
that he didn't want to start anything. He wasn't looking to steal another
man's lady and he thought he saw a wedding ring on my finger, but he
wasn't sure if it meant there was just a ring on it or if there was "a ring
on it." Then he told me that he just went through a divorce and that he
knew exactly how I felt. He warned me that my married friends would
not understand how I felt and that they might only speak in clichés
like "marriage takes work." He said he could be there for me. I didn't
write back.

I mean, I didn't write back on that flight. We eventually became
fast friends, platonic pen pals. And then one time when I went to pull
out my BlackBerry to text Kevin, I ended up summoning a black cloud.

4

TAKING LOTS OF GAMBLES

Gambling can turn into a dangerous two-way street when you least expect it. Weird things happen suddenly, and your life can go to pieces.

—HUNTER S. THOMPSON

Weeks before we went to couples counseling or even broached the subject of divorce, Matt and I just existed in our home together. We had a few tiffs that ended with one of us daring to tip over the whole house of precariously placed cards called our life—by saying, "I just feel like we aren't working out." Then we would return to our separate rooms and not elaborate.

Kevin and I had been e-mailing about once a week. He had been really helpful in pointing out all of the different types of people one can be post-divorce. Would I be a woman who doesn't believe in monogamy? Am I someone who thinks marriage is unnecessary or am I just in the wrong marriage? I never told Matt about why my friend Kevin and I e-mailed. He just knew that I had a new friend. But I have lots of friends and besides, Matt wasn't the jealous type. Now that I think about it—probably because he wished someone would just e-mail me and take me off of his hands.

In March of 2011 I had to do a weekend of stand-up at Foxwoods Casino in Connecticut. I ran it by Matt that I would go to New York City after that gig just to clear my head. I wanted to go to New York City to see if I missed Matt. I know that doesn't make much sense but New York City is where I always go when I need to think. It calms me. L.A. is too calm all of the time. It's the type of calm that gives me the creeps. It's the type of calm you look back on and say, "Wow, things were so calm right before that enormous earthquake that swallowed my apartment building."

My parents have found a pseudo retirement community at Foxwoods Casino. I'll never understand why two people in their seventies want to spend their weekends inside pulling the germ-riddled handles on slot machines—watching their hard-earned money turn into a series of lights, sounds, and rotating pictures of cherries. My mother assures me, "It's about the Wampum Points, Jennifah."

When I get overly critical of my parents' spending their time gambling and hanging out with people who smoke cigarettes in their mouth while breathing oxygen through their nose, my parents play the Native American Card. "Jennifah, we are supporting the Wampum tribe. Do you know what our ancestors did to these people when they landed on Plymouth Rock? We have to pay them back at the slots."

Or my parents will argue, "What? Do you want us to just sit at home rotting in our rocking chairs? Is that what old people are supposed to do?" No. I don't want my parents to rot, but in my fantasy they take up something that doesn't involve them collecting so many Wampum Points that they keep getting free off-brand iPad tablets or coffeemakers—the iPiddle and the Monsieur Coffee.

There's a comedy club inside Foxwoods Casino (and most casinos in this country). Normally I don't like performing for crowds of people who only decided to take in a comedy show because they're taking a break from betting on red and losing, but my parents, when not personally making amends to the Native American community for the sins of early America, have taken to acting as my publicists and agents. If they had a publicity firm it would be called Why Are You Writing About [insert name of comedian here] And Not My Daughter? Inc.

My mom convinced the booker of Foxwoods to let me perform for a weekend of shows—and she got me a great rate. I couldn't say no. And it would be a nice little weekend getaway with my parents. It's fascinating how when my parents are in their element, we all tend to get along great. I try to let go of the knowledge that these days their "element" involves befriending ex–Boston mafioso fatsos and their third wives who are younger than their first daughters.

I planned to meet up with Kevin in New York City. Just to have a drink in person. It wasn't going to be an affair or anything like that. I also needed to see my East Coast bestie Allison—much like I needed to be around Kevin to see if he moved my meter, I needed to look in the eyes of a woman who had known me since I was twenty-three years old and had seen me through so many boyfriends and so much love both requited and "un." She would be able to tell me for sure if I mean what I'm saying. She would brush off my suggestion that she's intuitive and say, "No, I'm not. It's just that when you're not happy your eye twitches and I notice these things."

After my late show, my parents and I hit up the *Sex and the City* slot machine. My dad never watched the show and so he had a lot of questions. "Jennifah, is that Mr. Big a good or a bad guy?" Oh, Dad. You've asked so much.

My BlackBerry was blooping. Kevin was texting me.

LET'S MAKE A PLAN.

I AM NOT IN NYC YET.

JEN, DON'T WORRY. I WON'T TRY ANYTHING.

I'LL MEET YOU FOR A DRINK BUT NOT SLEEPING WITH YOU.

I JUST SAID I WOULDN'T TRY ANYTHING. YOU'RE THE ONE TALKING ABOUT SEX.

SORRY. I'M PARANOID AND WANNA MAKE CLEAR—I AM STILL MARRIED.

My dad was getting agitated that I wasn't more supportive that he just got a bonus pair of shoes for Charlotte on his machine. "Jen, why are you always playing with your phone? Concentrate on the game."

My mother also got annoyed at my texting. She doesn't text. She doesn't know how but she claims it's because, "It's too expensive."

"No, Mom. You can get unlimited texting."

"No, Jennifah. Our phone company doesn't do that. You don't understand."

"Mom, you have AT&T. Just like me. There's unlimited texting. I should know. I have it."

"Oh, well. I don't know. Your father set up these phones and you know your father, he doesn't know about anything modern."

My mom was getting really angry at a machine that had betrayed her by, as she says, "leading her on" that it "was a hot one but then acting cold to her touch." It's hard to see your mom act like a frat guy toward a slot machine that was a total tease. "Let's go," she said in a total "this party blows" way. I gave up on *Sex and the City* and followed my folks to some machines that apparently would actually put out.

After five minutes of winning and losing on *Wheel of Fortune*, I went to text Kevin again. My phone was gone. I checked pockets I never used. I got on the floor and dumped out my purse like a crack addict looking for something in the lining. I ran back to those no-good slot machines. My BlackBerry wasn't there. I asked every cocktail waitress. I persuaded every person to stop pulling that slot and stand up to let me check the seat. I was in a panic. The Lost and Found said that they couldn't help find anything until the morning. I went to bed but I didn't sleep. I tried to soothe myself. *What's the big deal? I can get another phone. I've lived without a phone before. It's not like someone was going to see the phone and suspect me of having an emotional affair. That would be insane.*

Until it happened.

In the middle of the night, I thought to call my cell phone from my hotel room phone hoping against hope someone would answer it and say, "I'm downstairs! I'm a nice old woman who has your phone right here with me. I'll wait for you, dear." But instead someone answered who was a slick-talking younger man with a thick New York accent.

"Hello."

"Hi. Um, you have my phone? You're talking into it right now?"

"Yeah. I'm José. I'm in Queens. My dad found your phone tonight at Foxwoods."

"Wait, your dad was at a casino in Connecticut and instead of turning it in to the Lost and Found he somehow gave it to his son, in Queens?"

José laughed. "That's right, *Jen Kirkman*."

"Okay . . ."

"So, you're married, huh?"

"Um, yes."

"You have some texts on this phone that I bet you wouldn't want your husband to see."

Oh my god.

"I don't know what you're talking about. I was joking around with a friend."

This reminded me of the time that my parents found my cigarettes in my Jean Naté powder and when my dad picked me up at my friend Heather's house, he pulled my Camel Lights from his pocket and said, "Are these yours?" If they weren't mine, I would have said, "No. What is that?" Instead I started to sob and yelped, "WHY ARE YOU GOING THROUGH MY ROOM? THOSE AREN'T EVEN MINE. I MEAN THEY *ARE* MINE. THEY ARE PROPS FOR THE SCHOOL PLAY." The school play was *The Crucible* and I was trying to convince my dad that those women in Arthur Miller's masterpiece were not only witches but also chain-smokers.

The man on the phone, *my phone,* continued.

"Listen, I know you from *Chelsea Lately.* You're famous."

This was absurd because I was NEVER recognized from *Chelsea Lately.* Ever. People would approach me at airports when I was with my fellow cast members and hand me the camera saying, "You're so lucky to be friends with these guys! Can you take our picture?"

"I'm going to be in New York City tomorrow. I want my phone."

"I know you're going to be in New York City. You're going to see Kevin."

"I'll give you a reward. Fifty dollars."

"Fifty dollars? I want five thousand. And I should get more since you're rich and on television. And if I don't get that—maybe I'll just call your husband and tell him what I read. Or send it to one of those websites."

I was shaking. How would I explain to my husband that I had to withdraw five thousand dollars from our joint bank account? Just to get my phone back? What is so important about that phone, he would ask?

"You want the phone? Meet me outside of Radio City Music Hall at four in the afternoon."

I said yes.

I don't like having secrets. It makes me feel like a monster.

The only thing I knew how to do was lie facedown on my bed and weep. I wanted out. Out of everything. In the morning, I cried through breakfast* with my parents. I told them that I was feeling bummed out with my life and I didn't know what to do. I could never tell them the truth about why I was so sick over my missing phone. My mother tried to offer comfort by saying, "This is why I don't like all of that texting, Jennifah. It takes you out of the moment. And you were doing so well on that slot machine until you put your nose in the phone. Always, always keep your eye out for those bonus spins."

---

* Free croissants at the Players Club.

5

MAKE NEW FRIENDS BUT KEEP THE OLD.
ONE IS SOME GUY YOU BARELY KNOW,
THE OTHER WAS ONE OF YOUR BRIDESMAIDS.

It's the friends you can call up at four a.m. that matter.

—MARLENE DIETRICH

Once I got to my friend Allison's office in New York City, I told her the whole crazy missing-BlackBerry-with-text-messages-that-could-end-up-on-*TMZ* story. At the time, Allison worked at a television network situated in a Midtown Manhattan building guarded by a doorman who was a retired undercover cop. Like most doormen, in between signing for Amazon packages what he really wants to do is hear some gossip. Allison gave him an earful when she told him about my dilemma. He immediately called two of his buddies who were currently "on the force" and told them that he needed them for about an hour for an undercover sting. I got no further details from Allison, as she got no further details from the doormen. All I knew was that an hour earlier I was exiting a train from Penn Station and now—shit was going down.

Allison, a friend since my first day moving to New York City in 1998, was a bridesmaid in my 2009 wedding. She delighted in being a part of my wedding but I don't remember us ever talking about it from the perspective of "Jen, you have met the man of your dreams and I can't imagine your life without him." It was more like, "Check us out! I've known you since we used to traipse around the Lower East Side doing open mic shows and now you're doing this very normal wedding thing and I'm wearing a pink dress of my choice from J.Crew and carrying flowers with your kooky family whom I've adopted as my own."

Allison took a long lunch and we went somewhere to talk over a cheese plate and lots of wine. We have our own version of saying grace before we sit down to eat and drink. We take a moment and she'll ask, "Do you want advice or do you want me to just listen?" And I knew that this was going to be one of those talks where I would say, "Just listen. But then, yes, please, tell me what to fucking do because nobody has been answering my prayers." I told Allison that I'd even been rolling up little pieces of paper that have the question "What should I do, angels?" and putting them in this little dream box under my pillow every night.

"Well," Allison pointed out, "what do angels know about marriage? They're just flying around without any genitals playing harps all day. But honestly, if the only box in your bed getting filled is your dream box, there's your answer."

We were looking at a two-cheese-board, two-glass-of-wine situation. I was overcome with guilt, shame, and embarrassment. I don't know why people call it a "shame spiral." I feel it's more of a shame X-ray—a situation where you feel so transparent, like everyone can see through your chest and into the horrible person you really are.

I felt I was about to let everybody down. I got married in front of family and friends, and some friends had to participate in the ceremony. It feels like we all made a promise to each other. I made a promise to be the married friend. I made a promise to not make Allison fly to Boston, rent a car, put herself up in a hotel, and pay for her own pastel bridesmaid dress, only to look at her seventeen months later and tell her that all of that had been for nothing, and I couldn't make my marriage work. How could I expect to be forgiven?

I started to tell Allison everything. She stopped me. "You're building a case. You don't have to. Your feelings are valid enough." No one had ever put it to me that way before. She told me that she had a feeling I hadn't been happy in a while. I asked her, "Why didn't you tell me I seemed unhappy?"

"Jen, friends are here for when *you're* ready to tell *them*," she said. "But don't leave your husband for this other guy."

"No. It's not about Kevin. It's about me. I don't know me anymore. I want to be alone."

"Jen, you're the only woman I know who says things like 'as she's nearing forty she'd rather be alone than married.'"

"That's how I know this is really how I feel. Because it makes no fucking sense."

Allison said, "I know that this is the right thing because when you got married you talked about what you should be doing and what other people do. This is the first time in years I've heard my old friend talk about who she is and what she wants. We have walked up and down these streets for ten years as girlfriends and you sound like you're in your twenties again, in a good way. You were always so sure of who you truly were back then. And a lot of us who were a little older than you thought, 'Where does that twentysomething get off knowing what she's doing?' And when you get divorced so many guys that were probably bummed you were married are going to come out of the woodwork. You lucky bitch."

I looked at the second cheese board and lost my appetite. I was happy talking to Allison. I felt like myself again. And when I'm happy I don't abuse cheese. Cheese is a privilege.

I picked up the tab—which was the least I could do for Allison, who'd found me two undercover cops that I was off to meet before dusk, and who danced with my lonely cousin at my wedding.

6

MANHATTAN BURGLAR MYSTERY

Give me such shows—give me the streets of Manhattan!

—WALT WHITMAN

I was standing outside of the box office at Radio City Music Hall, not to buy tickets to the Rockettes but to meet the two plainclothes undercover cops who were going to help me get my phone back. It was a real sting operation. I couldn't believe that two professionals were willing to spend off-duty time helping an emotionally cheating woman retrieve her stolen BlackBerry. I was considering leaving my marriage but I still wasn't ready for an upgrade to an iPhone.

As I waited anxiously for the arrival of these two men, I considered slipping into a Sport Chalet to buy a bike helmet, something for protection in case bullets were going to fly. I didn't know if the undercover cops were carrying but if they weren't, what the hell separated them from just any guy on the street? A badge? Were criminals really afraid of badges? No BlackBerry Bandit is going to be spooked if a man flashes what looks like an elaborate belt buckle nestled inside of a leather passport cover.

Since I had no phone and only the Thief's phone number, I called him from a pay phone. He'd told me that he wanted a confirmation call from me that morning so that he could make sure that I was actually going to show up and not waste his time. His voice mail was full. I called three more times. I felt like a needy girlfriend. *Why won't he answer? Is he out stealing someone else's phone?*

My next call was to Henry the Undercover Cop to confirm our location. "Got it. See you at Radio City Music Hall," he said. "And never say out loud on the street where we are meeting."

I said, "I don't think this guy who stole my BlackBerry has bugged this pay phone."

He said, "Ma'am, let me do my job."

I tried to keep the mood light. "Perfect! If we can't find our culprit—maybe we can at least catch the first half hour of a show."

He didn't laugh. Instead he said, "Take note, but not actually. Don't write this down. Nothing goes in writing. Now, listen up. My partner and I will be on the southwest corner of Fifty-Fourth Street. He'll be in a gray coat and blue dress shirt. I'll be wearing a black suit and a tan trench coat."

I couldn't get past the "southwest corner" part. I have NEVER been able to envision quickly NSEW in New York City. When the Twin Towers fell on 9/11 and people said things like "The North Tower just went down," I had no idea which tower to mourn. I tried to fit in by saying things like, "What a tragedy, all of the officers at the longitude who didn't have to be at the latitude that day." Even as a New Yorker in her third year of living there in 2001, I'd get turned around when walking down Sixth Avenue and would have to ask people, "Which way is Lexington Avenue? Don't say a direction. Say left or right. Oh, never mind. Just point. Just turn me around like a child in front of a piñata and tell me where to swing."

I confessed to Henry, "I'm sorry. I don't comprehend directions. Can you stand somewhere that I don't have to find with a compass?"

I was five minutes early and I knew (or I thought I knew) that our operation was all about precision. I met Henry inside of a bodega per his instructions and while I was buying a cup of coffee I recognized him standing by the newspapers. I ran right up. "Hey. Henry?" He looked through me—like an ex-boyfriend with his new wife. He exited the bodega and even though I'm horrible with directions I'm great with subtle cues. I followed. He picked up a newspaper from a stand outside and put it to his face. He nodded at me to do the same. I did, dropping a magazine insert from the *New York Times* to the ground. Damn it, I should have grabbed the *Post*.

Henry whispered as we both held the newspapers up to our faces. "Don't look in my direction. I'm going around the block. Do NOT act like you know me. Walk behind me. But don't look like you're following me."

I whispered over the sounds of an ambulance, "But am I still meeting you outside of Radio City Music Hall?"

"Yes, but we can't be seen together and when you get to Radio City just stand there. I will be in the lobby pretending to read a brochure."

"Are you guys famous detectives or something? How would my burglar know you?"

"You never know who knows what."

You can say that again. Right now some random guy from Queens knew everything that I had texted in the last twenty-four hours to a curly-haired divorcé named Kevin.

I stood outside of RCMH. Henry was inside pretending to be interested in that year's upcoming events in the brochure and Undercover Cop #2 was across the street on the corner. Nobody else was around so we were in the clear. Henry loudly whispered to me, "Hey. Just to let you know. When José approaches you and asks you for the five thousand dollars, pretend to be about to give it to him and as you reach into your pocket with one hand throw your beret in the air with the other."

I tried to find Henry's face as he talked to me. He got snippy. "Hey, don't look in my general direction as you talk to me. Turn around and pretend you're looking up at the sky when you talk." Oh yeah, that'll look normal.

I was wearing a beret and I had just been instructed, like some seedy *Mary Tyler Moore* alternate cold open sequence, to take my hat off my head and throw it in the air when the man who stole my Black-Berry tried to shake me down for money. The hat would signal Henry inside to come and cuff José and then Undercover Cop #2, whom I really hadn't had the chance to get to know as well, would cross the street and join us for backup on the west, east, whatever corner.

Four o'clock. No sign of José. Fifteen more minutes passed and still no sign of José. I thought of José's full voice mail. I was confused. He was the one who had been so clear about *me* not wasting *his* time.

He asked *me* to meet here. A half hour passed and José was nowhere to be seen. Part of me felt a twinge, like, *Is this what it would feel like to be single? Maybe I do want to stay married.* I couldn't deal with a future of standing on street corners not having my calls returned—let alone not being met by guys who I am paying! I threw my beret in the air to signal to Henry that this was over. He came out of the lobby with some great information about the 2011 summer season of concerts at Radio City Music Hall.

It seems like José wasn't interested in meeting me. Maybe he had a change of heart. Maybe he sold my phone. I could feel in my gut that the drama had permanently blown over. He had no reason to mess with me and reveal anything he found out from my phone unless I wasn't willing to pay him. And I was willing to pay him. Well, I was willing to pretend to pay him and then signal a more than middle-aged undercover cop to take him down. Who knows? Maybe José spotted me in the bodega talking to Henry and could tell that something was afoot. Or maybe he just didn't want to spend a Sunday taking the train from Queens to Manhattan when he could be watching football.

I walked down the street with my new undercover cop friends who were going my way. We stopped at a coffee cart and purchased three black coffees in those blue-and-white paper cups that you see everyone drinking from on *Law & Order*. We walked . . . in some direction on Fifth Avenue as the sky was turning to dusk.

They asked me what I did for a living and I told them all about being a comedian and my recent gig at Foxwoods. Undercover Cop #2 chuckled. "At least you're not a rapper. Those guys are a dime a dozen these days. They can't even give it away on the street." He continued, "Everyone always needs a laugh these days, but you just don't seem funny."

I defended myself. "Who seems funny when they're on an undercover sting operation? I was too busy trying to think of the perfect way to toss a beret in the air and keep it natural looking. That's the biggest joke of all."

Undercover Cop #2 said, "Okay. Now *that's* funny."

He reassured me that usually people don't show up for money transactions because they figure it's better to just sell the phone. He said that José was probably just messing with me from the beginning because he had nothing better to do. Undercover Cop #2 really had a lot of opinions about who should be rapping, the human condition needing laughter, and what kind of schedules criminals keep.

Henry, who had really become a confidant that afternoon, asked, "There must have been something really important on that phone. What does your husband say about all this?"

"How did you know I was married?"

"Ain't that your wedding ring?" He pointed to my left ring finger.

"Oh. Right. Right."

"Listen," Henry said. "This may not be my business or nothing, but we've been detectives for a long time. Our job is to read people. A fortune teller will tell you that they can read you but they're guessing and bullshitting. It's magic. We've got intuition. Whatever is going on with you and this phone and whatever is on there that no one can see, I don't know. It seems like you're not all there, like you're grappling with a big decision. You have to follow your gut. And no one knows your gut but you. It's not a thing anyone can give advice about. We follow our guts for a living."

I loved him for saying that with absolutely no sense of irony as he adjusted his pants that had to make room for his gut.

And with the homeless guy who was on the corner as my witness, just then, a man started to play saxophone on the street as steam rose from the subway grate. We three looked at one another. I said, "Did we just have a conversation about me being alone in this city to make a decision and someone started playing saxophone? Is this really happening right now?"

Undercover Cop #2 said, "Sometimes New York just does its thing and we have to watch. You'll never see that phone again but at least you have this story."

At least I have this story. And I swear to God I didn't fucking make it up.

And I knew—it was time to go with my gut.

7

NOTHING GOOD EVER HAPPENS
AFTER THE SECOND ROUND

What lies behind us and what lies before us are tiny matters compared to what lies within us.

—RALPH WALDO EMERSON

Kevin and I met up in the Bowery for a drink. He shared with me his experience, strength, and hope with his divorce and I told him my tale of undercover cop-ery. Then, I mispronounced a word and he corrected me. I know that sounds like something to not be so sensitive about but when you're hanging out with someone in a let's-be-honest-maybe-we-have-something-here situation, a guy should not be so rude. The soldiers in my brain picked up their muskets and went to the front lines of battle again.

"Jen, if you're going to be single, relax. Someone correcting your pronunciation isn't a big deal. He didn't hit you."

"Yeah, Jen, but it's a red flag. Maybe he's condescending and overly critical."

"What if he's sometimes condescending but also a good person? Don't YOU have any flaws?"

"Yes. I have a lot of flaws but I want to START at perfection if I'm going to meet a new guy and then negotiate from there."

"Who says that this is your guy? You said so yourself, you're just here to talk about divorce."

I decided to let Kevin do the talking. I asked him questions about how divorce works, right down to paperwork and negotiations and how it all changes a person. He gave me the best advice anyone ever has. "No matter who you marry—when you divorce you both become different people, because when lawyers are involved they'll manipulate you both. It's all about money. And I mean the lawyers getting money. If marriage is 'just a piece of paper' to some people—those are the people who either will *never* get married or people who are happily married. It *is* a piece of paper. A legally binding document that costs money to get out of and it's impossible to keep emotion out of negotiation."

There's that moment in any night when it's time to go home. It can be simply because you have to get up and work in the morning and you don't want to be hungover. Or sometimes it's time to go home because you have to admit to yourself that the party isn't going to get any better. The love of your life is not about to walk in. Instead, someone is about to whip out a guitar and start a sing-along, or worse, suggest playing charades.

I knew it was time to go back to my hotel room—without Kevin. My decision was made. I was going to talk to my husband about getting a separation. I wasn't attracted enough to Kevin to want to have some night of passion or sin or selfish lust or adultery. But I wanted one more drink because I knew if I had one more drink it would lead to two more drinks. I wanted to let my guard down. I wanted to not be responsible for my decision—whatever that would be. I wanted to stay at the party and let my boring self go away. I couldn't decide whether to stay or go. I felt like the rest of my life balanced on this one decision. If I leave here and go back to Kevin's city art studio/sort of working apartment and do anything stupid, that would mean that my marriage has ended.

And I had my George Bailey moment—sort of. An angel named Clarence didn't throw himself in the river to stop me from jumping, but my friend Eugene walked into the bar. He was looking for just a couple more drinks before he went home for the night. He had been next door at one of those dinner parties that abruptly ends at ten and people start ordering coffee—shooing the waiter away at his offer of another bottle. I waved him over to join us. That's the beauty of male friends. They're so simple. You can say, "Eugene, this is my friend

Kevin. We have a mutual friend. We decided to meet up." They say hello. We carry on. Eugene doesn't grab me by the arm and say, "Who is this man! You're married, Jen!" The three of us had a drink and laughed and talked about—I have no idea.

Eventually Eugene decided it was time to head home and Kevin and I were left with my conscience and us. After some alcohol my conscience told me, *You're youngish. You're in New York City. Your husband hasn't checked in on you. What's one more drink?* Something inside of me was goading me along. *Just go back to his place and see what happens. You haven't been this free since you were twenty-nine. So many years of being spontaneous were missed out on. Go see what the inside of one more New York City basement apartment on the Lower East Side looks like.*

Kevin's apartment—which was technically just his workspace— had the décor of a madman hoarder stocking up on doomsday preparations, but really unnecessary ones like a box of hot glue guns and jars of india ink. Half-finished oil portraits sat on the couch just waiting for him to come home. They stared at me but didn't judge me. His bed was on the floor—not on a mattress box spring but just on the floor. My hotel was only blocks away and I had paid for a bed that was actually inside of a bed.

Kevin joined me on the couch—another piece of furniture that didn't need to go by society's rules of "having cushions." There was a frame, some throw pillows, and a flannel sheet. Perfect for a chat between two . . . strangers.

"You must really love him to be so torn about this. You must really respect him." Kevin sprawled out and put his head in my lap. I rubbed his really soft curly hair—which I didn't think I liked. The intimacy of just rubbing someone's head while talking—I couldn't remember the last time Matt and I shared that. My heart was breaking because this, THIS is what I wanted. I knew I didn't want it with Kevin, but the sensation of being loving and sensual made me feel like a woman again. She'd been stuck inside her mind and her cheese-weight for so long. I told Kevin that if my husband walked in right now, I would have to jump up and say something like, "It's not what you think! He's gay!" Or, "He's gay *and* has a headache and I was comforting him because gay

men are so noncommittal he couldn't find a boyfriend to do it for him!"
I mean, I knew what I was doing wasn't normal. If Matt had walked in
I couldn't exactly say, "Come snuggle with us. We're just talking about
fidelity."

I tried to picture what Matt was doing in that exact moment across
the country. He was probably binge-watching recorded episodes of
Breaking Bad. I was sure that with all of our problems he wasn't exactly missing me but he wasn't on a couch touching someone else's
hair. The worst thing he would be doing at home was emptying his
pockets and just leaving loose change on the coffee table with wild
abandon, away from my disapproving eye. Matt would never try to figure out his feelings by doing what I was doing—getting into a danger
zone just to see what emotions might get shaken free. Even though I
was not having ANY fun in the art dungeon, the simple fact that I was
there wasn't fair to Matt. I had to leave.

But first, I let Kevin kiss me. I had to feel what it felt like to have
a first kiss again. It was sweet, soft, and thrilling. I felt jolted back to
life. But it wasn't because of Kevin specifically. It just affirmed what I
thought I knew. There isn't anything wrong with my sex drive. There's
something wrong with my marriage. I didn't want Kevin. I didn't want
my husband. I didn't want anyone. I just wanted to get out. I didn't
even feel guilty and I hated myself for that. But I knew. I'm not in love.
With anyone. Hot tears welled up in my eyes. I tried to make a speech
but I was crying and making no sense. Kevin didn't try to stop me
from leaving. I ran outside and told him not to follow me, that I would
get my own cab but maybe he could watch from the window in case
there was a murderer or a sidewalk rat. I got in a cab. I felt strangely
independent and wild and sort of like I'd reverted to being twenty-four
again. I wanted to call Allison to tell her about my night and I actually
rummaged through my purse for a moment before I realized, *Oh yeah.
I don't have a phone. It's somewhere in Queens with a guy who really
needs to clean out his voice mail.*

A day later, I was on yet another mood-lit Virgin America flight,
knowing that this time I was flying home to leave my husband. When
I got home, I wanted to tell Matt everything about Kevin and how I'd
come to my realization, but I just couldn't. Instead I sat on our bed

and told him that I didn't think things were working out and I had this strange feeling that we shouldn't be married anymore. I said that maybe we should go to a marriage therapist to see what she thinks. Matt looked at me with such huge relief and said, "I've been feeling the same way. Things suck. Thank you for saying this. I might never have said anything, I guess because I'm from Boston and I'm Irish." I assured Matt that his hometown and heritage had nothing to do with it. He would never have said anything because he's a nice person, a caretaker, and someone who doesn't like to make other people sad. I felt such appreciation for who he was at his core as I crawled under the covers. I smiled at how we were going to be so nice to each other as we embarked on our new journey: to sue each other for alimony.

8

"C" IS FOR COOKIE, "D" IS FOR DIVORCE

When two people decide to get a divorce, it isn't a sign that they "don't understand" one another, but a sign that they have, at last, begun to.

—HELEN ROWLAND

After listening and nodding and drinking her coffee throughout our first session, our marriage counselor said, "Well, Matt and Jen, I think there's a lot of work to do and you two need at least a year here with me." The woman was so goddamn emaciated I didn't even think she had a year left with that body. I couldn't imagine what more Matt and I could have worked on. The only thing left we hadn't worked on was a papier-mâché project together. But that wasn't going to save a marriage. Although I'm sure there's some hippie art therapist out there who would disagree with me.

There was something so irretrievably gone between us that, from a lot of our private talks, we figured out had maybe never really been there to begin with. Neither of us being great with confrontation, we fibbed to our new therapist and said, "Sure. We'll call you about an appointment next week." Matt and I left her office in silence and as we waited in the hallway for the elevator, my stomach lurched. I headed for the trash bin, leaned over, submerged my head in the hole, and puked my guts out. The proof was in the pudding. Or more like the truth was in the garbage can. I couldn't stomach any more marriage.

Matt and I shared a look and he laughed and said, "Well, I guess that's how you feel."

"You can't do another year. Can you, Matt?"

"No. You must be hungry now that you've emptied out. You want to have lunch?"

And so even though I'd just thrown up and we were breaking up, Matt and I went to an atmospheric Italian restaurant and sat at a sidewalk table on Canon Drive in Beverly Hills. We had two glasses of wine, lots of spaghetti, and two rounds of the bread basket. We laughed a lot. We talked about all of the times that we probably should have broken up. Right before we moved in together. Right after we moved in together. Right before we got engaged. Right before we got married. We even gently ribbed each other about how our life post-marriage would be. I fantasized that we would be like Courteney Cox and David Arquette—best friends. Matt felt like when you're done, you're done. He wasn't sure he wanted to be best friends with me. I wanted to start seeing other people during our separation. He said that he didn't, but I was free to. Then we decided to just stop talking about the future because we weren't in each other's future. We did take a moment to toast that this was the one decision we made as a couple that took zero input from our families and that for this little ritual we were about to undertake, we didn't have to hire a justice of the peace, wear uncomfortable clothes, or invite dozens of our least close relatives.

For once, something in this marriage—the divorce—was just about the two of us.

The feeling we had was anxious relief, like the relatives of someone who is dying on a morphine drip and then suddenly springs back to life for a couple of days. Even though you know they're dead in forty-eight hours, you're grateful they're alert just one more time.

Luckily, my separation coincided with an already planned week off from my writing job, because the first week alone in my apartment (Matt had opted to move out and find somewhere new to start over), all I could do was sit in bed. I couldn't fathom calling everyone I know and explaining that there was nothing really to explain. It was over. I sent out a mass e-mail to all of my friends and said, "Please don't ask if there's anything that you can do because I don't know what I want anyone to do. I know that I'm in bed. And I'll be here and if you can think of anything that I need, can you just please come over?"

In those moments I saw who my friends were (and weren't). Most people didn't get back to me right away. Some still asked, "Let me know if there's anything I can do." Whereas my friend Janie e-mailed me to tell me that I just had to get an Apple TV—and she came over and installed it for me. I never would have thought to ask anyone but a husband to do something like that for me. What an awful feminist I am. My friends Tami and Tara, newlyweds themselves, called me and told me to come over. They said I didn't have to get out of my pajamas but I had to get out of bed. I went to their condo and we drank wine. And—just like I had said to Tami when she came out of the closet after insisting she wasn't gay—Tami said to me, "I was waiting for you to admit that this particular marriage wasn't who you are." My friend Sharon bought me a vibrator and left it in a shopping bag on my doorstep with a note that said, "Your new boyfriend for a while." (Yes, it was brand new. No, girls don't share those things.)

A TO-DO AND TO-DON'T LIST FOR THE NEWLY DIVORCED

1. When breaking the news of your split to your friends, even if you're closer with the man in a heterosexual married couple, do not tell him first about the divorce. It will seem like you're hitting on him when he goes home and tells his wife that he just had lunch with his newly divorced friend who is a woman. Tell his wife first. This way nobody thinks you're out to steal her man *and* she gets to tell her husband, which is a form of guilt-free gossip. You've given a married couple something fun to do for one night.
2. You don't have to talk to your ex-mother-in-law. You don't have to have a good-bye with her. You don't have to prove that you're not a bad person. She's going to think you are anyway. She probably already did.
3. Enjoy your insomnia. You don't need as much sleep when divorcing. It's like being elderly for a week.
4. Lay off the coffee. You may not know it but you're acting manic. No, seriously, you are. You say it's happiness but it's a temporary form of mania. Enjoy the weight loss.
5. Don't think this weight loss will last forever. When you feel better your body will stop burning calories. And that's when you'll be

ready to start dating. So, keep that wedding-registry waffle maker in the closet for now.

6. It's okay to throw away everything from the marriage. You have your memories—unfortunately the bad ones too. Who are you saving the photos from your wedding for? Your nonexistent children? The children you'll maybe have one day with another man? Just this once, don't recycle, don't be environmentally friendly. I took my wedding dress, rehearsal dinner dress, shoes, marriage license, and photographs still in their nice leather-bound books and tossed them in a Dumpster somewhere in the city of Los Angeles. I hope there is a homeless woman walking around right now in a lovely floor-length J.Crew chiffon gown. You look good, girl.

EIGHT THINGS YOU SHOULD NEVER SAY TO YOUR NEWLY DIVORCED FRIEND

1. **"DON'T WORRY! YOU'LL GET MARRIED AGAIN!"**
Let your friend digest their excruciating paperwork and lawyer's fees and their natural inclination to ponder whether the institution is for them at all. How about instead of telling your friend what their future holds, you just ask them a nice question like, I don't know, "Did you know that the candida medication Diflucan is sold over the counter in Canada but only by prescription in the United States? Why are we the land of the free but we don't have easy access to yeast infection cures?"

OKAY, WELL CAN I ASK, "DO YOU THINK YOU'LL GET MARRIED AGAIN?"
How can anyone know if they want to get married again when they aren't even in a relationship? Just know that marriage is the furthest thing from a newly divorced person's mind. This isn't due to heartbreak or cynicism but to the strange and disturbing new reality that your divorced friend now sees marriage AND divorce as two very real possibilities and will always carry that reality to their next romantic endeavor. Do you think a sinkhole will swallow you? What do you mean, you don't know?

2. "WHAT WAS THE FIGHT THAT CAUSED IT TO END?"
Marriage isn't a toddler friendship where you suddenly decide to
end all playdates because Suzy didn't share her blocks one time.
One fight does not end a marriage. This question implies that
you're trying to figure out what went wrong so that *you* can figure
out what *your* fight with your spouse meant last night. Don't worry.
Divorce isn't contagious. You're fine.

3. "WE WOULD HAVE INVITED YOU TO DINNER TONIGHT BUT IT'S
ALL MARRIED COUPLES. YOU WOULD HAVE BEEN SAD."
First of all, no one likes to hear in retrospect that they weren't invited to a thing. That's just shitty. But it's especially shitty to think
that if only they were legally bound to someone, they could have
had a seat at your dinner table. Maybe it's not about a sad divorcée
at all? Maybe it's *you* who would be uncomfortable. Are you afraid
that inviting a divorced person to a couples dinner might be like
inviting a political radical to a black-tie fund-raiser? You think we
might show up, kick open the door, strut around with pamphlets,
and start "tellin' the truth about some things, man? Turns out—it
is just a piece of paper, man!" We're not going to do that. And of
course, even people who know divorce is for the best get sad. So
it's shitty of you to point that out and then try to keep a sad person
from an event that has *food*.

4. "WELL, WHY DID YOU GET MARRIED IN THE FIRST PLACE?"
How come YOU got married? Love. Or what you thought was love.
What do you expect a divorced person to say to this? "I'm sorry, I
don't have a crystal ball and can't see the future"? Or maybe "We
just wanted some presents!" To be fair, today I have more than ten
knives for ten different kinds of cheese. That never would have
happened if I hadn't gotten married.

5. "DO YOU STILL SLEEP ON 'YOUR' SIDE OF THE BED OR DOES IT
FEEL WEIRD?"
What feels weird is you thinking about me in bed. And also what
was even weirder was being married and not wanting my husband

in my bed. That's what's weird. Once the divorced person is in that bed alone, it's just a bed. And a bed is a wonderful place to do what we all love to do—sleep. And occasionally eat. Without a plate.

6. "OH."

This is what usually gets said to the divorced person after she tells her married friend that she had her first post-marriage sex. We aren't asking our married friends to high-five us, but we are just trying to share what we're going through. And trust us—we feel awkward about it too. Just say, "I hope you're having fun." We're going to have to go through some sex before we settle down again or become monks. As long as your divorced friend isn't giving gory details there's no need to get all puritanical on them. If you do, then you have to wear a Pilgrim hat and belt buckle and really commit to the part.

7. "IT JUST UPSETS ME TO HEAR ALL OF THIS SINCE I LOVE YOU BOTH."

Yeah. It must be hard for people to hear about their friends divorcing—but guess who it's harder on? The divorced. Don't even try to steal our feel-bad glory. This is *our* moment not to shine.

8. "ARE YOU SCARED IN THE HOUSE ALONE?"

Because we weren't until you brought it up.

***** BONUS ADVICE*****

DON'T SAY TO A DIVORCED STRANGER, "I'M SO SORRY."

Sometimes divorce isn't a bad thing. Sometimes ending a marriage can feel so oddly right that when divorced people see that strangers are more affected by the news than they are they question themselves. *Am I a divorcée* and *a sociopath?* Instead, just say what every person wants to hear. "You look thin!"

9

JEN COUGAR MELLENCAMP

Older women are best, because they always think they may be doing it for the last time.

—IAN FLEMING

I have complicated feelings about what does and doesn't empower straight women—especially when it comes to women acclimating to the social/sexual habits of men in the name of "If they can do it—why can't we?" I'm talking about being a cougar—an older woman who dates a younger man. Sure, older straight men date younger straight women all the time, but they don't have some name for it where they're compared to a lithe yet desperate-seeming animal that crouches in the brush, hiding, either waiting to be preyed on or nuzzling her cub. For men, dating someone twenty years younger is just called being a man. There is no slang from the animal kingdom that stands for the "man with the hair growing out of his ears who doesn't want to face mortality with an age-appropriate mortal."

For the longest time, I never understood the phenomenon of desiring to rub up against someone half your age. When I was a young twentysomething I thought older men were gross and if one of them ever hit on me I would have found it menacing, not sexy. Even thirty-five seemed like a lot of mileage when I was twenty. I wasn't turned on by chest hair peeking out of a shirt, wrinkles around the eyes, or a guy who has to keep getting up to pee in the middle of the night due to an enlarged prostate. As a teenager imagining some of my adult male celebrity crushes—well, I could have never gone through with the fantasy if it became real. (Sorry, David Bowie and David Letterman.) But as *I* hit my late thirties, I noticed I was attracted to men my age and even (gasp) some who were in their forties—formerly known as "gross older men." (Probably because I got older and chest hair started peeking out of my shirt too. Not really—but I have spotted a few gray pubic hairs this year. And yes, I'm sure they're mine. They're rooted. We'll discuss that later.)

As women age there is pressure to stay youthful by altering our faces. Instead of looking younger, with the kind of plastic surgery that the average noncelebrity can afford most women just end up looking Asian. There's nothing wrong with looking Asian, but if you were born a white lady from Palm Beach, Florida, I'm sure it can get a little disconcerting for everyone at the family reunion. Society doesn't ask men to modify their faces (though pioneers like David Hasselhoff and Kenny Rogers have insisted on doing so); instead, they just have to trade in their age-appropriate arm candy for less leathery, perhaps more of a soft pleather, twentysomething arm candy.

The problem with being a forty-year-old woman and dating a twenty-five-year-old guy is that you're *dating a twenty-five-year-old*. Remember how shitty it was to date twenty-five-year-olds when you were twenty-five? They'd bring their friends along on a date—or never even ask you out on one in the first place, thinking you'd be overjoyed to sit and watch them play video games or noodle around on their out-of-tune guitars and stupid bongos. Sure, they were all yours once it was time to get to the fucking portion of the evening and that was great too except that sometimes they were *just fucking* and you were *loving*—because, you know, you were a twenty-five-year-old girl full of hormones and promise and hormones that felt like promise.

But take a been-there-done-that nearly forty-year-old divorcée who really just wants to get laid and pair her up with a twenty-five-year-old who also just wants to bone and can't relate to any of the girls his age who want something meaningful, and you've found a situation where two people can really be useful to each other. The cougar doesn't even have to capture her prey. The cougar will, however, apply anticellulite cream to her ass cheeks, tell her Pilates teacher to go really hard on her today, get a body wrap to decrease water weight, and skip lunch *and* dinner for a few days. She doesn't realize it but none of this is necessary because the cougar possesses what the cub wants, a maturity he can trust and a wisdom about things like what the world was like the day that Kurt Cobain was found dead.

The cougar won't fall in love with him right away or cry when he wants to go back to his studio apartment instead of sleeping over at her fancy condo and she will certainly be too busy to want to see him again the next day. And lastly, the cougar provides a house that's as comfortable to hang out in as his mom's home, populated with couches that aren't futons and lamps that . . . well, just lamps.

Three days after my separation, at age thirty-seven, Ryder the twenty-three-year-old bassist turned me into a cougar for one night.

When I first met Ryder, the twenty-three-year-old bassist with the gauge earring in each lobe (the rubbery ones that stretch out the pierced hole in the earlobe and look not like jewelry but like something industrial that could be popped onto a faucet to stop the leak), it was the summer of 2010 at a vodka bar in West Hollywood, California. I have an aversion to vodka. I think it tastes like earwax. At that time in my life I didn't like gallivanting about, especially not for vodka, because that meant that *I* would have to go along with *me* and I didn't like myself very much. I was forty-five pounds over my normal weight. My goal was to just stay inside until the weight decided it was so uninterested living in my body that it would just pack up and liberate itself on its own. My then husband Matt and I were having conversations about our mutual doubts about staying in our nondenominationally blessed and legally contracted union. I was sort of hoping my husband would do the same thing as my newfound poundage. We'd been married for one year and unbeknownst to me in that summer of 2010 this Town Hall–approved platonic friendship had only ten more months left. The reason that I dragged my Smirnoff-loathing ass out was to perform in a comedy show, for free, in the small cabaret toward the back of the otherwise thriving Bar Lubitsch. It's not as pitiful as it sounds. Or maybe it is if you're the two-car-garage, two-point-five-kids-and-one-husband type who likes to stay in and play board games rather than go tell jokes to strangers who may or may not have known that a stand-up comedy show was going to spring up during their date as they canoodled in a pleather booth.

If you had told me that while I was onstage at this legal speakeasy doing nothing resembling speaking easily, someone I would eventually find attractive was watching me and that this was his first impression of me and I'd be single again in a year and have a chance to make sweet, hot, and awkward love to *and with* him—I would have probably just hid under my car in the parking lot instead. And yet, Ryder, the twenty-three-year-old bassist, sat in a booth in his painted-on pants with zero gut spillover, observing my set with what I can only imagine was childlike glee.

It's all my friend Sharon's fault. Unlike married me, who only hung out with my husband and our vast array of cheese boards, Sharon was social. She was also in the show and brought a bunch of her musician friends. They came out to support her since she had sat through so many of their acoustic café "concerts." Ryder was a friend of Sharon's friends. All of them were in the music industry and all of them were from Silver Lake. Silver Lake is the Williamsburg, Brooklyn, of Los Angeles. If you still don't understand what that means, think of it this way—if Los Angeles were a high school, Silver Lake would be the overgrown outskirts of the football field where the burnout musician boys and the girls who write poetry for them live and everyone wears skinny jeans—even on their arms.

After the show Sharon asked me to stay and have a drink with the Silver Lake-ians. I said no, I had to get home and be married and stuff. She motioned to a table of people that looked like they should be in a black-and-white photo from the seventies with Debbie Harry, Lou Reed, or Joey Ramone in their midst. I saw the boy who I would come to know as Ryder smoking a cigarette in his white T-shirt. His arms—where biceps should be—were unable to fully fill his sleeves. He was dainty and sexy and mellow and young. I changed my mind. I didn't have to go home right away. I could have *one* drink, right? Hello! I was married but not dead! Nothing in that marriage license framed on my wall said anything about not bumming a cigarette (even though I had quit years before) off of an aspiring musician.

"Sharon! Introduce me to your friends!" I said, suddenly the life of the party that I'd just decided to throw for myself on the patio of a vodka bar.

I met Producer Armen, Some Chick Named Something-Or-Other Who Was Just Staring At Her Phone, Guitarist, and then . . . Bassist Ryder.

Ryderhadsunglassesonatnight. Ugh, don't make me say that again. He had sunglasses on. Indoors. At night. But they weren't expensive sunnies. Just cheap plastic black ones that maybe he was forced to purchase in an emergency blinding sunset from a gas station on a road trip to one of his out-of-town gigs.

When I took a seat next to Ryder, he said, "Damn, girl. You're funny." I couldn't believe he thought my unfocused ranting was funny, but then again he was wearing plastic sunglasses at night. What did he know about anything? But who cares? He was fetching. He looked like a guy I would have wanted to date when I was twenty but didn't. I was naive and inexperienced when I was twenty and didn't realize that guys probably wanted to get it on with me and the reason they weren't asking me out was because they were discouraged and dismayed at the words "RIOT GRRRL" I had written on my forehead in black Magic Marker. And I don't even know if half of my classmates knew that I wasn't a dude myself because I often wore long underwear underneath cargo shorts with combat boots. It was the 1990s and the fashion statement I was making I guess was, "Look, any second I might have to be shipped to a frozen tundra to take a feminist studies class about the sexual politics of the meat industry. I have to be dressed and ready."

After ordering some kind of vodka drink that was so full of sugar I couldn't taste the earwax—I was a goner. I ordered a few more. I was self-aware enough to know that I was having a secret conversation with myself in my head wherein I was bullshitting myself. I was looking for any reason to continue talking to someone I was so attracted to— something to justify sitting so close. I remember thinking that Ryder was pretty smart for his age and I should take in some of his savvy in order to better get to know the very demographic that every television show targets. Maybe I would one day write a hit Ryder-inspired TV show and make millions of dollars and send him a brand-new pair of expensive Ray-Bans as a thank-you. Other points in Ryder's favor: He was facing the proper way at the table. He could hold his glass without dropping it. And when he drank and swallowed he didn't choke because the liquid went down the wrong tube. I was Dorothy Parker to his Alexander Woollcott. It was a regular Algonquin fucking Round Table.

The girl who I referred to in my head as Some Chick Named Something-Or-Other Who Was Just Staring At Her Phone came to life, lifted her head, and joined the conversation. Ryder put his arm around her.

"There she is."

"Sorry, baby," she said. "I was texting with my sister. Ugh. So much drama."

My heart dropped. "Baby?" Then again, she was wearing a floppy hat, a faded sundress, and lots of string bracelets. Maybe she was just a friendly nonsexual child groupie. What kind of old lady was I being, assuming that "baby" meant that she was Ryder's girlfriend? That's how young people talk! It's a seventies revival! Everybody is baby, and cat, man. And maybe even cat-man.

"That's okay, Daisy. Just let her cool off."

Ryder ran his fingers through her hair and gently swept her long bangs out of her face, tucking them behind her multiply pierced ears. That intimate move could mean only one thing. He's her stylist! Sigh. I know, I know. At that point I had to admit to myself that Daisy was probably his girlfriend. I sat with my boring clunker of a name. "Jen" short for "Jennifer"—the most popular name in 1974. The year I was born. The year that Ryder and Daisy were still orbs in some outlying universe—they weren't even sperm and egg yet. They did not exist. I wished one of them didn't exist in this moment.

My heart slumped. I reminded myself that not only was I married—I was a good sixteen years older than these people. I had already lived my youth. I had my fun. I went to bars when I was underaged too. There was an underground drag queen bar in Boston that just wanted to make a buck before the drag shows started and if you were willing to start drinking at six p.m., they would serve just about anyone. So, yeah, I've lived, Daisy! I've split a bottle of champagne with my friend Wendy served to us by a man with dazzling French-tipped nails. This was way before *RuPaul's Drag Race* was a TV show. So watch it, young lady. I'm the Madonna to your Miley Cyrus. People my age paved the way for you to sit in a bar illegally.

Ryder leaned over to me. He put his arm around both of his girls. Oh. What was this? Some kind of subtle threesome offer? Is this what the kids were into? It reminded me of the scene in *Cabaret* where Liza Minnelli is crocked on champagne, smoking a cigarette out of a long holder, dancing for her boyfriend (played by Michael York) and their new friend the baron. Eventually the three of them end up swaying together in a circle to old-timey trumpet music on the phonograph. Their noses touch and it's clear—everybody who can stay awake is totally going to bone.

Ryder interrupted the classic film in my head and whispered in my ear, "Jen?"

Just that murmur—the sound of some other man saying my name in a hushed tone—or let's face it, any man saying my name—sent my stomach into another free fall and it conked out somewhere in my underwear. I looked at him with searching eyes, just like Liza Minnelli's Sally Bowles. Every second an adventure. What could be coming next?

"Yes, Ryder?"

He whispered, "Can you go and buy Daisy a drink? I'll totally pay but she forgot her fake ID and I don't want to go up there again with mine because I think I should lay low too."

First of all, how was I going to stand up and walk away with my intestines in my granny panties? And next—what am I? Some middle-aged guy who lurks outside of a liquor store in his hometown that he never left hoping some fledgling foxy high school girl will ask him to buy her some wine coolers? I looked over at Daisy. I figured now was a good time to introduce myself.

"Hi, I'm Jen."

"Daisy. Hi."

"How old are you?"

She smiled, "Nineteen?"

"Is that a question?"

Ryder answered, "She's shy about her age. She doesn't think people will take her seriously. But she's an old soul."

Said the twenty-three-year-old.

"Old soul." What a meaningless expression. If Daisy were such an old soul she would be at home watching *Jeopardy!* repeats and then dying alone in her bed. I had no choice but to decide to be a good sport and get up from the table to get this brunette olive-skinned goddess her drink—mostly because the hot tears were starting to brew in the back of my eyes and I didn't want Daisy to see me cry. It didn't take a lot for me to cry in those days—a few drinks, feeling my extra forty pounds as I tried to cross my legs under a table, and the presence of young people who have their whole lives ahead of them. At the bar I ordered Daisy her vodka/soda. Maybe she *was* an old soul. She could handle the hard stuff better than I could.

After my third glass of vodka, burnt sugar, and mint leaves I wanted to smoke a cigarette. Not just any cigarette. The one in Ryder's mouth. I watched his lips around the cigarette the way us women think that guys are watching us when we eat a banana. I wanted to eat him. I wanted to open my jaw and swallow him inside of me until all that was left as evidence were his cheap sunglasses on the ground in front of me, and if Daisy later approached me and asked, "Where is my boyfriend?"—I'd wipe my paw over my mouth and burp. I took the American Spirit from his hand, pretending to be a free American spirit myself. I put the cigarette that had been on his lips to mine.

"Damn, girl. I would have given you your own."

Ryder opened his pack and pulled out another. He lit up and started over.

He said to me, "You're aggressive."

I decided to act like my aggression was something that he was too young to understand—make it his shortcoming, not mine.

"Ha, that's just what women my age are like. You'll see someday."

He stared at me. Daisy was back to texting on her phone.

He shook his head. "I don't know, man. I just don't like when someone seems like they could be mean."

I backpedaled, stubbed out my cigarette, and dropped the older-woman-with-bravado thing. "Oh, I'm not mean," I cooed. "I'm just a comedian."

"Well, I guess I'm just a musician. We're sensitive."

Daisy tossed her phone down in frustration and burrowed her head into Ryder's arm like a toddler who had missed her nap. There was some more burrowing, a hushed-tones consultation, and once again I was asked to move over—this time so that Daisy and Ryder could take their measly two-hundred pounds of combined body weight and breeze out of there like sexy shadows.

"Nice meeting you, Jen."

"Yeah, thanks for the drink, Jen," Daisy whispered.

Sharon was already socializing around the bar. I remained at the table with Armen the Producer. He leaned in.

"Can I buy you a drink?"

"No. I have to go back home to my husband."

He said lasciviously, "I've seen you hanging out all night. You don't want to go home."

Ewwww. I sobered right up.

"Yes. I do."

There are never cabs to be found roaming Los Angeles but I walked outside as one was at the stoplight. I hailed it down and yelled, "Taxi!" When I got in, the cab driver said, "You didn't have to wave and yell. I could tell exactly what you wanted." *Why couldn't I?* I thought.

I got home to find my husband sprawled out on the bed. I climbed under his arm and managed to sleep for about an hour before waking up with a racing heart. Two drags of a cigarette and a few sugary alcoholic drinks and my aging, agitated liver lectured me.

"Hey. Lady. That kid was right. You're aggressive. I had to wake you up to let you know what you put me through tonight. I can't even begin to process all of this before morning."

"I used to be able to smoke half a pack of Camel Lights every night and drink way more than this."

"Yeah. It wasn't fun then either but at least I had the strength to get it done. What you just did tonight is the equivalent of me putting stacks

of to-do files on someone's desk at five p.m. just as they are going for their car keys."

"I'm sorry. I know. This hurts me too. It's not like I do this all of the time."

"At your age, you better do it none of the time. Treat me right and we can have a pleasant albeit less fun rest of your life together."

I tiptoed out and headed to my laptop in our home office. I returned e-mails and then just happened to wander over to Facebook. I put in a friend request to Ryder. I don't know what I wanted from that. I pictured him and Daisy holding each other under what I assumed were very low-thread-count sheets. I went to the bathroom to pee. I apologized to my kidneys for what they had to filter. I returned to the computer and Ryder had already accepted my friend request and sent me a private message. "Nice meeting you tonight. Come see my band sometime. You're funny." I wrote back, "I will definitely come and see your band sometime. Thanks for liking my comedy." That was it. We never wrote each other again until ten months later.

THE BEAT GOES ON—RYDER PART II

It was May 2011. Matt and I had split up a week earlier and we agreed we could see other people. I had lost so much weight in the past year—most of it from stress, nerves, and adrenaline. I have no weight-loss secrets for anyone. You know those people who we all hate who say, "I just forgot to eat," and you ask yourself, *How the hell do you forget about cheese plates and pumpkin-stuffed ravioli and ice cream and fun-sized Snickers and organic cacao-flavored "healthy" cereal that instantly becomes unhealthy when you eat the entire box in one sitting?* I know. I know. But when you're going through a divorce you actually do forget to eat. For some reason the biological mechanism in our bodies that is supposed to signal hunger shuts down. Perhaps it's nature's way of saying, *"You may lose a lot of money getting unmarried, so, just like a contestant on* Survivor, *you might want to learn how to live on less."*

Walking through the door of my place on this first Friday as a separated woman, I didn't know what to do with myself—which was weird because Friday night used to be my "alone" night until my then husband got home from work. I would get in my pajamas, order in, and usually indulge in some classic DVDs of *Maude*—a divorcée heroine. But now—knowing that nobody was coming home—it suddenly didn't feel that decadent to have an alone night. (This is an attitude that would take a few months to go away . . . but eventually I settled back into a routine of making Friday nights my recovery night because I'm a grown-ass woman and I do what I want.) Maude's "God will get you for that, Walter" wasn't keeping me company. Sharon sent me a text. "Remember that guy Ryder? I saw him and his gang tonight at a party. His band is playing next Tuesday night."

"That's a school night. I work early Wednesday mornings."

"Jen, you should come. Don't just stay home all the time like you're married."

I walked into my home office to get my laptop. I caught a glimpse of myself in the mirrored closets I always hated because they're cheesy and scream "rented apartment," but I didn't cringe this time. Whoa. Who was that in the mirror? I was thin and back to my God-given brunette hair. No more Courtney Love blond or bloat. I wasn't too bad for a thirty-eight-year-old divorcée. Hell, I wasn't bad for a twenty-eight-year-old divorcée. Sharon was right. I couldn't just stay home. Matt said I could see other people and I was incredibly horny. It was time I started seeing people. Maybe I would meet someone at Ryder's show. Maybe I would meet some thirty-eight-year-old divorced man who also liked alt-folk-country-rock in a bar setting?

I logged on to Facebook as a surrogate Friday-night hangout with people. While scrolling through pictures of my friend's kids losing teeth and smearing food, I saw a notice in my Facebook in-box. It was Ryder. I considered seeing a gastroenterologist because that old stomach dropped again. What did Ryder want? Did he finally find the courage to tell me that I was a mean old lady who had no business contacting him on Facebook almost a year earlier?

I thought about how stupid I felt around Ryder that night at the vodka bar and how I had always regretted sending that friend request at two in the morning. What kind of married loser contacts a young, hot musician on Facebook when she knows he's at home with his also-young, also-hot girlfriend? I felt I couldn't face him at his concert. I clicked on his message and braced myself. It simply said, "Jen. I hope you can come to my show next week! I will put you on the list! I can't wait to see you again! How are you?"

Whoa. Whoa. Whoa. Why was Ryder insisting that I come to this show? He has that beautiful girl—wait a minute. Let me do some Internet "research." Click. Ryder's home page. Relationship status: "It's Complicated." *Oh, it's not that complicated, Ryder. I'll show you how easy it is.* Uh-oh. There I went again. The old—I mean young— feelings rushed back to every nerve center in my body. I might finally have my chance. I wrote back. "Hey, Ryder. I'm great. I mean, sort of great, I'm single again and it's weird! How are you? Oh, I may not be able to come to the show Tuesday night because it's hard for me to commit to plans in advance but please put me on the list anyway?" That last part was my attempt at playing it cool even though I wrote back in a record 2.5 seconds. Then without even taking a breath I wrote ANOTHER very un-cool Facebook message. "Let me give you my e-mail address. I hate messaging on Facebook—sometimes they disappear for no reason." (I completely made that up. In fact, I have messages from 2007 that I swear I've deleted and they show up again and again in my in-box.)

Luckily, Ryder was as uncool as me. Within a few minutes I got an e-mail from him. The e-mail began, "Jenny, Jen, Jen! It's Ryder! This is my e-mail address!" Hang on. Needle-scratch on the record bought at a vintage store in Ryder's neighborhood. "Jenny-Jen-Jen" is what my older sister Violet has called me since I was a little girl. Wow. Within three minutes I decided to do some very complicated math. Ryder and I meeting almost a year earlier and me feeling sexually excited for the first time in a long time, plus him randomly contacting me almost a year later when I was newly single and calling me my sister's very private nickname for me equaled that he is my soul mate, and the reason my husband and I met and split up was so that I could meet Ryder. Age is just a number. Don't judge us. Ever hear of a little couple named Ashton and Demi? (Ryder and I happened before those two imploded and Demi ended up checking into rehab for a condition known as "Being Fifty and Dating a Thirtysomething Is Stressing Me the Fuck Out. I Want a Pizza but I Can't Have One.")

Ryder and I volleyed for a bit over e-mail. His last one said, "Don't leave after the show. Make sure to stay for a drink." I knew enough not to write back. I knew it was important to maintain some mystery. Maybe he would wonder, *Why didn't she write back? She must be on a yacht with some dashing billionaire as only a charming divorcée does. Oh, wow. I'm jealous. I'll have to play the bass extra-hard next Tuesday night to try to woo Jen.* I lay in bed and tried not to have excited insomnia. Besides, I was a mature woman. I had to face facts. Did I really think that I was the only one that he was listing? Come on. It's a numbers game. I drifted off to sleep on my side of the bed—not ready to stretch out and take up the entire mattress just yet.

Tuesday night I stared into my closet and realized that the beauty of a wrap dress is that it helps cover you up when you're packing on some extra pounds, and if you're thinner—the feeling of pulling that belt around your waist more than twice is so satisfying. It can give a false sense of underweightness. *Wow. Should I check myself into a hospital? Can my body even function at this weight? Well, I'll deal with that tomorrow. Let me go out tonight and have one more last night of fun.* My short-sleeved brown wrap dress was the perfect call for my night out seeing Ryder's band. It was more sophisticated than all those other jean shorts–wearing floozies on his guest list and yet kind of seventies—so I didn't seem like your mom but maybe your friend's hot mom.

I walked into the Hollywood bar and Ryder was right in front of my face. "Jen, you came!" Big hug. "I'm about to go onstage. Will you please come watch? And get a drink. It's on me. I have a tab at the bar."

I sat off to the side. And I'm not just saying this because I wanted to have sex with Ryder—his band is good. And he's a good bassist. I looked around the room trying to find the other women who were on Ryder's list. I stood alone on the side of the room, nodding my head to the beat when I thought Ryder might be looking in my general direction. And he was. He looked up and winked at me. WINKED, like he's goddamn Engelbert Humperdinck or something. After their set I retreated to the bar. I felt like it was too emasculating to watch Ryder dismantle the set. I sat at the bar nursing my pinot grigio that sadly the bartender would not let me put on Ryder's "Pabst Blue Ribbon Only" tab.

Ryder approached me again. "Jen, I saw you watching the show! Did you like it?" He took my hand and led me back into the show room. He really wanted me to watch the headlining band. They were great. But if I wasn't sitting knee to knee with an exquisite young man whom I'd coveted for almost a year I might have paid more attention. Ryder whispered in my ear, but this time not to ask me to buy his underaged girlfriend a drink.

"What do you think of the lead singer?" he asked.

I whispered back, "He's incredibly charming and he kind of reminds me of Robert Smith from the Cure."

Ryder's young breath tickled my ear. "Wow. You have a thing for Robert Smith of the Cure? That makes me kind of happy because now that I know you're into someone as gross as Robert Smith I think I might have a shot with you."

This was my moment. I took a deep breath and whispered back in his ear, "Oh, you have more than a shot with me."

I don't know if Ryder heard me because the guy in back of us at that moment swiped his arm like Moses parting the sea and separated Ryder and me. His arm made an audible smacking sound that could have easily roared above the sound of my cheesy divorcée come-on. "Quiet, you two! Or go into the bar area!" Ryder—whether responding to my careless whisper or perhaps his wrist fell asleep—placed his hand on my knee as I tried to pretend that I cared about the music.

After the show, Ryder tried to order me another pinot grigio on his tab and I gave the bartender a nod when Ryder's back was turned to put it on *my* tab. I gave a second hand signal to indicate "let me sign off on that tab when the kid isn't looking."

I stood next to Ryder as we watched the show from a safer distance—no threat of being swiped at, just leaning against the bar and reflecting. *I really have this divorce thing down. I thought I was going to spend my entire thirties just gaining more weight, shutting down emotionally, and not trying new things. I was way too young to have done that. I never imagined that I would get a second chance at being single*

and would have this lust at first sight. I wasn't projecting my future happiness on him; I was simply noticing how attracted I was. That's normal. Then I thought, *When our extreme lust dies in thirty years because
I'm an old woman and he's more age-appropriate as my caretaker not
lover . . . well, we will deal with it then.* I just felt so free. I hadn't even
told my parents I was separated yet. It wasn't anybody's business and
I wasn't in trouble. I was just a woman, out on a weeknight, sipping a
pinot grigio and planning a young man's conjugal visits to my old age
home in between his band tours.

Ryder reached over and let his finger touch the palm of my hand
while he was answering some questions from other girls about how long
he'd been a bassist. That little move of staying connected to me while
talking to another woman is what women all over the world are complaining to their spouses about. "You can't just take me to a party and
then walk around talking to everyone else!" Ryder wasn't coming off
as a player. He seemed truly sweet and sincere. A boy with good Mid-
western values. (What. His Facebook page said that's where he's from.
It's not like I went to the library and did a book report on him. I'm not
obsessed!) Ryder leaned in to whisper to me, "Jenny-Jen. I'd rather talk
to you than everyone else. Do you want to go sit down at a table away
from it all?"

First I had to signal the bartender to get a mop and bucket because I was officially a puddle and I didn't want any of these girls
in their kitten heels to slip on me, then Ryder and I held hands and
walked ten feet to a table where we could no longer hear the music.

"I'm so glad you came. So, you're divorced now?"

"Yeah. Separated. With the intent to divorce but you know, legal
stuff, and it takes a while and I don't want to bore you with details."

"You could never bore me. You're handling it so well. My parents
are divorced and it was an ugly scene."

Ryder thought I was handling it well! And I fully bought into the
fact that going out to see a band—something I would never want to
do on a Tuesday night—meant I was a new person. I didn't know that
I was in the midst of a cliché. I was the same person who was in sort
of a mid-divorce crisis. Trying new things isn't necessarily always the
beginning of the perfect next era of your life. Every new era has its

awkward adolescent phase. Nobody congratulates anyone for trying crack. "Good for you, Melissa! Get out of your comfort zone. You're always so responsible by eating gluten-free and taking weekend excursions to local beaches to test the pH levels of the water and writing to your congressperson about pollution. But I'm so glad you smoked some rock tonight and just put yourself in that dangerous situation in the alley when you bought the drug and then took the first toke. This shows that you're a well-rounded person! The ocean will be there tomorrow for you to protect after you've been up all night chewing on the insides of your cheek."

Being out with Ryder—I had to admit that deep down I just wished this could be my new life. So far it felt manageable, fun, and if the next stage of my life could begin NOW—after only four days of being unsure—that would really work for me. That is the kind of streamlined simplicity my life needs. I tuned out the fact that he was saying things, not dumb things but just young things, things like, "Noam Chomsky should be taught in schools, man, but people don't want to do what's best—only what's easiest. No, actually what they should be teaching is more art and music and that the banks actually steal our money—not protect it. But they call it 'interest' to trick us into thinking they care." Look, he's not wrong, but you know what I mean.

I couldn't stay out all night. I had things to do; starting with Ryder. I asked him, "Do you want to get out of here?" I even turned myself on saying it.

"I have my truck parked here but it's out of gas. I can leave it parked overnight but I have to get back here early in the morning before it becomes bank parking."

This is why I don't like dating anyone with instruments, children, or cats. There's always some need to "get up early, check on them/drop them off/feed them" situation. And it had been so long since I'd been single I forgot to bring my "emergency gym bag." That's when you carry your gym bag in your car with a change of underwear, deodorant, eye-makeup remover, makeup, a blow dryer, and clothes. The average guy who knows nothing about fashion accepts that what you're wearing the next morning are gym clothes but they're actually stylish-enough-to-wear-in-public cotton clothes. This way the guy doesn't think you packed an overnight bag which would immediately scare him into thinking you're trying to marry him, when all you're trying to do is take precautions so that everyone at the office doesn't look at you and think, "She got fucked last night."

I don't know what you call something that's like a nightmare but even worse because you can't wake up from it because you already ARE awake and in it, but that something was suddenly in Ryder's lap. A big-boned blond girl who was so drunk that her body had taken on that Muppet-like floppy quality walked over and splayed herself all over my boy toy. I was concerned that she might be breaking his penis. I was planning on using that later.

"Ryderrrrr," she cooed. "You guys were sooo good."

She swayed to me.

"Weren't they sooo good?"

Our eyes locked. It was Daisy. A rather heavyset, now-blond, no-longer-youthful wispy-twig Daisy. It's like we had both used the last roughly three hundred days to morph into each other's former bodies. Daisy recognized me too.

"Heyyy. I knew you were coming tonight." (Loud whisper) "Ryder told me not to bother you guys . . . but I didn't know this was you. Congrats. You don't look your age at all and shit."

Ryder tried to lift her off of his lap like a mall Santa who wanted to keep the line moving.

"Okay, Daisy. We're just finishing up a drink."

"I'm getting another."

Daisy stumbled off. I guess she was more emboldened to drink underaged and get away with it now that she suddenly looked like she was as rode hard as Britney Spears.

"Are you guys still dating?" I asked Ryder, trying not to sound jealous but more like an open-minded, inquisitive, neutral therapist.

"Nooooo. We broke up, like, six months ago. But we still live together. I don't have any money so I can't afford to move out. But it's starting to get awkward."

"I can imagine it would. You're sneaking girls to your room at night and out in the morning? What? Do they have to climb out the window so that Daisy doesn't get jealous?"

"Well, um, we live in a one-bedroom. So, I can't take anyone home."

"You sleep in the same bed as your ex-girlfriend!?" I said in a completely closed-minded, judgmental, like-an-old-woman-who-doesn't-understand-how-kids-today-handle-ending-relationships way.

"I know. It's okay. We're like best friends but she gets a little drunk when she knows I have a date."

I softened. A date? He thought we were on a date? Awwww . . . CRASH. Daisy was back and this time like a dinosaur with an inner ear infection causing her to lose her balance and a huge purse acting like a Triceratops's tail. Everything was on the floor. Our drinks. The LED candle. The table itself.

Ryder took me aside. "We have to get her home."

"We? Just call her a cab."

"No. She'll just get home and go back out again. I have to put her to bed."

I put both Daisy and Ryder in my car and drove them to his/her/their apartment building. I felt like I should be driving them to school. I called to my adopted alcoholic daughter in the backseat. "Honey? If you're going to throw up can you try to aim it in that Trader Joe's recyclable grocery bag?"

I pulled up in front of my potential lover's apartment that he shared with his ex-girlfriend. Ryder and Daisy walked inside their home-slash-hell and stayed inside there so long it was quite possible that they had made up, gotten back together, had make-up sex, conceived a baby, birthed it with a bathroom doula, had it baptized, watched it graduate high school, college, and eventually welcomed it back home for Christmas with a baby of its own, delighting in what a long and happy life they'd had together. I looked at my watch. I had to work in the morning and the morning was no longer a next-day concept. It was seven hours until I had to be awake and eight until I had to be at my desk writing jokes about celebrities who forgot to wear underwear when exiting a car and politicians who didn't know that their invitation to a college girl to see their penis was not a private message on Twitter.

I thought, *I'm a grown woman. I should drive away and let Ryder know that I don't put up with this nonsense.* But the other part of me thought, *Yeah, but he can't come back after me. His truck is broken down at the venue and I am not waiting one night longer to see what it's like to kiss another man.* I felt the same as an angst-ridden teen writing in her diary. "I'm so ready! When am I going to kiss a man???"

Finally, Ryder bounded out of the front door and down his steps, looking back as though a monster might be chasing him. Driving home with Ryder in my front seat, I realized he was the first man—er, boy-man—who had been in my car since my separation. Every single thing I was doing became "the first XYZ with a man since my separation." I would have to stop counting because there were many, many firsts that night. (No, I'm not talking about anal.) (Wait, that sounded like I meant that I totally do anal all of the time. No. No. I mean, I've never done it and don't plan to.)

I suddenly felt slightly disheartened that this was how I was spending my night. I had been a responsible, normal adult. Technically, legally I still had a mother-in-law and here I had waited for someone sixteen years younger than me to put his live-in ex-girlfriend to bed before he could come over. I was immediately re-heartened when I started to unlock the door to my apartment and felt Ryder's arm around my waist. I think he was about to try to kiss me but I didn't want my neighbors to see. They didn't know that Matt had moved out and I didn't want them to think I was having an affair. I rushed Ryder inside and one look at an adult living room temporarily threw him off of his kiss game. "Wow. This place is dope!" He was particularly taken with my china cabinet.

"This must have been really expensive."

"Oh, not at all. It's, like, a thousand bucks."

I forgot to account for twentysomething inflation. A thousand dollars in my years was like ten thousand in his. I explained that it was a wedding gift. But still the sight of a piece of furniture that cost the same as the rent that he and his girlfriend were paying was leaving him speechless. I wanted to say, "Listen. At some point people have a thousand dollars. It doesn't mean we're rich. You'll find out when you're older." But I didn't want to remind him of my age.

Ryder poked around my living room, admiring my *Sassy* magazine with Kurt and Courtney on the cover. "Oh my God. Where. Did. You. Get. This?" he asked in wonderment.

"I got it in the mail. At my parents' house. In Massachusetts. In 1992. When I was seventeen."

That issue had survived my adolescence from the day it arrived on my doorstep and my mom tried to throw it away, not wanting her seventeen-year-old daughter to admire two very obvious (to her) junkies who were wearing "rags" on the cover of a magazine.

"Jennifah, why does he wear that old gray cardigan? Your grandfathah had one of those sweaters. It doesn't even fit him. And look at her hair. It's like a rat's nest that was left out in the rain."

That issue survived my college years, moves to three different neighborhoods in Boston, one move to Brooklyn, and a move to Los Angeles where it found four different homes—to arrive safely on my glass display-style coffee table in West Hollywood.

"Man, I wish I had known Nirvana when they were actually around."

I laughed. "What, were you not always this cool? Were you listening to New Kids on the Block or something?"

"No. He was dead."

"What?"

Ryder's words confused me even more than when I found out from Kurt Loder that "Kurt Cobain was found in the garage above his sun house with a self-inflicted shotgun wound to the head." I was in disbelief. I had a twenty-three-year-old in my home. He was three when Kurt Cobain took his own life. Meanwhile, I was not three when Kurt Cobain took his own life. I had been getting my period for five years at that point. I was nineteen. TECHNICALLY old enough to have a baby. In fact I was sixteen when Ryder was born. I was old enough to have birthed Ryder TECHNICALLY if I had been some kind of Teenage Whore (nod to you Courtney Love/Hole fans out there).

This is where I differ from many guys. I don't find it sexy to "teach" the kids about where I was when Kurt Cobain died. I didn't want to be some baby boomer telling a girl who's the age of his coworkers' daughters about what Woodstock was like. I didn't want to answer Ryder's questions about what "the vibe" was like on April 5, 1994. I thought it would be much sexier to stop talking about a dead rock star and start getting it on. But I didn't want to make the first move. I already felt like a cross between an alpha male and his great-aunt. I needed to submit a little. I offered him some wine, hoping to maybe lube him up a bit more, to bring him back to the moment when he had his hand on my knee at the bar. I asked what I thought was a simple question.

"Would you like some wine? I'm going to have a glass."

Ryder looked around as if needing to see proof of this wine I was talking about.

"Wait. When did you get the wine?"

"What?"

What kind of question was that? Oh. Wait. Was my young date actually a little wine connoisseur? "Do you mean what vintage year is the wine?" I asked.

He said, "No. I mean how do you know you have any wine? We didn't stop at 7-Eleven on the way home or anything."

I wanted to hold him in my arms and protect him from the world. I wanted to say, "Oh, no, baby-sweetie. When you're a grown-up, you can just have wine waiting at the house! You're mature enough not to be tempted to drink it and sometimes you're just so old and tired that the mere task of opening it seems too much and you just look at it on your wine rack—happy to know that it's there. Especially when you live alone. It's like having quiet roommates who you know will be a good time once you open them up. And when you're all grown up you don't have to buy wine at 7-Eleven or cash your work check there either." But I refrained. I was nervous that he would follow me into the kitchen, see my wine refrigerator, and his mind would explode all over my white stucco walls.

He asked me if instead of pouring the wine into one of my goblets, I could just put it in a red plastic Solo cup. He explained that he didn't want to drink out of the goblet because he was afraid that he would break the glass. I explained that I didn't want to have people drinking out of red plastic Solo cups in my home because I was afraid that I would have a flashback to bad college keg parties. I further explained to Ryder that not only did I have twelve goblets, I had twelve champagne flutes and twelve white wine glasses as well. I could afford to break one. I wasn't about to throw a thirty-six-person dinner party with three types of wine anytime soon or ever. In fact, I think we had only used the same two wine goblets over and over since we got that stupid hutch. But at least glasses were there and ready in case I ever became a completely different person and held a wine tasting party. Who knows? That's what adulthood is all about. Being prepared at a moment's notice to start acting like how you were told you were supposed to act; hence a vegetarian owning a gravy boat.

When I handed Ryder the wine he took the glass out of my hand and then took *my* glass out of *my* hand and put it on my coffee table—maintaining eye contact with me the whole time. Silence is sexy. And so is Led Zeppelin. Ryder put his iPod on my dock. (Not a euphemism.) And the sounds of "Ramble On" rambled in. I was confused. Why was he playing music? I thought we were about to kiss or something—until he came over to the couch, grabbed my face, and kissed me. He was putting on music to kiss to. I had totally forgotten that people could and even bothered to do that! I whispered to him, "I haven't done anything like this to music in a long time." He whispered back into my ear, "Aw, baby girl. That's about to change." Suddenly *he* seemed like the mature one with something to teach this lady who, sure, had a hutch complete with gravy boat and six different kinds of serving spoons for salad, but who hadn't remembered that sex could be playful, fun, and set to the rhythm of John Bonham's drums. I wanted to send my soon-to-be ex-husband a thank-you text for joining me in fucking up a marriage enough to make this moment possible.

There's nothing like a first kiss and there's nothing like the first kiss you have after you took a vow and assumed that you'd never have another first kiss. I don't care how in love any couple is—if you asked them if they thought on the altar, *This kiss signifies that I'll never have another first kiss*, I bet most would say that they did. And most people are happy about that, which is the difference between a marriage that ends and one that is endless.

I took Ryder to the bedroom. I mean, he walked alongside me. I didn't tell him, "It's time to pick out your jammies and go night-night. Let me brush your teeth!" I was relieved to find out that sex hadn't changed in the seven years I'd only been having it with one person. Maybe there was a wandering finger nearing my butt, but like JFK and the Cuban Missile Crisis, I negotiated that he did not get to bring that thing in that area. As he hopped under the covers to spend the night, I rolled over and looked at my alarm clock. It was six a.m. I had to be up in one hour. It seemed like the sun was rising extra early just to judge me. I immediately regretted telling all of my coworkers that I was going to see a band last night. I could have called in sick if that information wasn't out there. Now it would be obvious that I was calling in hungover. Actually I think I was still drunk. I told Ryder that he couldn't stay behind when I left for work because I wanted the door dead-bolted and I didn't have an extra key to leave him. "Dude, I have to get up at seven anyway to get my truck." I went from Baby Girl to Dude in the morning light.

Ryder convinced me to just stay up for that extra hour instead of trying to sleep. I wanted to tell him that I invented that trick back in college but I didn't want to begin another round of him asking me questions about the 1990s. It was bad enough that I didn't have any food in the house to offer him for breakfast and so I had to breastfeed him. Do you know how hard it is for a young man to latch when it's not his mother?

He said to me, "Can we do this again? Can I, like . . . text you if, you know, I feel like doing this again?"

"Of course," I said, being the laid-back cougar that I had become, just chewing on some blades of grass.

As he watched me dress for work, I was flattered that he said, "You're hot," but I wasn't used to a man being fully awake and just . . . watching me. There's something to be said for having a husband who is still sleeping when you have to bend over naked—the least flattering pose for a naked body.

I walked into work three hours later and my writing partner, Chris, said, "Why do you look like you're all cracked out? You smell like wine."

I said, "I showered!"

He said, "Well, the second round is now making its way through your pores."

My drunk wore off and my hangover began around noon. I decided to go home. I simply explained that my ragged appearance was from a night of crying after I had gone to see a band and I wished to go back to bed. I was splitting up from my husband, after all.

Back in bed by one p.m., I wondered why Ryder hadn't texted yet. He wanted to "do it" again but why wasn't he texting to make "do it again" plans? I called a friend, who explained that a booty call happens in the moment. I knew that. I was separated—not my mother. But I thought that maybe because I was an older woman he would respect that I can't just drop everything last minute and that I need to kind of make a plan to be spontaneous?

I went to his Facebook page. Facebook for me was mostly just a place to keep in touch with my extended family and put the occasional "like" on my friends' pictures of their kid's first day at school, first tooth loss, first time wearing red, first time looking slightly to the left, baby's first exorcism—the whole laundry list of parental pride. I was becoming self-taught in the fact that Facebook is also a great way to police someone, which I think is a word I'm more comfortable using than "stalk." Facebook can show you what time the guy who wants to "do it again" with you last logged on, and according to this website—he was online now. Just like me! So if he could be on Facebook why couldn't he be texting me to say, "I can't get enough of you and your wine goblets. When can I come back over, baby girl dude?"

I started to look at his Wall. He was friends with so many women. He was either quite the feminist or . . . a twenty-three-year-old dude in a band. His Wall looked so different from mine. People (like my cousin) wrote things on my Wall like, "Are you coming home for Christmas this year?" My friends wrote things like, "Here's the picture from our five o'clock dinner we had last night and you held my baby! Maybe you are maternal enough to have kids! Lol!" Ryder's Wall was like a bathroom wall. Women just writing their e-mail addresses, phone numbers, and then other random things, like emoticons. I sat there wondering, *Who is Charlene and what does . . . 'Call me I'm still at the 323' and then a picture of a watermelon mean?*

I sat there wrought with confusion. Did he just sleep with me because I was drunk? Did he think of me as a cougar? Was I the last stop on some twentysomething scavenger hunt? Was he fucking with me when he was fucking me? I called my friend. She assured me that young men these days sleep with older and younger women and they aren't comparing. They are still men and happy to be getting some. But my mind wouldn't stop. When he was watching me get dressed did he really mean I was hot? Was I as hot as a twenty-year-old with thigh gap, or was he studying me—appreciating me like an ancient work of art? Analyzing me the way a young boy gets dragged by his mother into a communal dressing room and experiences seeing his first underwire bra and saggy thighs?

Then I spotted the T-shirt that he'd had on underneath his button-down shirt hanging off my doorknob. A-ha! Finally. An EMERGENCY. I had to contact him. I had to tell him. He's a young man. I don't know how many T-shirts he can afford to have. He could be out there freezing to death. Los Angeles is a dry heat but come afternoon, brrrr that desert chill. I texted Ryder.

"Your T-shirt is here."

He wrote back. TWO HOURS LATER. Do I even really need to tell you how I spent those two hours? Napping. With my ringer turned UP so that every "bloop" of any possible text from that bassist would wake me so that I could immediately respond to what would probably be his text saying, **I KNOW I'M YOUNG AND STUPID BUT YOU'RE THE WOMAN FOR ME. CAN I MOVE IN AND JUST CALL YOU BABY GIRL AND MAKE YOUR STOMACH DROP FOR THE REST OF YOUR LIFE?** Ryder's actual text read:

OH, THAT'S OKAY. I HAVE A MILLION OF THEM.

I started to text back: **OH, OKAY. ROCKEFELLER!**

Or was that too old of a reference? Shit. I erased what I wrote and typed, **OH, OKAY. FRESH PRINCE OF BEL-AIR!** Shit. Was that also too old of a reference? Shit. Delete. What if he thought I was just trying to tell him that his shirt was here and he's sitting on the other end of our iPhones thinking, *Why hasn't Jen asked me to come back over?* Maybe he needed me to take the lead. I texted back:

OH WELL, I'LL KEEP IT HERE IN CASE YOU NEED A MILLION AND ONE.

Send.

Funny. And an immediate unfunny follow-up:

IN FACT, WHETHER YOU NEED IT OR NOT YOU SHOULD COME OVER AND GET IT. I WENT HOME "SICK" FROM WORK TODAY. I NEVER SHOULD HAVE GOTTEN OUT OF BED IN THE FIRST PLACE.

He texted back. ONE HOUR LATER.

SORRY I HAVE BAND PRACTICE TONIGHT. HOW ARE YOU?

I wanted to text back . . . How am I? I'm horny! You came over with your 0 percent body fat, kept me up all night breaking my levee to

Led Zeppelin, and you want to know how I am? Mortified! I'm a career woman! I write for television! I have a book deal! I'm a stand-up comic! I'm ON television. *How am I?* Horrified that I am texting a twenty-three-year-old who is giving me the same treatment he's giving all of the other "women" on his Facebook Wall—the SILENT TREATMENT.

Band practice. Pfft. I dated guys in "bands" back when I was his age. I'm not some groupie over here. You know who has time to practice? People who don't tour doing gigs!

I got out of bed and headed to the living room. I picked up our undrunk red wineglasses and gave them a good scrubbing—with a proper wineglass brush of course. I started thinking about how all of this texting was so beneath me. Texts are for quick communication between two people who already talk on the phone. "I'm running five minutes late!" That's a text. You don't text an adult woman who is in possession of a china cabinet, "How are you?" and expect her to be happy that you asked. I thought of how I felt sorry for/superior to the girls on his Facebook Wall. All of these young, attractive people home and hiding behind computers, phones, and social media. I'd had to figure out with my super-sleuth abilities that of course he was fucking other people. It's not that I took our night together as a bond of commitment, but I thought that I at least took the number one slot for that week. I never expected to be a one-hit wonder and get kicked off of the charts in one day. I wanted to get back on Facebook and befriend every single one of those poor girls who were throwing themselves at Ryder. I wanted to write things on their Wall like " 'A woman needs a man like a fish needs a bicycle'—Gloria Steinem." But I realized that at their age they were all where they were supposed to be. I was the only brick that didn't match the rest of the wall. I put my wineglasses on my specific-for-wineglasses-only drying rack and headed to my computer. I logged on to Facebook and unfriended Ryder. Then I went to my friend Margaret's page and hit Like on a picture of her daughter with her finger up her nose. I left a comment. "Call me sometime. I'm still at the 323."

10

I'M OKAY, YOU'RE OKAY

Sometimes we just need to be told that it's OKAY. Here's some random advice that I wish someone had told me so that I wouldn't have been so self-conscious doing all of these things. It was always okay.

Listen. Remember when you were little and you dreamed of being an adult because your stupid mom never kept sugary soda in the fridge? Remember when you were a teenager you thought to yourself, *When I get out of here, I'm going to do whatever the hell I want.* Are you doing that? If your inner teenager would be embarrassed by your adult behavior now—you're not truly doing what you want. Okay, maybe you should take those posters off your walls. Your inner teenager is wrong about how cool they look. And besides, Poster Putty *is* bad for the paint job or wallpaper. Your mother was right about that.

It's okay to not want monogamy for some periods of your life.

People will tell you that being non-monogamous can't be done. It can't. For some people. What non-monogamy can do is offer you the wonderful relationship-sparker called "jealousy." If your partner is allowed to see other people—maybe you won't have that extra bag of chips. You'll keep your gym membership and you'll throw out that pair of underwear with the moth holes. Non-monogamy can keep relationships sexy and open and honest. And it's also okay to date around! Just don't join one of those swingers' clubs or nudist colonies. Even non-monogamous people find that too much.

It's okay to not spend holidays with your family sometimes.

Your mother cries because she thinks the turkey is too dry and that you don't love her anymore. Your father becomes obsessed with snow plowing instead of socializing. You fly from somewhere you decided to live to go to the place you moved away from only to see old high school friends that you don't have anything in common with anymore. You visit your extended relatives who say things to you like, "Do you see any gay people where you live? What do you do when you see two guys holding hands?" Instead, do what I did. Go visit your family on the Fourth of July. There's a lot less drama because nothing is expected of anyone. I did this once and it ended up pouring rain all day. We flipped on the television and the Hallmark Channel had a movie marathon called Christmas in July. We built a fire in the fireplace and watched some C-list actors perform their hearts out in watered-down stories about women who ask Santa Claus for boyfriends. Without the pressure of having to buy gifts or feel merry and bright—it was the best holiday we ever spent together.

It's okay to stop visiting your friends if their kids are loud and obnoxious.

Your friends who have toddlers can't come to your house because it's a pain in the ass for them—that doesn't mean you have to make a bunch of extra effort to go to them. You never bargained for hanging out with a three-year-old on a Saturday night, so don't get roped into it if you don't want to. Were you ever friends with your mom's friends? No. In the seventies, moms had their friends over during the day so that they wouldn't have to drink alone. Friends of a mom came over to smoke a cigarette and ash in the playpen and say things like, "Tell Thomas to stop playing with my platform shoe." My advice is just let some friendships have some breathing room. When their kids are teenagers, you can see your friends again. Just make sure to bring over extra alcohol because their teenagers have added water to Mom and Dad's stash.

It's okay to stay in a hotel in the same city you live in because you want to watch TV in bed.

It's called a staycation and it feels indulgent, wrong, and like something we shouldn't be doing while there are still starving children in the world. I don't have a TV in my bedroom. I do this so that I get a good night's sleep away from distractions. Yeah, I know I have an iPad, a laptop, and an iPhone in my bed but that's just in case I have to text, write something down, or watch HBO GO in the middle of the night. Lounging in bed and watching TV is my favorite indulgence that I never do. When I don't have time to take a real vacation, I stay at my favorite hotel, the Sunset Marquis in West Hollywood, for a night. There's a recording studio in the basement. The room keys have pictures of Joan Jett or Morrissey. Despite its rock-star status, the place has a great get-away-from-it-all vibe. It's quiet. Except in the late afternoon when Eurotrash toddlers make noise in the shallow end of the pool.

This is the type of vacation that may not be socially acceptable. Nobody gives you a hard time about getting a hotel room in Bora Bora. Of *course* I would need to get a hotel room in Bora Bora. I don't live there! But people might think I don't need to pay for *another* bed in Los Angeles since I already have a nice two-bedroom condo. I've often thought about the fact that if I stay in a hotel in the city in which I live, I should offer up my home to a homeless person that night. But I just think it would be so cruel asking them to leave the next day. I could just get a homeless person a room at a hotel, but I have to be honest. I have trust issues. I don't know if said vagabond could really resist not drinking everything in the minibar. That's a lot of charges on my credit card for incidentals. But every once in a while, staying in a hotel is a great way for me to get away from myself. And it feels okay to lie in bed watching *Keeping Up with the Kardashians* or *19 Kids and Counting.* Two reality shows about people with too many children whose first names all begin with the same letter. It's okay to indulge once in a while. Just make a donation to UNICEF or something to balance out your karma.

It's okay to drop your old friends from grade school.

Just because Facebook exists it doesn't mean you have to accept Becky Stalling's friendship request. You guys weren't in World War II together—no matter how much Chad calling you both out on stuffing your training bras in gym class felt like the hell of battle. You and Becky have nothing to bond over anymore and you probably never did. Every girl stuffed her training bra. Go meet a new friend who understands your past but also relates to you now.

I spent way too much time getting angry at a middle school friend's Facebook post. I took it personally when Susan copied and pasted a poem to her Wall called "For All the Moms." I shouldn't call it a poem because that's disrespectful to actual poets like Dr. Maya Angelou and Dr. Seuss. This unfortunate epic rhymed words like "bag" with "bag"—as in, *"To all the moms / went from selfish to selfless / when they gave birth / and decided to trade in their Prada bag / for a diaper bag."* It continues—as it rhymes "hair" with "hair": *"Your sacrifice is important / although it may go unappreciated / but be proud that you gave up styling your hair / for not having time to wash your hair."*

Susan couldn't just let the composition stand alone. She wrote underneath it, "To all the moms. Enjoy! And don't let the women without children make you feel badly for not keeping up with the Joneses!" I spent days reading this post to people. "I mean, listen to her. First of all, if I was a mother or were a mother or however the fuck you say it, I would still have a designer bag. And I bet Prada is the only brand name she knows. Prada doesn't even really make a purse that's great for a working woman. Marc by Marc Jacobs would make more sense. *And* she doesn't have time to wash her hair? What about at night when the kids are asleep? She can go to bed with wet hair and wake up with some great waves. I do it all the time. But I guess I'm just a materialistic bully who makes moms feel like they're inadequate because they don't get manicures! And by the way, does she even know what my life is like? No. She doesn't. She only *thinks* she does. That's why she asked me to get her niece a job on a set in Hollywood. Her niece lives in Massachusetts and has zero production experience! And she thinks I can just make a call and get this little shit a job? There are so many other little shits who at least are making the effort to *live* in Hollywood before trying to get a job in Hollywood."

My friends only had to stare at me for me to realize I was spinning for no reason. Maybe the post was aimed at me. Maybe it wasn't. I mean, of course it was but I'm just trying to sound rational. Anyway, in the middle of the night, while Susan was probably getting no sleep because she's a martyr, I mean mother, I simply unfollowed her. I did frantically text a few friends asking if Facebook sends some kind of notification when you're being unfollowed by your godless friend in Los Angeles. And guess what? So far, it's gone unnoticed. Or maybe she did notice and didn't care. More importantly, I realized, I don't care. I don't actively hate this girl. I just really couldn't see another post about moms or pictures of throw pillows that say "Live Laugh Love."

What I'm worried about is that I'm not likeable. Why do I need to be liked by people whom I don't like? I like me, which should be enough. But I have to be honest, sometimes that doesn't feel like enough. I'm kind of an asshole sometimes. But I'm going to stick by my side. That's how selfless *I* am.

It's okay to call yourself "spiritual but not religious."

Spirituality saved my life. I'm not an addict, but I sat in on various twelve-step meetings and found the stories so inspiring. After I started meditating daily on the serenity prayer, I got out of my own way. Grant me the serenity to accept the things I cannot change, the courage to change the things I can, and the wisdom to know the difference, *indeed.* Also my religion is Don't Compare and Despair. You want the life someone else has? That's because you can only see their outside and you're comparing it with your inside.

It's okay to talk honestly about sex.

If you don't have anyone in your life to talk about sex with, I'll talk about it with you. I think that when some people get into a relationship they become protective of their sex lives. They see sex as a sacred bond between two people. It IS. But there should be freedom to talk about your sacred bondy sex with your friends. Some people in their thirties—when they are still looking hot and flexible (they can still put their legs behind their head *and* plan a trip on a moment's notice without having to parcel out seven days of medication)—settle down with one person to ensure that they have someone to grow old with. Other people sleep around or date or keep their options (ahem, legs) open. Both are valid lifestyles. But both types of people can feel pressure to lie about how fulfilling their sex lives are. Lots of married people don't tell their single friends about the sex slumps they're in for fear of being seen as unhappy or boring. Most single women aren't afraid to admit that a guy didn't call them back but lots of single women are too afraid to say, "I think he didn't call me back because my vagina is weird-looking."

When I was married and people asked me how much sex I had I used to lie. One time, during a particular monthlong no-sex marathon, I told a friend that my husband and I got it on three times a week. When I told her that we were separating the first thing she said was, "What? But you have sex three times a week!" I lied at the time because I didn't want to face the truth. So, if a girlfriend asks you how often you and your lover/boyfriend/husband/girlfriend/streetwalker have sex—it's a cry for help! She needs to know if what she's going through is normal. Don't dismiss her question by lying and saying that you and Bob have sex five days a week, right after the local news, and you wake up walking with a limp. Tell her the truth. That you have sex every other week and that neither of you has the energy lately to stay awake for the eleven o'clock news. When you admit to not having sex that often, talk about what the sex is like. Are you doing it just to get it done so that you can say, "Well, we do it once a week." What do you do once a week? Two quick pumps with a T-shirt on? Are you satisfied? Do you just pull your sweatpants down a little bit to save time because you have to get up early in the morning? That's okay. Every relationship goes through phases. We all just want to know that what we're doing is normal—yes, even that weird stuff with the strawberry-flavored body gel.

Here are a couple of things I wish I'd been told before I had to go figuring it out for myself.

I think once you're of a certain age and there's not a lot of time to waste, it's okay to have sex on the first date. How else are you going to know if you're attracted to someone? If you wake up and can't stop thinking about him and want more—that's good. If you don't care, you just saved yourself another boring dinner. And if we're talking heterosexual relationships, guys aren't that different from women. Stop thinking withholding sex makes him want it more. He'll just get it somewhere else. Once he sleeps with you, if he likes it, he'll want to again. Whether you just went out for the first time that night or you made him wait a respectable three weeks.

If you're in a relationship and it's date night, have sex before you go out to dinner. Who wants to bone after they are filled with dinner rolls? You're just asking for an accidental wind breakage situation when you mount your man/woman/streetwalker at the end of the night. And having sex before dinner gives you a secret to think about during the meal—*and kicks up your metabolism.*

Some guys like it when you take your little vibrating thing out of your nightstand drawer and offer to make their inner thighs tingle, or something. But they'll never ask, so you have to bring it up. No. I won't elaborate. My future boyfriend could be reading this book and I don't want to ruin any surprises.

Oh. And your vagina? It's not weird. And if a guy tells you that your vagina is weird—he better be gay.

11

NO NEED TO BE ALARMED

If there's anything worse than a woman living alone, it's a woman saying she likes it.

—THELMA RITTER

iving alone can be intimidating, and I know it sounds cynical but part of me thinks that deep down people like to couple up and move in together because two people fighting off a home intruder is better than one. And a ghost most likely won't haunt a couple in the same way that a spirit likes to prey on single people who are curled up in front of their fireplace alone.

I got to keep the apartment in my divorce but I also inherited a newfound fear of my once beloved floor-to-ceiling picture window in the living room. Why *wouldn't* a deranged groper throw a brick through this window and just walk right in? Absolutely nothing is stopping him (or her). With the help of a friend who ordered the same Mace for his daughter, I was equipped with many canisters of the probably illegal stuff. I figured if I burned the eyes of my assailant, whether or not it was legal would be the least of my problems. Besides, if I got arrested for defending myself against an attacker there is no way that story wouldn't get turned into a Lifetime Original Movie. Win-win.

But I worried that, should someone smash my front window, I would have to get pretty close to him to scare him with Mace, which is why I also purchased a state-of-the-art Taser that makes a horrifying electric zapping sound, lights up when I pull the trigger, and can hit a "perp" up to thirty feet away. I'm not a paranoid person. I don't think that anyone is after *me* specifically. I'm just convinced that there are sickos out there. When I decide to give away a piece of furniture, a chair for example, instead of selling it, because I'm too lazy to deal with Craigslist or yard sales, I'll just put it outside on the curb at night and it's usually gone within an hour. That means that someone walked by who wasn't necessarily looking for a chair but decided that they needed a chair just because they spotted one on a curb. By that same logic I am convinced that someone could walk by a window and decide that this is the night he'll bust through that window and attack a lady. I'd like to think that it's the writer in me who comes up with these murderous scenarios and it's not that I have some latent desire to ditch my normal cotton/poly blend shirts and instead wear someone else's skin.

One morning I smelled marijuana coming from my living room, because it was actually coming in my living room windows from outside. I opened the front door and found three kids, about thirteen years old, sitting on my stoop and just puffing on a joint, passing it around. I thought for sure that even the act of me opening the door would startle them and scare them away, but this must have been some good mellow shit that takes away reaction time and fear of adults. They stayed put like lizards on a rock in the sun.

"Hey," I said. "Do you live here?" I knew they didn't because *I* lived there and I knew that the two gay guys who lived in the other ground-floor apartment of the fourplex hadn't adopted three teenaged children. Not that I wouldn't fully support their right to. The little shits didn't even respond with words, just nods of no.

"I'm not going to work until you get the fuck off of my steps!"

Remind me never to write dialogue for badasses in movies. If I'd been in charge, John Wayne wouldn't have said, "Hey, pilgrim, you're gonna need a couple of stitches," but rather, "Hey, I have somewhere to be but you kids make me not want to leave my stoop unguarded!"

They didn't move. I said, "I'm calling the cops. Get out of here."

I slammed the door. I picked up the phone but didn't want to call 911. This wasn't a situation like cold Chicken McNuggets or any of the other reasons I've read people in Central Florida call for emergency assistance. I had the phone number to the local police precinct written down *somewhere. Where was it?* I knew that I'd put it in a place for safekeeping but now it was so safe I couldn't find it. I went to get my Taser, and then stopped myself. I couldn't pull a Taser on teenager. I wanted to but couldn't. Since I never got it registered I would essentially just be calling the cops on myself.

When I got back to my stoop to issue one last severe suggestion that they leave—the teenagers were gone. Ha! I *did* scare them! They just didn't want to show me how shaken they were. It would have been admitting defeat. Then I walked down my steps and saw them only a few yards away; slowly, casually, *confidently* sauntering down the street on their way to school. I hadn't scared them. They had simply accomplished their goal of getting sufficiently high to start their day. I was never a factor in how long they sat on the stoop. It pissed me off. When I'm pissed off and feel like I'm not being taken seriously as an adult I pity myself and think, *Angelina Jolie is younger than me. She seems like she's been on the earth since the beginning of time—not her looks, but her presence. She's adopting kids, working as a UN ambassador, keeping that Brad Pitt and his wine vineyard in line, all while wearing her famous black T-shirt, aviator sunglasses, and bony arms. If she walked outside you bet those kids would have run. She's Tomb Raider and I'm Stoop Failure.*

The only delight I took in those brats and their wake-and-bake was that they were tiny, pimple-faced, innocent-looking *kids.* That delights me because somewhere their parents are bragging to other parents about what great children they have. "Oh, my Ashley would never do anything wrong. I'm so sorry that your Steven was caught skipping school." I may be an undesirable member of the community because I'm a divorced, childfree renter, but "Hey, Mr. and Mrs. Goody Two-Shoes who did everything right in life by owning, marrying, and procreating, YOUR KIDS are getting HIGH on MY STOOP!"

I decided that it was time I get a home alarm system. Because I'm a renter I couldn't equip my vulnerable windows with protection from some of the standard places like ADT that have their own private security force who zap your unwanted guests for you. I went with a company called SimpliSafe. They sent me a giant Bluetooth sensor that I hid behind my TV and a bunch of mini-sensors to tape on the windows as well as a keypad for the front door. They threw in a panic button that I stuck under my nightstand. The only issue was that with SimpliSafe, a tripped sensor or a panic button hit in a state of panic wouldn't produce privatized police at my door but simply a call from SimpliSafe headquarters. If there was a real problem SimpliSafe would then call the police for me. That's certainly nice of them but it's a lot of steps in what I assume would be a situation where time is of the essence.

A few times I did trip the sensor and SimpliSafe promptly rang my home phone and asked me for my password, which was "Judge Judy." I picked that phrase figuring if anyone ever broke into my home, hearing me say "Judge Judy" into the phone might scare him or her off. But as President Obama says, "Let me be clear." This was not a safe word, but a password. Me saying "Judge Judy" to a SimpliSafe phone operator lets them know that I am indeed the owner of the alarm system. It does not mean "All is well here." Then after I say "Judge Judy," verifying my identity, they ask, "Why was the alarm activated, Ms. Kirkman?" Usually my answer was, "I went to take the trash out and then it went off and I couldn't run back in time to stop it." But if there is a bad guy in your house you can't say, "Oh, well, I would love to tell you that I set the alarm off by opening my door and taking out the trash but actually there's a bad guy here with some rope and he's about to tie me up." So when I would breathlessly say, "It was just me taking out the trash," they never once thought to ask, "Ms. Kirkman, are you telling the truth? Say the words 'Whatchoo talkin' 'bout, Willis' if anyone is in your home and you're lying." They always took my word for it that it was just me setting off my own alarm, which never made me feel simply safe.

The night that I stayed home to try to figure out how to hook up my home non-invasion system was a bigger disaster than a creep smashing my window. I'm terrible at reading instructions. I zone out after the first sentence and usually just try to figure it out myself— which, as you can imagine, is not a strategy for success. Around eight p.m. on a Friday night I affixed my keypad to my door, turned on the sensors, and before I could pick a password—the thing started wailing. At least I knew that if someone broke in the alarm was so annoying that he would immediately leave. It's like how I feel when I walk into a store in December and that awful Paul McCartney song "Wonderful Christmastime" is playing. *Not worth it. I'm out of here even though I could have finished all of my holiday shopping in one place.*

The instructions on the box had promised me that this system was "incredibly easy to set up" and even "idiot proof." It didn't say anything on the box about what to do in case of a poltergeist that causes the alarm to go off before it is even programmed or how to stop it without a password because one doesn't exist yet. I called the 1-800 number and was greeted with SimpliSafe's answering service.

"Answering service? What does that mean?"

A cheeky operator said, "Ma'am, answering service means that I'm a service and I'm answering your call."

"Well, I can't turn my alarm off."

"Okay, ma'am. Well, you can call back during SimpliSafe's normal business hours, Monday through Friday, nine a.m. to five p.m., and a service technician can help you then."

"Wait. So you're a service that answers the phone only to tell me that no one can answer the phone?"

Silence.

My upstairs neighbors started pounding on the floor, their floor. My ceiling. It could not go on like this all weekend.

"Ma'am, just put your password in and it should stop. Any other technical questions can be answered nine to five—"

"Yes. I know I can call back on Monday—that is, if I take the day off from work."

"Just put in your pass—"

"My. Password. Hasn't. Been. Picked. That's why I'm calling."

"That doesn't make sense, ma'am."

"Maybe I'd have better luck calling Ghostbusters since you don't fucking seem to—"

Click. She hung up.

Nobody hangs up on me.

I called her back.

"Hello, SimpliSafe. This is Sherri. How can I help you?"

"Sherri. This is Jen. I was just hung up on—"

Click. She hung up on me again.

I called back again.

Sherri skipped the official greeting and answered, "What."

"Sherri?"

"Don't you dare use foul language with me, ma'am. Jesus didn't make your mouth so you could use foul language."

"Sherri. I'm sorry. I'm tired. I live alone and I'm divorced. I'm just trying not to get stabbed. I have a big picture window. My neighbors are mad—"

"Hold up, ma'am. You're divorced?"

"Yes."

"Me too. I was the first one in my group."

"Me too."

"Okay, ma'am. If Jesus can forgive, I can forgive."

"Okayyy . . ."

"I have access to the help manual and I'm not supposed to do this except in real emergencies but you're going to have to listen to me. Are you ready?"

"Yes."

I positioned myself by the keypad, ready to take her orders.

"You got a couch? Sit on it."

Confused, I sat down.

"Now, ma'am, take deep breaths."

"Sherri, what does this have to do with—?"

"DEEP. BREATHS!"

"Okay. Okay."

"Now. Was he good to you?"

"Who?"

"Your ex-husband."

"Yes. He was great in a lot of ways but I don't think marriage was for me."

"Oh. Well, I was cheated on. If your next husband ever tells you he's just taking on an extra shift at work, don't believe it."

"Okay. Good to know."

"All you have to know are two things. First, love is love. You can find love in friendships and mostly love exists in abundance in the world but people act like there isn't enough of it. We're in charge of that. I can love all I want. Can't stop me."

I sat attentively awaiting her next piece of wisdom. Sherri actually made me feel better.

"And what's the second thing?"

"Star. Star. Star."

Star star star? I tried to figure out what that could mean.

"Like, as in astrology? You mean, look to the stars? Believe in something bigger than me? Or is it more like a message of follow the North Star to my own personal freedom?"

"No, ma'am. Hit star star star on the keypad and that will silence the alarm."

"Oh."

I got off the phone with Sherri, thankful that she bent the rules for me. And I realized that we have our Oprahs and our Deepak Chopras but every once in a while inspiration is just a flawed alarm system and a phone call away. I would buy a Sherri's Words of Wisdom Page-A-Day calendar in a heartbeat. And even though it was only a code, I'm choosing to believe in the wisdom of Star Star Star. Can't stop me.

12

RENT (NO, NOT THE BROADWAY MUSICAL)

It's easy to underestimate the real cost of home ownership.

—SUZE ORMAN

Hi. My name is Jen. And I'm a renter. Wow. Unlike alcoholism, admitting that I'm a renter doesn't feel like the first step toward recovery. I still feel shame. I do not own my home. In fact I don't own the following things that came with my rental: the refrigerator that makes three kinds of crushed ice; the washer and dryer; the dishwasher; the garbage disposal; the toilets; the rainfall showerheads in both bathrooms; the dimmer lighting; or the hardwood floors. None of these things are mine. Actually, I don't even rent a house. I rent a condo. I want to rent. I know I don't have "equity" but I also don't have "debt." Your friends will tell you that you need to start investing in something that can give back to you. Then they'll tell you about the homes that they own; that the pipes are old, there's mold in the ceiling, and every other day the sewer drainage system backs up but that it's all "worth it." When is the worth it part? When you're seventy-five and finally own your home outright only to leave it to move into assisted living?

I only live in my home about two hundred days out of the year and I'm so glad that I don't even have to think about it when I'm not there. If the building loses power—it's not my problem. If my garbage disposal backs up, I tattle on it to the building manager and by the end of the day it's fixed. A doorman is sitting at the front desk twenty-four hours a day. If an ex-boyfriend comes to tell me that he loves me—he cannot get upstairs. I leave photos and names with my doorman for the two exceptions. Just in case. My mailbox is inside, safely secured behind locked doors so no shitty neighborhood kids can hit it with a bat or fill it with shaving cream on Halloween. I have an elevator. Do you have an elevator in your house? You do? Well, screw you, then. Okay, but, Jen, you don't OWN it. You're throwing money away, you say. No. I'm just giving my money to different people. Homeowners give their money to a bank once a month. Once a month I give my money to the nice blond lady downstairs, who then gives it to a bank.

I'm an independent woman but not that independent. There's a gym in my building and a coffee machine in the lobby. It feels like living in a hotel, and since I do that for half of my year, when my home feels like a hotel it feels like home. Houses are scary. There are creaky stairs for ghosts to walk on; attics and basements for monsters to hide in. You never see movies where a ghost haunts a brand-new condo. There's nothing satisfying about a ghost dimming the lights or changing the setting on the central air-conditioning. And since I was the first one to live in my place—there's no history. If a ghost tried to haunt me claiming that she lived there first, I could totally call bullshit.

Another bonus about my living situation is that the doorman who works the night shift is studying to be an EMT and he knows the Heimlich maneuver. I made a pact with him that if I ever call downstairs and I sound like I'm choking it's because I'm choking and he has full permission to enter my apartment and maneuver the crap out of my Heimlich. If I keep on living alone, I will probably die in this condo. I'll definitely hit my head on the tub someday and then three days later a cat will eat my face. I don't have a cat, but when a single woman dies alone I hear that cats magically appear.

After living on the first floor with an enticing-to-murderers big picture window and then another apartment with a loud toddler clomping around upstairs—my brand-new condo in Los Angeles was a welcome haven and heaven. The building manager took pity on me when she saw how shell-shocked I looked from sleepless nights because of someone else's baby. She offered me a great price on a top-floor unit—no babies above me unless there are some ninja SWAT team babies that climb rooftops. So far so good. I haven't heard any.

I've never been a talk-to-my-neighbors kind of girl. If I'm home, I'm usually sleeping, showering, or completely zoned out on the couch, not in the mood to talk to anyone. I would have sucked at living in the 1940s when people had nothing to do except knock on each other's doors and borrow sugar or be friendly. I like to know my neighbors' names, and starting to figure out their schedules comforts me, but that's it. I sit at home thinking, *Okay. Michelle next door is home. If I smelled carbon monoxide I could knock and ask her if she smells it too. I could also ask her, "Wait, does carbon monoxide even have a smell?"*

Back at the old West Hollywood building, I threw a swinging New Year's party complete with homemade sangria. Our neighbors, who had planned to stay inside and have a couple's night, got bored with each other by eleven p.m. and knocked on my door wondering if they could join in and bring some of their Veuve Clicquot. When I'm tipsy I'm everyone's best friend. "Come on in! Oh my God! It's . . ."

"Dana and Steve."

"Right! Dana and Steve! I love you guys! I never see you!"

I'm not lying when I talk like this. I'm accessing the deepest part of me that truly loves all people.

The next morning I woke up with the foggiest memory that I'd gone out of my comfort zone. A text from Dana said, **JEN! SO NICE TO HANG LAST NIGHT! LIKE YOU SAID, YOU TEND TO HIDE AT HOME WITH CANDLES LIT SO WE WILL BE KNOCKING ON YOUR DOOR A LOT MORE OFTEN, FRIENDLY NEIGHBOR!**

I pretended to have diarrhea for at least eight months until they got tired of knocking.

The beauty of New Condo was that I was one of the first people to move into the building. There was no bumping into next-door or across-the-hall neighbors carrying boxes or new lamps. No forced new friends like in college. I lived alone in my little corner of the sixth and top floor for months. Until I opened my door one day and seconds later the door down the hall whipped open as if someone had been standing behind it waiting, listening for a sign of life from my place. I was face-to-face with a sort of odd duck of a man who looked like he wasn't born but rather drawn to life like a *Simpsons* character. He had too much phlegm in his nose, mouth, throat, and teeth.

"Hi! I'm Billy! What's your name?"

"Jen."

"Hi, Jennifer. I'm Billy."

He seemed drunk. He seemed off. Not mentally challenged, but off.

"Well, nice to meet you. I heard you open your door so I decided to say hi."

I went on my way down the hall as he shouted, "Let's have wine sometime. Stop by anytime or I'll stop by your place. Stop by later for wine!"

I didn't turn around. I kept walking. No. No. No. No. No. No. No. This could not be happening. I hoped that was the last I would see of Billy and that nobody would be having wine. Why did the nice building manager lady have to put him down the hall from me? A wildly private single woman? Can't he live down the hall from a nice family and bother them? That's what people make families—to have backup against the weird neighbors of the world.

Two nights later I was home, reading in bed at nine p.m. A luxury I hadn't had with the loud toddler above my head at the old West Hollywood place. I heard a knock at the door. Not one knock but a nonrhythmic series of knocks, and my doorbell was ringing too. Not once but in tandem with the knock. Knock. Knock. Ring. Ring. Ring. Knock. Knock. Knock. Ring. Knock. Ring.

I assumed it was FedEx. That's usually how they knock and I was expecting a package. I opened the door without consulting the peephole. It was Billy.

"Do you hear that?"

"No."

"Your next-door neighbor's smoke alarm is going off and it's driving me crazy. Can you talk to her?"

"I don't know her. Everyone's smoke alarm goes off the first time they use the stove. This is a new building. It's going to be fine."

"Am I bothering you?"

"It's fine but I was in bed reading."

"I'm going to go outside until it stops."

I nodded and shut the door. He seemed high. He smelled like pot. He still sounded like a drunken cartoon. I really hoped he was just an anxious first-time mover and he would calm the fuck down. I didn't like where this was heading so far.

Exactly twenty-four hours later, the off-rhythm door knocking and doorbell ringing started again. I tiptoed to my peephole. Billy. I watched him turn around and walk back into his apartment, go inside, and come back out with pieces of paper and a Sharpie. He pressed the pieces of paper up against my door—they covered the peephole so I could no longer see him but I could hear the loud squeak of the marker writing something on the paper. When he put pen to paper it sounded like a hammer to a nail. Everything he did was loud. I started to pine for a ghost—at least with ghosts you aren't quite sure if they're really there. There was no question that Billy—who didn't seem "all there"—was really there.

I ran into my bedroom, shut the door, and called my friend and former coworker from *Chelsea Lately* Chris Franjola. He lives in the building next door. I whispered, "You have to come over here but covert-style." Chris and I hatched a plan. After Billy tired of taping things to my door and knocking, Chris took the elevator up to the sixth floor. I instructed him to creep down the hall and if he saw Billy not to move. He was only to enter my apartment without Billy seeing him. I left my door unlocked. Chris made his way in and I gently shut the door so that Billy wouldn't be able to detect any sign of new life at my place. Chris was to pretend that he was my boyfriend who was pissed at all of this door knocking. He waited ten minutes and said, "I don't think he's coming back."

"Oh, Chris. You've never been a woman. Our instincts are never wrong. He's coming back in five minutes."

I was right. Billy started furiously knocking again. It was Chris's turn to open the door angrily and deliver the performance I had written for him.

"Who are you?"

"Oh. I'm Billy. Is Jen here?"

"She's in bed, Billy. WE were in bed, Billy. You don't knock on this door like that this time of night or any time of night."

"Jen told me she just reads in bed alone every night."

Chris started to waver. "She said that? That's pathetic-sounding."

I kicked Chris from behind the door whispering, "No I didn't. Keep going."

Chris continued. "If you don't stop bothering her, and us, we will have to call the police and we don't want to have to do that."

"I . . . I just wanted to give Jen tickets to a comedy show. Here."

Billy handed Chris the pile of papers that had once been taped to my door and retreated.

They were printouts of free tickets that Billy had for shows at the Hollywood Improv, a place where I regularly perform.

After Chris left, I sat in bed worrying that perhaps I, er, Chris had been too strong with Billy. Maybe Billy was back in his apartment feeling sad and wondering why he never fits in. I felt like a prisoner in my own home—racked with sympathy for Billy and guilt and pity for myself. I was having a classic codependent victim/martyr break-down. I sent an e-mail to my building superintendent and basically told on Billy. I told her that I want this to be a home; I'm on television sometimes and can't have people stalking me. I told her that I would consider breaking my lease if something wasn't done. She wrote back that she totally understood and she would love to talk to me about it further face-to-face if I could come to her office. Ugh. Isn't e-mail supposed to have saved us all from personal confrontation?

When I was a young Catholic girl I had to go to confession twice a year, and in the 1980s my church decided to forgo the kneeling behind a screen anonymously talking to the priest for a FACE-TO-FACE confession. It's like therapy without a comfortable couch or prescriptions. I don't like face-to-face. I don't even like open-faced sandwiches.

I reluctantly knocked on the building superintendent's door the next day. I brought her muffins because it seemed like something that nice, well-adjusted people do. She explained to me that Billy spends his days in her office talking nonstop and offering her free tickets to comedy shows too. I'm not a fan of "it happens to me too" as a solution for a problem. I told her that that sounds horrifying, and might I add at least she gets to leave work at the end of the day. This man LIVES down the hall from where I LIVE. She explained that he's harmless.

I explained to her that I'm not afraid he'll murder me. I'm afraid he'll talk to me.

She said that he had an accident years ago. He fell into a gravel pit. She claims he was only injured physically and spends most of his days with in-home physical therapists and some medical marijuana. How does one fall into a construction site gravel pit and NOT HAVE IT AFFECT THEIR BRAIN? He totally seems like someone who fell on his head. It made so much sense now. Medical marijuana doesn't make you knock on someone's door all night—hauling some rocks knocking about in your noggin does.

She told me that she would talk to Billy and explain to him that not everyone likes visits from neighbors. I thanked her and when I got back to my apartment I realized that I never put the muffins down in front of her. I kept them in my lap and absentmindedly brought them back to my apartment. I'm a monster.

Two days later, as I was walking out of my door Billy opened his down the hall. He said, "I have to talk to you, Jennifer." He was angry and his phlegm was boiling inside of his esophagus.

My stomach dropped. Face-to-face.

He said, "Your boyfriend was rude to me the other night. Very rude. And I complained to the building manager about it. You will be getting a warning soon and might have to move."

Suddenly I was just so *over it*. A montage went through my head of the years and years of crazy roommates I had had—from the girl who cried loudly at seven a.m. waking me up like an alarm clock that needs Prozac, to the weird hippie couple who boiled leaves from the city street to make tea, to the cockroach infestation of 2005, to my ex-husband and his many attempts to get me to use a clip-on reading light in bed, to the loud toddler stomping above me. Enough was enough. I was finally going to live free, live alone on my own terms, and I was not going to have any kids smoking pot on my stoop or a construction-site accident victim making me feel uncomfortable.

My eyes focused in and I said, "Billy. That is not true. My boyfriend wasn't rude. [I tried not to sound like I was lying about having a boyfriend.] I was there. I heard him. YOU were rude. You do not need to ring someone's bell late at night. I don't want tickets to a comedy show and I didn't come to this building to make new friends. I came to have some peace and quiet. You can tell the building manager on me all you want. I'm not moving. And you will not be making me uncomfortable in this hallway anymore."

He coughed. "Okay." And went back into his apartment.

I walked down the hall feeling like an adult. I stood up for myself. I set a boundary. I had summoned my inner Angelina Jolie and I didn't even have to get a bunch of painful, tribal, white-woman tattoos to do so. Once I was alone in the elevator heading down, I burst into tears. There's no hard-and-fast rule about the face of bravery. Those tears didn't mean that deep down I'm not someone who can handle "face-to-face" combat. They just meant that standing up for oneself is a nuanced process and I would be inhuman to not shed a tear for someone who once fell headfirst into a gravel pit. Maybe I would leave those muffins at *his* door.

13

YOU CAN PICK YOUR FRIENDS, BUT YOU CAN'T PICK YOUR FRIENDS' NOSES. ALTHOUGH SOMETIMES YOU CAN HAVE SEX WITH THEM.

Rare as is true love, true friendship is rarer.

—JEAN DE LA FONTAINE

I disagree with the basic premise of many romantic comedies that presuppose that a man and woman cannot add sex to their friendship without complication or falling in love. In most movies, hearts either get broken or the friends-turned-lovers come together in a big scene on a significant historical bridge or on the viewing deck of the Empire State Building. It's always somewhere involving heights where these souls decide to spend the rest of their lives together. I blame the thin air and altitude for casual lovers and close friends coming to the conclusion that just because they've slept together it means there has to be pain, consequences, and eventually marriage and a baby carriage. I think, no, I *know* that having a Friend With Benefits *can* work out. And by work out, I don't mean it leads to taking an elevator to the top of a 102-story skyscraper and exchanging "I love you"s. I just mean, as the Rolling Stones told us, ". . . if you try sometimes, you just might find, you get what you need."

My therapist says that a Friendship With Benefits situation is taking a huge sanity risk by having sex with a man who is emotionally unavailable for a traditional relationship. This is due to the production of a chemical called oxytocin that makes women bond with every man they sleep with whether they like it or not. But I know that there are women out there who have been in a place in their lives where they too are emotionally unavailable for a "real" relationship (ahem) and I'm a strong advocate for a Friend With Benefits seeing us through.

I don't believe in stereotypical gender norms that men can "just have sex" and women can't. I also don't believe that sex without a relationship is "just sex" either. And I don't believe in oxytocin. I mean, I believe that oxytocin is *real*. I know it's not Santa Claus. I obviously don't doubt that it's a hormone that actually exists, but either the science of how oxytocin works is partial bullshit or some women are just outside of the chemical equation.

I've done some research on oxytocin—the key word here is "some," but here's what we've got. **Oxytocin** (/ˌɒksɪˈtoʊsɪn/; **Oxt**) is a mammalian neurohypophysial hormone.

What?

I'll say it in laywoman's terms. Oxytocin plays an important role in sexual reproduction (both sexes) but in particular during and after childbirth. It's released in large amounts after the distension of the cervix and uterus during labor and after stimulation (no, not kissing—lactating). Okay. So far, this hormone doesn't apply to me. I'm barren by choice.

But recent studies show that oxytocin plays a role in various behaviors like orgasm and social recognition. It's sometimes referred to as the "bonding hormone."

I have another hormone called "common sense." If I'm with a man—even if the sex rocks my world and I feel like snuggling with him afterward—if I know that he's the wrong guy for me due to our different lifestyles, values, and the simple fact that I don't think he would be a good boyfriend, I do not get attached. Something in my DNA—call it my commonsenseytocin—just naturally kicks in and I can get out of bed and make it to my morning Pilates class without an urge to cancel. In fact, I think that the men and women we *should* have a Friends With Benefits situation with are the ones who *don't* provide us with a sense of security. Safety, yes. I'm not saying sleep with a runaway convict. (Although it seems to have worked out pretty well for Kate Winslet in the movie *Labor Day*.)

If I know that my FWB is someone I would not want to "pair-bond" with romantically, then it's easy to see it as just sex because I've already decided that it can't be more. If you're sleeping with a good guy who thinks you're girlfriend material but just doesn't want a girlfriend you better make sure that you really don't want him as a boyfriend either or else you'll get crushed. You'll feel constant dread and anxiety wondering why he isn't falling in love. This will only serve to make you feel unlovable. If you're truly thinking (and not in a defensive way), *I don't want to be your girlfriend either*, then it's the perfect non-relationship.

Sure, there have been exceptions, moments I've lost my mind for someone only to feel perplexed a few weeks later with *What was I thinking?* I've had dalliances with acquaintances, knowing they were emotionally unavailable. I can admit that in those cases the oxytocin was probably flowing through me like hot lava through a volcano about to explode but, full disclosure, I had feelings I wasn't admitting to at the time, hoping the guy might magically change his mind.

Popular romantic comedies do not help support my campaign for the acceptance of Friends With Benefits. Every movie seems to start with two friends, let's call them Guy and Girl, who go on depressing dates with other people who don't understand their jokes. Then Guy and Girl meet up for breakfast and commiserate about their awful love lives. Guy is a player who says crass things about his date like, "Her boobs weren't big enough and she wanted to get married." Girl disapproves of this dirty playboy platonic friend of hers but feels she's really learning about the male psyche through her brutally honest friend. Guy, despite his penchant for big-boobed, emotionless girls will say something sweet to Girl that lets the audience empathize with him while they yell at the screen, "You two should sleep together! Even though he seems emotionally stunted he's perfect for you to marry because he's sitting right there!"

Someone must be putting oxytocin in the movie theater popcorn because moviegoing audiences aren't happy until Guy and Girl end up together, even though it's clear they really don't have much in common. They have a good rapport and enjoy eating together, but even though Girl didn't respect Guy during the first half hour, suddenly that doesn't matter. They have sex and now they realize that they always loved each other . . . and that's the reward that everyone wants. Monogamy.

Why do Friends With Benefits who remain just Friends With Benefits make some people so uncomfortable? It calls into question the one thing that separates a marriage from a friendship—sex. And if other people have figured out how to have the sex, friendship, and freedom, maybe married people simply don't want to know. Married people will explain that their marriage is more than just fornication—bragging about how they have intimacy without being intimate that often, as though there's maturity involved with not having much sex. Do you ever get the feeling that to your married friends you're some character in a video game who is jumping but just can't reach that next level of enlightenment? We know that when they first met the sex was what made them giddy about each other. Nobody meets someone and proclaims, "I'm so turned on that I'm going to show up at his house in flannel pajamas and we're going to sit on the couch and not have sex, but have *true* intimacy by eating pizza!"

I'm sick of hearing that something is going to go wrong if you have a fuck buddy. Okay. Something *might* go wrong. So what? Something might go wrong in *any* relationship. That's life. Look at life itself. Life itself "goes wrong" because each and every one of our lives ends in death. I'd say that's pretty much the definition of *something went wrong*. Yet we still get out of bed every day. Maybe one of my girlfriends will suddenly start acting like a scheming liar. I'm not going to not have friends for fear that it might *go wrong*. So goes the same for a fuck buddy. Who else are we supposed to have sex with until we meet someone who is relationship-appropriate? Strangers? And don't tell me that the Universe will provide us with the perfect partner once we clear all extraneous men and women out of our lives. I promise your next great love will find you, even if your fuck buddy is in your apartment once a week.

I had a successful Friendship With On-Again/Off-Again Benefits for almost twenty years with a male friend who I'll call "Gypsy." I'm calling him this because though he and his grandparents are all California natives, he's always talking about how his ancestry is made up of Jewish Gypsies of a nonspecific Eastern European area. And he's also somewhat of a gypsy in the Stevie Nicks sense. He's a true artist, whether he's painting a watercolor interpretation of his dreams, playing multiple instruments on tour with a band, or using the Internet not to watch porn but for researching the best places to live in the world if you want to have access to a full-time shaman.

I've never fallen in love with this man and he hasn't fallen in love with me. We know that we aren't "the one" or even "a one" for each other but it works because we can ignore each other for weeks, sometimes months, and nobody gets offended. We've never been at a loss for words around each other and we keep no secrets. I could tell Gypsy anything and he would never judge me. He would laugh and tell me something even worse about himself. We have an intimate friendship but neither of us wants the other to become their domesticated mate. I never want to live with Gypsy and come home to him burning spaghetti and asking me, "How was your day, honey?" Truthfully, having lived that scenario with a few men—even men I've *loved, loved, loved*—I found that level of togetherness to be overwhelming. I like people asking how my day was—just not the second that I walk in the front door. I'm easily overwhelmed if I don't have a few minutes alone every day. If I come home to too much mail waiting I can lose my patience and yell, "Just wait a goddamn minute, please. Stop pushing yourself on me, you envelope! I'll open you after I've taken off my shoes and cleared my head."

During the years that I was married, Gypsy and I simply had platonic lunches together, not those hedonistic sex party lunches that you've heard go on all over Los Angeles. When Gypsy had a hot Hot Yoga–teaching girlfriend he refrained from sex with me as well as from eating, opting only to drink the Master Cleanse for a month. When we were both single at the same time we were there for each other during bouts of loneliness and horniness. When we occasionally lost touch there was no teary good-bye or break up. And *that* is the benefit of being friends. We just knew that we'd see each other around. Our Friendship With Benefits arrangement took much care, respect, communication, and acceptance from the hot-and-heavy beginning through to the platonic conclusion. In a lot of ways it was like a marriage without the whole "I have to talk to his mom" or "throw his dirty underwear into my load of whites" expectations.

Right now our switch is set to off and we just text each other about our failed romances. There's nothing better than a male pal telling you that he hates all men on your behalf. Although Gypsy isn't someone I would put on my Christmas cards—"Happy Holidays from Jen and The Fuck Buddy"—he's been one of the most special men in my life. Gypsy and I are both in Los Angeles now but our origin stories take place in Boston and New York City.

GYPSIES, TRAMPS, AND THIEVES (OR HOW I CAME TO HAVE A FUCK BUDDY, IN TWO PARTS)

PART 1: BECOMING BUDDIES FIRST

I hope you make a lot of nice friends out there. But just remember there's a lot of bad and beware.

—Cat Stevens

When I was twenty-one, the love of my life (so far) Blake dumped me. I of course took it really well and waited a whole three hours before I knocked on the front door of his apartment with a plan to explain to him that although I respect his freedom of speech and really found his opinion on "not loving me anymore" fascinating—he was wrong. Luckily for Blake, he wasn't home. His roommate, my friend, who you know as Gypsy, opened the door. I was mortified. I didn't care if *Blake* thought I was desperate and psycho. I couldn't have our *friends* think I was too. What I didn't know was that this was the beginning of a twenty-year close friendship and occasional benefit-ship with Gypsy—someone I never thought about *in that way.*

Gypsy said, "Come in. Come in. You need a cigarette and some tea."

"You don't think I seem crazy?"

"No, Kirkman. I think you seem sad."

Gypsy poured water into a frying pan, which is the closest thing to a teakettle that an apartment occupied by two twenty-year-old guys has. He carefully poured it into a mug. He looked around. "Shit. We're actually out of tea. How about some whiskey?"

I sipped my whiskey and hot water in the living room. Gypsy stretched out in a beat-up La-Z-Boy and I sat on a neighboring papasan chair.

"What if Blake comes back? He'll hate that I'm here."

"You're my friend too and you're my guest now."

Gypsy grew up in Beverly Hills. He had a 1970s style that didn't seem costumey. He would simply not look right in a T-shirt and jeans. He was made for bell-bottoms and floppy hats. Gypsy lit up a Camel Light and told me that he just had a breakup as well. His girlfriend, the hippie painter, had dumped him. I found this so hard to believe. In my mind they were the perfect couple. I sometimes heard them having sex and it always sounded so intimate and whispery. I thought they had figured out the meaning of life and were just keeping it secret.

I asked Gypsy what happened. He said he couldn't explain it to me but Joni Mitchell could. He took out the record *Blue* and put the needle on "A Case of You." Joni sang, *"I am a lonely painter. I live in a box of paints. I'm frightened by the devil. And I'm drawn to those ones that ain't afraid."*

"Oh," I said while nodding and pretending to get it.

"Your breakup is more of a Cat Stevens song," Gypsy said thoughtfully. After "A Case of You" was over, he pulled *Tea for the Tillerman* out of its sleeve and let Cat Stevens sing "Wild World" for me. *"You say you wanna start something new. And it's breakin' my heart you're leavin'. Baby, I'm grievin'."*

I couldn't believe it, but just a few stanzas into that song and I was feeling better. It was so thoughtful of my friend to find me the perfect breakup tune. Gypsy and I sat in silence as "Wild World" ended and "Sad Lisa" began.

ROMANTIC COMEDY MOVIE VERSION OF HOW THAT DAY ENDED:

Gypsy comes over to me and takes my hand, leading me to stand up. We slow dance. I catch a whiff of his musk and realize that it's always been Gypsy whom I love. Blake comes home. "Gypsy, what the hell are you doing?" Gypsy says, "I'm doing what you could never do for her. I'm appreciating her."

Blake comes closer. "You throw yourself at my roommate in *my* apartment, Jen?" Gypsy says, "This is *our* apartment. Not yours. In fact, your name isn't on the lease. Technically this is my *dad's* apartment." Blake angrily tries to throw a punch but trips over the warped corner of the Oriental rug. He's humiliated. Gypsy says, "Just go. Unless you want to stay and continue making a fool of yourself." After Blake leaves, Gypsy takes the needle off the vinyl and changes the record out. "Don't look," he tells me. "I have a surprise song for you. Listen to the lyrics." I wait in suspense until I hear Stevie Wonder's "I Believe (When I Fall in Love It Will Be Forever)." Gypsy takes my face in his hands and says, "I believe." We kiss. Roll credits.

REAL-LIFE VERSION OF HOW THAT DAY ENDED:

After a few more songs, my fear of Blake coming home outweighed my confidence that I belonged. I drove my dad's Oldsmobile Cutlass back to my parents' house, crying hysterically when "Angie" by the Rolling Stones came on the classic rock radio station. I didn't see Gypsy again for two years.

PART 2: NEGOTIATING THE BENEFITS (OR HOW WE CAREFULLY ADDED SEX TO A FRIENDSHIP)

She was pleased to have him come and never sorry to see him go.
—Dorothy Parker

In 1999 the Internet was on the verge of becoming more important to us than Sony Discmans or dual cassette player stereos. Us twentysomethings referred to it as AOL because mostly that's all those giant typewriters with screens were to us—ways to send e-mail through America Online. Even then e-mail was used sparingly—something you drunkenly composed and sent when you knew it was too late to call a friend but wanted to let her know about this amazing night you'd had. There wasn't Wi-Fi back then, so if you were on the Internet you had to be at home connected to a modem that made loud screeching noises like your computer was in heat as it took a good five minutes to connect to the web. That's where the notion that everyone online is just some creep in his or her mother's basement comes from. You actually had to be in a basement because it was the best place to keep that unsightly equipment and muffle the sound. With the invention of laptops, now you can be a creep in broad daylight at a coffee shop.

I was suspicious about the Internet before I started using it myself. I looked skeptically at Brian—the guy in college who always wore the extra-long striped Doctor Who scarf even in warm weather. He was constantly at the library (so was I but I worked there) using the one computer and typing away sending e-mails. I used to stare at him and whisper to my friend Liz who shared checkout desk duty with me, "Look at him. He's *writing* to his friends? What a weirdo. Why doesn't he just pick up the phone and talk to someone? What kind of sociopath doesn't want to talk on the phone?" Today, I only want people to call me if somebody died—even then I imagine it's way easier to just text me the time/place of the funeral and I'll write back "K." Followed by a sad face emoticon, of course.

I was also a bit suspicious about this sudden new technology. "I bet the government reads our e-mails." Now that we've found out that the NSA *does* read our e-mails, people posit, "Well, they're only scanning them for terrorist buzzwords. It's not like hired hands are sitting in offices reading our private exchanges." I disagree. Of COURSE they are reading our private exchanges. Do you really think some low-paid hired hand sitting in the basement of the Pentagon is using his access to your Gmail to hunt for words like "terror plot" instead of words like "I don't usually send pictures of my pussy but . . ."

So it was definitely out of character that in 1999 I landed a job working for an Internet start-up company in New York City. The company was called Funkytalk.com and the goal was to be one of the first "reality TV shows" on the Internet. I was being paid to travel America, blog about my experiences, and perform wacky pranks on camera. No website had successfully integrated video before and lots of bandwidth or whatever it is that makes it all work didn't really exist in giant quantities yet. Nobody watched videos on their computers. When the funding fell through to keep videos alive on Funkytalk.com, the once-ambitious multimedia website just turned into a webzine.

I was assigned to write a romantic relationship he said/she said advice column with my male office mate Austin. We were forced to make up the questions ourselves because we apparently had zero readership. Our higher-ups were obsessed with the notion of a grassroots campaign to get young people interested in coming to our website. A few write-ups about Funkytalk.com in *Time* magazine and the *Wall Street Journal* weren't turning into web "hits." I was assigned to spend my days on Internet message boards trying to make natural online conversation with people about Funkytalk.com. Nowadays people can smell that kind of thing a mile away. "Hey, guys! I'm new here so I'm just wondering what you all think about energy-saving lightbulbs? There's a great new company that's on the verge of saving the world with their bulbs made from cow dung. Anyway, LOL! What are you kids up to? I'm young too!"

I trolled one particular message board where people used to go to hook up and I not so casually dropped that there was this great sex advice column they should check out! I got a reply from a guy who nicknamed himself "Sid Kindness," a take on the Sex Pistols' famed heroin addict bassist, Sid Vicious, who killed his girlfriend Nancy Spungen in New York City's Chelsea Hotel. "Sid" wrote on the message boards that he would check out my column and signed off, "Cheers, love."

My advice column had my work e-mail address at the end of it so that people could write in. Within an hour I had an e-mail from Sid himself waiting in my in-box. He had written me a long correspondence saying that he has difficulty with meeting girls. He asked me all about myself; quality questions such as, "Where did you grow up?" and "How long have you been a writer?" and not creepy inquiries like, "How big are your boobs? May I nickname them?"

I had just broken up with my boyfriend Patrick and was happy to be getting male attention. Patrick and I had dated for a year but the communication in our relationship started to get rocky when I told him that I was leaving to go on a four-month adventure across America with Funkytalk, and wasn't able to temper my excitement with the slightest, "But I'll miss *you*." I jumped to conclusions and took Patrick's sadness at my leaving as him trying to "hold me back." I hastily broke things off by asking him to go for a walk in Brooklyn's Prospect Park where I just said, "We have to break up," and then ran off. Like, literally ran away as though it were a game of tag.

Nowadays, Patrick and I are great friends. I'm grateful that he forgave me for my terrible lack of breakup etiquette and I forgave him for rebounding with a woman who at the time was my sworn enemy. We share in common a divorce (not the same one, obviously), and we're both fiercely independent comedy writers who would rather work late than change diapers.

Sid wrote that he thought I was pretty (my picture accompanied the column) and that he didn't have a picture of himself that he liked enough to send but promised me that he looked just like the lead singer of Blur. I wasn't that familiar with Blur, and the Internet being what it was in 1999, I had a hard time finding a picture of the lead singer. I had to have a friend describe him to me. It turns out that there are *two* singers in Blur, Graham Coxon and Damon Albarn, and I wasn't sure which one Sid looked like. I was hoping for Damon and instead of asking Sid *which* lead singer of Blur he resembled I just fantasized that of course it was the cuter one.

I wrote back and told Sid all about myself. I hit Send and since I had no idea how to check my work e-mail from home I found myself going to bed earlier so that the next morning would come faster so that I could get to work and see if Sid had written back. He wrote back! He gave me his phone number and asked for mine. Later that night I got a call on my landline. I picked it up and heard "Alloisjentheyyah?"

"What? Who is this? I can't understand what you're saying."

"Alloisjentheyyah?"

Having never traveled abroad at that point in my life I had only heard the prim-and-proper, crisp British accents in movies. I'd never heard a regional UK accent before. It didn't even sound like the English language. I was confused. It took me a minute to realize that this was most likely Sid calling. He sounded like he had a swollen tongue and was just mastering language in general.

I hung up the phone. I was actually scared of an accent.

He called back. I let the machine pick up and record whatever the hell it was he was saying. *Beeeeep.* "Alloisjentheyyah?" The next day at work I wrote back to him that I thought my phone had a bad connection. He e-mailed that he wanted to come to New York City to visit me and it would be better to talk face-to-face anyway. I told him about how I lived in a two-and-a-half-room apartment in Brooklyn with a roommate and her friend. Sid wrote back, "Your flat sounds a little cramped!" I've always found it maddeningly adorable when people who use different slang from us Americans respond back with their word ("flat") for what I just said ("apartment"). Sid offered, "I'm going to get a room at the Chelsea Hotel. I've always loved the history of that place. You can come and visit me there?"

My office mate and advice column partner, Austin, caught wind of what I was using my work computer for most of the day. He was concerned. "You're having a romance with someone you've never met? That's creepy."

"I'm sorry if I'm on the forefront of technology. I used to think that e-mail was creepy. And now look at me. I'm able to fall in love with someone from England without having to fly there."

"Jen. It's creepy. And you're not in love."

Sid signed off of that day's e-mail exchange with, "I'm going to look into flights. I think I want to stay at the Chelsea Hotel! You should meet me there for a 'drink.'"

I logged off. I felt uneasy once he took it this far (and mentioned the Chelsea Hotel.) Twentysomething me wanted a long-distance British boyfriend who looked like one of the (again, hopefully the cute one) lead singers of Blur, but I kind of wanted to meet him, you know, in London. Not online.

At this point I hadn't seen Gypsy in almost two years. I was now living in Brooklyn on the corner of Prospect Park West and Eighteenth Street. He'd been living on Seventh Avenue not even a mile away. We had been neighbors for six months and had no idea until one Sunday afternoon my cell phone rang. I don't even think we were up to the technology of flip phones yet and texting was as sophisticated as spelling out a word on a push-button phone. Gypsy couldn't have used

Facebook at that time to find me because Mark Zuckerberg hadn't even hit puberty yet.

"Kirkman? Aren't you living somewhere in New York City? It's a Sunday afternoon and I'm in Brooklyn by myself having mimosas at an outdoor café."

"Gypsy! Are you gay now?"

"No. I'm a musician just waiting for my trust fund to fully kick in and the cheapest happy hour drink is cheap champagne and orange juice."

And within ten minutes I was joining Gypsy mid-mimosa. It took me no time to get down there because I didn't have to put on makeup or worry about the right outfit. I didn't have to impress Gypsy. He'd seen me crying with snot running down my face listening to Cat Stevens. On our second drink, Gypsy told me that he still missed the artist girl but she had moved on to someone else. I updated him on my love life from the breakup with Patrick to the e-mail from Sid—my British online wannabe boyfriend.

Gypsy reacted with bold statements like, "He sounds like a serial killer. He loves the history of the Chelsea Hotel and his name is Sid? He's definitely at least interested in murdering *you*. Don't write that guy back ever again. There are tons of guys in New York City who would date you. You don't have to fly in guys from England."

"I wasn't flying him in. Fine. I get your point. It was just so exciting to be liked."

Gypsy invited me to go back to his place to eat ice cream and watch *Fletch*. Then we ordered a pizza and watched more movies. Both of us got up a couple of times each to pee and each time we came back to the couch, we landed an inch closer to the other. We were being very polite and welcoming to two invisible people if they had shown up and wanted to sit on either side of us. I didn't want to leave. I wasn't feeling attracted to Gypsy in that "do me then murder me in the Chelsea Hotel" way but something was keeping me from getting up and calling a cab. I think he felt the same way because after we ran out of movies to watch (this was before Netflix) we watched stupid infomercials as though our lives depended on it.

He wasn't asking me to leave. Maybe he felt bad for me? I

tentatively suggested that maybe I should go. Gypsy suggested that cabdrivers are all on speed at that hour and even though I only lived a mile away I should be careful. I offered that he could let me stay on his couch. He offered that I could stay in his bed. He asked, "That's not weird, right?"

"Not weird at all! You're like my brother! Why would that be weird?"

Maybe it would be weird since grown-up brothers and sisters do not sleep in the same bed? I threw in the "you're like my brother" as extra protection in case Gypsy was asking me to share a bed platonically. I didn't want him to think that *I* thought that *he* thought we were going to have sex or that I wanted to.

We crawled into bed and I made sure that, unlike our seating arrangement on the couch upstairs, I gave him plenty of space and I slept so close to the edge of the bed I had to stay half awake to make sure not to fall out. All of this just to let my friend know using body language that I *did not want to have sex with him even though I was very curious about having sex with him.*

Never underestimate the very old heating system of an apartment in Brooklyn. By five a.m. I had a sunburn and beach hair from my salty sweat. I peeled off my clothes and got back under the covers in just my underwear. I wasn't trying to be sexy or even sexy in a not-trying way. I was way too tired to leave. Shortly after that, I was woken up again, this time by the sun streaming in my face. No guy has ever mastered curtains that actually block sun out of their windows. Maybe they design it that way to annoy their one-night stands into getting up and leaving right away.

Gypsy woke up. I pretended to be asleep. What was I waiting for exactly? Did I really think he was going to roll over and say, "We should have sex"? Morning is the worst time to brew up anything but coffee. He got up and I heard him brush his teeth in the bathroom. I couldn't decide if he was brushing his teeth because he anticipated kissing me or if he was just trying to start his day. If it was the latter, I was as good to him in that bed as a dead hooker is to a politician.

The bathroom door opened and then Gypsy was back under the covers. He gently tapped my ear. "Kirkman, you're naked." I had sort of forgotten that detail. "Kirkman, don't you think we should have sex?" The calling me by my last name was throwing me off. I felt like we should be tossing a football around.

"Really? I never thought about it."

"I thought of it when the sun was setting and we were walking and your eyes looked pretty."

"REALLY?"

"Yes. And if this convinces you to not meet up with someone from England who is going to chop you up into little pieces—even better."

This is where Gypsy laid out what would become the blueprint for our sex life.

"It won't change anything. What's good about this is we are friends. Just friends. I know you think I'm too flighty to have as a boyfriend. I'm bad at commitment anyway. I like you too much to put you through my issues. It's perfect. We will never fall in love. We can have sex and now that's another tool in our toolbox. We can use that tool when we want or we don't have to but we know it's there."

"So we stay just friends but have sex when we want?"

"Yeah. And we stop when one of us gets a boyfriend or girlfriend."

He didn't invent the concept of Friends With Benefits but it was truly new to me. I stared at the ceiling. One of us was going to have to make the first move. "Okay. You start," I said. And he kissed me. A million neurons fired as the molecules of our relationship changed forever. I was ambivalent about the kiss. His beard bothered me, but he knew just where to touch me as though he'd been born with the manual for my engine. Once the sex started there was a humor to it at first—catching each other's glance and laughing at the fact that it is so bizarre to see your friend have an orgasm. Then we had sex again except this time there was no laughing.

"Kirkman. I had no idea we had it in us."

"Can you not call me Kirkman? I mean, weirdly now that you've been inside of me you would think we would be less formal but I feel like I'm supposed to high-five you back when you do that."

He held my temples with his hands and gently tapped his finger on my forehead. "There's a lot going on up there, Kirkman. Shit. Sorry. I mean Jen." There was affection and an acceptance between us. I walked home down Seventh Avenue, not doing a walk of shame but a swagger of pride. This really nice friend of mine thought I was sexy. I don't have to be on the Internet trolling for love from a guy who definitely did not look like anyone from Blur and probably didn't even look like the cousin of a roadie for Blur.

Gypsy called me that night and invited me to go bowling with a group of his friends. Admittedly, I felt a little disappointed. Bowling on a Saturday night? If we're bowling, we can't be making out. I mean, at least not simultaneously. I felt a little bit angry. What had changed in twenty-four hours? Did he not want to sleep together anymore? I started to feel resentment. Resentment can do only two things—stay chilled in the refrigerator until you throw it away, or you can pour alcohol over it until it reheats itself into a fury that is too hot to hold on to and therefore the only choice is to unleash it—in public at a bowling alley.

Gypsy wasn't giving me any special attention at bowling. No wink. No hand on my knee. He was acting like my platonic friend, cheering with every spare I threw. With every gutterball he threw, I cheered, doing a little "in your face" dance to only him even though we were on the same team. He took me aside for a minute alone to ask me, "Are you okay? You're being really aggressive toward me." I took that as some kind of antifeminist statement. My resentment spouted. "Sorry I'm not some quiet hippie chick who finger-paints in the park!" (Now that I think of it, I'm *still* really sorry that I'm not some hippie chick who finger-paints in the park. That sounds relaxing.) Gypsy looked at me like he was a priest struggling to get into the mind of a possessed child before performing an exorcism. Where had Kirkman/Jen gone? Why was she talking in a deep growling voice and projectile-vomiting insults?

The next morning I felt like a piñata after a kid's birthday party. I was empty and confused as to why I was on the front lawn—aka alone in my own bed. How had I killed my Friends With Benefits situation so quickly? And now I was left to call him and have one of my famous confrontations in Prospect Park.

I asked Gypsy to meet me for coffee. I wanted him to call it off to my face. I wasn't going to let him get away with that thing that guys do where they just act like nothing ever happened and us girls go completely mental wondering what we did. This was on *him*. We walked through Prospect Park with our to-go cups and I told Gypsy that I didn't understand what the whole bowling thing was about. He explained that the bowling thing was about going bowling because he knew I liked bowling and so he invited me along. God, guys can be so simple. Gypsy was confused that I had taken an invite to go bowling as a rejection. He meant it to be inclusive and he hoped we would go home together and have sex after. He said if I had suggested it, he would have skipped the bowling altogether to have more getting-to-know-each-other sex.

I would advise anyone embarking on a Friendship With Benefits to not do what I did. It's not oxytocin—it's ego that takes over when you do the most intimate thing you can do with a person and then decide that it would be improper to try to also communicate feelings to that person. I should have just said to Gypsy, "Bowling? What about boning?" But instead I had to act cool and when I was about to crack from the pressure that I'd put on everything, I watched my dignity go down the gutter. Because neither of us said anything—I had no idea that Gypsy wanted to have sex again and he had no idea that I didn't feel that I could initiate sex again because I feared looking needy. A great tip for anyone who actually wants to look needy—try to not look needy and you'll achieve your desired effect.

We talked about our feelings. We worked it out. We promised never to hold anything in again, to strive to be fully honest, and to keep checking the temperature of our Friendship With Benefits to make sure that each of us was still benefiting and our friendship had the perfect amount of space to flourish.

ROMANTIC COMEDY MOVIE VERSION OF HOW THAT WEEKEND ENDED:

I get up out of bed and trip on his mesh laundry basket—embarrassed that Gypsy saw me. I say something like, "Well at least you put out a net." I get up to leave and go home. He grabs me and spins me around to face him. "I don't want a pop-up laundry hamper to catch you. I should be there to catch you. Every time. I love you and I'm ready to jump right in. Forget this Friends With Benefits stuff. You're the one, Jen. You're the one I want and I'm not going to treat you like a white shirt that I separate from the pile. I want you to mix into my life."

REAL-LIFE VERSION OF HOW THAT WEEKEND ENDED:

I walked around with Gypsy in the park. I knew in my gut that he wasn't what I wanted for a long-term boyfriend but I wouldn't mind another go around. I went back to his place and didn't leave until the next morning. I got back to work and deleted the e-mail in my in-box from confused Sid wondering why his Nancy wasn't getting back to him.

14

DOCTORS WITHOUT BOUNDARIES

The most exquisite pleasure in the practice of medicine comes from nudging a layman in the direction of terror, then bringing him back to safety again.

—KURT VONNEGUT

I mean, some doctor told me I had six months to live and I went to their funeral.

—KEITH RICHARDS

I never thought I would have a story about my primary care physician/gynecologist in Woodland Hills, California, Dr. Beverly. I only see her annually for my Pap smear, blood tests, and so she can hit my knee with the little rubber hammer. Nothing was different when I went for my first post-divorce checkup. My insurance was the same. I had the same old allergy to penicillin, the same old mild asthma, and the same old disdain for the way parents allow their children to completely take over the waiting room.

The receptionist, Dina, asked me if there were any changes to make in my file. Temporarily forgetting that marital status is a thing that needs to be indicated on a patient's record, I said no. She ran down the list just to make sure.

"Phone number still . . . ?"

Yes.

"Address is still . . . ?"

Yes.

"Still married?"

No.

She looked up at me in shock and whispered, "I'm so sorry." People in the waiting room looked up. The best way to get everyone's attention in public is to whisper. They were probably wondering why the receptionist was giving me the news in front of everybody and the fish tank that I was dying. I whispered back, "It's okay. It's just a divorce. And it's not a secret." In a regular voice I asked if she could just cross that "M" out and circle the "D." Dina fumbled with my paperwork and said, "No. No. I need to fill out a whole new sheet for you. Your husband was your emergency contact." I was tempted to keep him as my emergency contact. If they ever found a lump in my breast they could call him. "Your wife has cancer." "I don't have a wife." "Well, somebody here has cancer. We thought you should know."

I understand why doctors and dentists need our address (to send us bills and reminders to actually pay those bills). I understand why they need our social security number (to send our information on to the collection agency when we forget to actually pay those bills). What I'll never understand is why they need to know if we are divorced, married, or single. And why are those three statuses even considered the same category? Marriage is a legal contract. Divorce just means that the legal contract no longer means squat. "Single" is a big tent word. Under this tent you've got your sluts, speed daters, people in committed monogamous relationships, people looking for love, people who have stopped looking for love, celibate monks, even noncelibate monks. Single is not a type of relationship. Single is a type of person. It's fluid and can change in an instant. And sometimes exchanging fluids is involved.

Does the treatment differ depending on your relationship status? If I had Ebola would they just let me bleed out of my eyes in a corner? "She has Divorced Ebola. We don't need to begin treatment right away. Take care of the Married Ebola cases first! They have someone to live for!"

I labored over whom to put as my new emergency contact. My entire family lives in Massachusetts, so if I get some horrible flesh-eating virus none of them could bring me clean underwear for at least twelve hours. My friends with kids can't come and get me without losing valuable time futzing with a child's car seat, plus those kids have germs. I figured the only time I would be in my doctor's office is Monday through Friday during business hours so I put my manager Kara. She's been my comedy manager and friend for more than eight years and I know that she answers her phone. If she doesn't, her assistant will. And she has an interest in coming to help save my life because she gets 10 percent of the rest of my life and she's got big show business dreams for me. This choice confused Dina the receptionist. "And Kara is . . . your spouse?"

"*No.* We're not *married.*"

"I'm not judging."

"That's my manager."

"Okay, I don't have . . ." she hesitated, "*manager* as a drop-down option for emergency contact. I have . . . other?"

"Sure. Put other. I'm sure we won't ever need this anyway."

"And you can always change this if something *changes* with . . . Kara."

"Yes. If I get a new comedy manager, you will be the first people I call."

"Again, I'm not judging."

"What are you getting at? Even though I said ten times that Kara is my manager you still think that Kara is my lover, don't you? Do you think her feminine wiles caused my divorce or do you see me more as the one who had an awakening and left my husband?" I knew I shouldn't have worn a Ramones T-shirt to a doctor's visit. I looked like a post-punk lesbian, which is fine. Dina wasn't judging.

I sat in the waiting room looking at the sign that said ABSOLUTELY NO CELL PHONE USE. BE RESPECTFUL OF OTHERS. I glared at the toddler playing a toy piano loudly. This kid's penchant for hitting the C key over and over and over is somehow considered within the definition of respect for others?

Once in the exam room, my doctor was feeling my divorced boobs. "And you're doing breast exams in the shower every month?"

"Yes," I lied.

My doctor went down her checklist. "Smoker? Did you ever smoke?"

"I haven't smoked since I quit when I was twenty-seven," I lied. She didn't need to know that I had spent the last six months of my marriage having two cigarettes for dessert.

"Anything else you wanted to ask me about today?"

"Um, yeah. Can we throw in some STD tests?"

Dr. Beverly cocked her eyebrow. "Are you at risk for something?"

"No. I figured it would be nice to get a piece of paper that says I don't have any diseases in case a new partner asks."

"How many partners do you have?"

"Well, I mean, no it's not like that. I mean, I have a friend with benefits. But I plan on having a relationship and, um, if I meet someone I would love to show them, since, um, they don't know me very well, that I don't have anything. Because I don't have anything."

I swear I saw a look of disappointment. She said that she was sorry for my divorce and that my grief shouldn't cause me to act out and engage in risky behavior. I explained to her that I hadn't done anything risky. I did not sleep with anyone who had a disease. I did not have any diseases. I just wanted it documented. In the single world, that piece of paper that proves you don't have herpes is like a college degree because a lot of times people won't let you in without one.

I flashed back to when my ex-husband and I were just embarking on becoming boyfriend/girlfriend. We both decided to get STD tests and show each other our results before we slept together. I remember discussing this with that very same doctor. She had asked, "Do you want to get married?" A silly question to ask a thirty-year-old who had only been dating someone for a couple of weeks, but I thought I was all grown up back then and I said, "Yes. I think I'm going to marry him someday." Now that I admitted to two partners since my split she was looking at me like SHE needed to get tested just from being around me.

A few days later I received a terrifying e-mail. No, not a Paperless Post invite to a shower for someone's second baby but an e-mail from my doctor's office with the heading: "ABNORMAL RESULTS FOUND." The body of the e-mail included a PDF file showing check marks in every negative box, HPV, Herpes, HIV (yoo-hoo, fellas!), but one marked ABNORMAL. Hepatitis C. I had hep C? I was dizzy. I immediately began to google hep C. The only two people I'd ever heard of that allegedly had hep C are Pamela Anderson and Tommy Lee. They didn't even get it from making that sex tape. Pamela claims that she got it from sharing a dirty needle with Tommy at a tattoo parlor. I've never even been NEAR a needle except to take this stupid blood test. Other things came up in my Google search for hep C, like how unhealthy nail salons can be. I thought that if I did have hep C no one would ever believe that I'm not some dirty whore but instead I got some dirty pedicure. I thought of the two guys I had been with since my divorce. They most certainly did *not* have hep C. They probably didn't even have *vitamin* C in their bloodstream. They weren't even hep dudes in the 1960s "cool cat" sense of the word. How did I potentially have this? Was I born with it? My friend Sarah tried to put my mind at ease by reminding me, "I've been much sluttier than you and I've never had hep C. If I don't have it, you don't have it." My friend Sharon soothed me, "Some asshole I dated cheated on me with a porn star. If I don't have it, you don't have it."

Back in the waiting room at my doctor's office I used my cell phone even though it was frowned upon. If preschoolers could bang on that damn out-of-tune toy piano then I could continue to research hep C. I finally found a message board discussion group where worried people shared their stories of hep C false positives—people who test positive who in no way have or carry the disease. According to experts, antibodies that the immune system has produced to combat infections other than hep C can be what's known as "cross-reactive": the initial test winds up picking up on these antibodies' presence and can incorrectly come up positive. What really determines whether one has hep C is what's called an RNA test. I hadn't had an RNA test.

Sitting in my doctor's office, I wondered why I had to be in the paper gown. More humiliation? Did she want easy access so she could yell at my vagina face-to-face?

When she walked in I pounced and told her I read that 50 percent of patients come up with a false positive on the first round of testing. That's why it's recommended that people only get tested if they're in high-risk sexual situations or doing anything involving needles. I don't use needles, not even sewing needles. I have a fake Christmas tree so that I don't even come in contact with pine needles.

The doctor took another vial of blood for the RNA test. She said there were no false negatives or positives with this test. And then she said, "We can determine which treatment is best."

Her statement dumbfounded me. "Why are we talking about treatment when we haven't even handed my blood over to the lab yet?"

"Let's just act as if you do so that we can get in the mind-set of treatment."

Isn't that guilty until proven innocent? Good thing my doctor wasn't a lawyer. She would suck at representing the plaintiff. "Your Honor, although my client shouldn't have to go to jail for the crimes she didn't commit, I still believe her to be a filthy tramp and may I suggest a good old-fashioned stoning as her punishment?" She told me that she would call me personally on Friday morning with the news if I was negative or about to join Pamela Anderson and Tommy Lee as yet another name that comes up in a Google search for people with hep C.

The night before finding out my hep C results, I wasn't able to take my mind off of what that phone call might bring. I did laundry, organized my clothes by color, consolidated lotions in my bathroom, and threw out expired eyeliner just to take my mind off of things. But my mind kept taunting me. *"When you get the official word that you have hep C, Jen, this is how you'll spend every Friday night instead of ever being able to be with a man again!"*

I wanted someone by my side when I got the phone call with the results. I wanted to sleep in someone's bed. I texted Gypsy, who had moved back to Los Angeles earlier that year. He was more than happy to have me over, even with the news that he was being diagnosed with "no chance of having sex with me." We sat and looked through old photographs. He was doing a little organizing himself—scanning pictures so that they could also never be looked at again in digital form. We found a picture of us hanging out in that living room back in Boston where we first bonded over Cat Stevens, Joni Mitchell, and broken hearts. Even if I wasn't potentially suffering from a contagious sexually transmitted disease I knew deep down that I still wouldn't have wanted to have sex with Gypsy that night. Our pheromones had cooled that year. He let me wear his favorite T-shirt and sweatpants that he's had since high school. Every once in a while I would remind him that if I did have hep C, he might have it too. Gypsy was unconvinced that anything was wrong with me but he offered, "If you and I both have hep C we can get married."

"No, Gypsy, it's not a *baby*."

I felt cozy and sort of like what married couples always say they feel like at year twenty. Maybe that hot passion had faded but what was left was a deep familial fondness. The new benefit of being Gypsy's confidante was that we were almost family—a fucked-up family of two who have fucked each other, but still family.

I woke up fully clothed next to Gypsy, my alarm and my phone ringing all at once.

"Hello. This is Jen. Is this Dr. Beverly? What is it? Just tell me!"

"Hello. May I speak with Jennifer, please?"

"Yes. Yes. Yes. This is Jennifer. What. *What?*"

"This is Dr. Beverly. I am calling about your results."

"WHAAAAAT ARE THE RESULTS?"

"Is this a good time to talk?"

"YES. IT IS THE BEST TIME EVER TO TALK. WHAT. WHAT. WHAT?"

"You're negative. You do not have hepatitis C. You are not a carrier of hepatitis C. That first test was a false positive. But if you continue to engage in any high-risk behavior it is important to get tested yearly."

What was it with this biotch? "Doctor, I am not engaging in any high-risk behavior. I don't even watch episodes of *Intervention* where they show junkies using needles! I'm sorry that I didn't stay with the same man until death did us part but I am not going to be shamed because I am a single woman who occasionally has sex!"

I hung up the phone and crawled back into bed. Gypsy said, "We might have the longest-running relationship of anyone we know, though."

"That's true. Our secret is we're not in love and we mostly see other people."

"Jen, maybe it's not *love* love, but I have so much love for you."

"I not *love* love you too." I snuggled up on Gypsy's shoulder so relieved that I wasn't going to have to attend any hep C–themed charity lunches with Pamela Anderson and that my skin wasn't going to turn yellow.

Gypsy and I remain platonic friends. Our FWB dissolved years ago. And I have a new gynecologist, Dr. Karen. I went to her for a second opinion and admittedly to get a little validation that Dr. Beverly was an uptight prude. When I told her the story of my "hep C" scare she rolled her eyes and said that she's treated far too many divorced women who were feeling judged by their former doctor. Dr. Karen isn't a sanctimonious goody-goody but unfortunately she is quite a straight shooter. Once I got my feet up in the stirrups she said, "You know you have some gray pubic hairs, right? I can't pluck them but you might want to."

Well, I don't have an STD but I do have something that *will* ruin my sex life and eventually kill me—AGE.

15

DROPPING THE BALL (OR A GUIDE TO STAYING AT HOME ON NEW YEAR'S EVE WITH DIGNITY)

The only way to spend New Year's Eve is either quietly with friends or in a brothel. Otherwise when the evening ends and people pair off, someone is bound to be left in tears.

—W. H. AUDEN

The best party I've ever been to in my life was on a neighbor's multiacre front lawn. The DJ—clearly enamored of me—put up with my request that he play Eddy Grant's "Electric Avenue" twice in a row. I danced with wild abandon, not even doing clear-cut dance moves. I sang along at the top of my lungs. "We gonna rock down to E-LEC-TRIC AV-E-NUE!" I fell down, tripping on the hem of my long summer maxi dress. I got back up and continued to flail around, not concerned with the grass stain that was making a home in my dress fabric. The fun only ended when the police told the DJ that that was enough. It was almost midnight and Eddy Grant was cut short, "And then we'll take it—" Silence. The friendly policemen said that we could continue the party quietly inside or just . . . go home. I turned to my parents. "Time for bed, Jennifah." I was ten.

We were three doors down at the Clearys' house. It was some kind of summertime party—somewhere in between the Fourth of July and Labor Day. It was the first time that I had ever stayed up past ten p.m. and was allowed to be out with adults. My parents weren't freewheelin' hippies. They were already in their twenties, married with kids, during the whole free love era. It was just one of those things . . . a neighborhood family barbecue turned into . . . well, the kids are having fun and it's nice out and we don't want to leave and I guess it's okay if Jennifah goes to bed late tonight and sleeps it off tomorrow. It's not like she's drinking. I was dead sober, boobless, and boyfriendless. I have never had so much fun at a party since.

I know that the theory that New Year's Eve is just another night, that it doesn't mean anything and is actually the worst night to go out because you have to deal with people who don't usually go out, has been studied, analyzed, and reported on already. But even though most people say that New Year's Eve isn't a big deal these people still allow themselves to be sucked in every year and they end up at parties talking about how they don't really care about being at a party.

When you get home from work some nights and heat up a microwave dinner, eating it anyway even though it's not fully cooked, and sit in front of the TV, do you ever think to yourself, *I bet I'm really missing out on a meaningful party that's going on somewhere right now?* No. You don't. You're so happy to be without pants and wiping melted cheese on your couch instead of using a napkin. But if you did that on New Year's Eve you would set yourself up for scrutiny and pity not only from others but yourself.

I stayed home on New Year's Eve this year and I did it for all of us. You too can spend a holiday alone and it doesn't mean that you're lonely. I even kept a diary of my night so that you can follow along should you choose to opt out of mandatory fun this December 31. As a visionary, I don't mind if my vision is appropriated. This is an empowering how-to guide for the woman who isn't afraid to spend some time with the love of her life—herself.

December 31—4:00 p.m.

I have it all planned out. I will go on a forty-five-minute hike so that I can watch the sun set. (What others might call "walking" through a carved-out trail in the woods that has the occasional incline and dip, people in Los Angeles call "hiking." But I am not, as you may have pictured, wearing Vasque Summit GTX boots or brandishing an aluminum trekking pole.) With an air of superiority over the people of Studio City who were probably taking disco naps to get ready to stay up all night, I think to myself, *This is truly the end of the day, if we are going to go by nature, not midnight as The Man with his clocks and urge to control time would have us believe.* Technically—if we were all farmers—we would be in bed at sundown and up at sunrise. Maybe this is the year that I will be more like a farmer. I live in a condo so I can't quite have crops or chickens but I think I will look into getting a planter for my patio and maybe I can grow my own green beans. That's one less person supporting the industry of green beans being flown in from other areas, sprayed with chemicals for that long-lasting crunch, packaged in plastic, and causing local business and the environment to suffer. Or maybe I will just go to more farmers markets on Sundays. I remind myself that since I am an independent thinker, on what is a night no different from the rest except for the meaning we project onto it, there is no reason to start affirming what kind of agricultural approach I will employ in the New Year.

December 31—4:10 p.m.

I park at the base of the trail. Hmmm. It's already pretty dusky out already. It will most likely be quite dark by the time I finish up the hike and head back to my car. I'm carrying Mace right next to my inhaler in my pocket. There are other people hiking, it's not like I'm going to get attacked by this woman in front of me walking with her delicate, shaking Pomeranian peering out of her backpack. But the New Year's Eve Murderer could be hiding in the woods. That's what he would be known as in the papers after he ends my life, her life, and her little dog's too. Would my Mace really be enough to take him down? A serial killer who hides in the woods would probably have a machete. And what if I accidentally grabbed my inhaler in the throes of terror? He would be caught off guard for a moment but then after catching a whiff of that Albuterol mist he would feel the air flowing freely into his lungs, adrenalized, having even more energy to wield his sharp object and then steal my iPod. On second thought, with these clouds looming it isn't really a sunset kind of night. And that's what this was all about—the ritual of watching the sun disappear as I say good-bye to the year, not that I need to say good-bye to the year because tonight is just another night. I think I'll go home. I'll hike in the morning as a New Year's Day beginning! Or just a beginning of a day—since it's also just another day, right?

December 31—4:30 p.m.

I turn on the Christmas tree and light pine-scented candles because my "O Tannenbaum" is plastic and from a tree farm named Target. I enjoy my cozy holiday environment. Going out would just waste the last socially acceptable night to have decorations up anyway. I make myself some hot apple cider. Well, I pour some cider that I bought from Trader Joe's into a pan on my stove. But I even have cinnamon sticks to plop inside the mug to add a little spice. Who thinks of these things? Me. I'm adorable. There's no need to drink alcohol on New Year's Eve if I'm spending it with myself. That would be awful if I needed booze to enjoy my own company or get myself to open up or be attracted to myself. Besides, if I drink now, I could lose all judgment, keep drinking, and that could lead to drunken texting. I don't feel like telling any platonic male friends that I love them but not in "that way" but well *maybe in that way*. Remember that one night when we got drunk and fooled around—that was fun, right? We could do that again sometime I bet and keep our friendship intact. Why have we never talked about it? Oh, you have a girlfriend now? Oh, cool. Well . . . enjoy your kiss at midnight, you two!

December 31—4:31 p.m.

I settle in on the couch to watch a movie before I decide what to do about dinner. I'm finally using the gigantic shag-rug-like blanket that could fit four people. How many days did I sit at work wishing that I could be on the couch doing this instead? I'm doing it! Fun! Oh shoot. That reminds me. I forgot to clean out my mini-fridge at work before

I left for the two-week vacation. Oh, that's not going to be pleasant to come back to in a few days. I think there's half of a tuna wrap waiting for me.

December 31—4:33 p.m.

My DVD player is making a whirring noise every time I hit Play on the remote and then nothing happens. I immediately wish I had a boyfriend so that he could take a look at it.

December 31—4:34 p.m.

In case you're wondering why I'm using a DVD player like I'm some grandma or something instead of streaming a movie, it's because I'm watching a screener. A screener is what big showbiz types like me call DVDs that we get in the mail during the holidays, just before awards season. My membership to both the Writers Guild and the Screen Actors Guild allow me to get this year's Oscar-nominated films delivered to my door without having to do anything like sit in a movie theater with the unwashed masses who are slurping Diet Coke out of buckets.

December 31—4:37 p.m.

The DVD player is now completely dead. I continue to wish I had a boyfriend so that he could run out real quick and buy a new DVD player and then also some ice cream. No. Frozen yogurt. No. Ice cream. Definitely ice cream.

December 31—4:45 p.m.

My DVD player miraculously starts up again. It whirs like a vacuum cleaner. I *think* vacuum cleaners whir. I have a housekeeper. Don't judge me. I immediately break up with this boyfriend in my mind. He would just take up too much room on the couch and would probably not want to watch a Julia Roberts/Meryl Streep vehicle. I'm so happy that Fake Boyfriend and I are over. Please don't feel badly for me spending New Year's Eve without him. Everything happens for a reason.

December 31—5:00 p.m.

I can't quite get comfortable. I feel like I'm going to throw out a joint in my neck if I lie on a throw pillow. I decide I have earned taking a pillow from my bedroom and bringing it to the couch. In the movies people always sit up straight on the couch eating ice cream and wearing makeup when they watch movies alone. I'm keeping it real. Besides, if I were sick I would have no problem lying on the couch with my bedroom pillow. This is just like being sick—except for the being sick part. And I'm still fully dressed like an adult should be at five o'clock. This is perfectly acceptable.

December 31—5:05 p.m.

My clothes feel too restricting. Jeans don't go with a Tempur-Pedic pillow. It's time for pajamas. What? The sun is fully down. It's fine. Also they're silk and monogrammed. This remains perfectly acceptable.

December 31—6:55 p.m.

Huh? What happened? What time is it? I check my phone. Credits are rolling. There's drool on my pillow. I fell asleep and missed the entire movie.

December 31—7:00 p.m.

I consider restarting the movie but conclude that it's too depressing to watch *August: Osage County* by myself on New Year's Eve. Damn it. I mean, not that it matters that it's New Year's Eve!

December 31—7:05 p.m.

I look at the cut-up vegetables in my refrigerator. I'm too tired from my nap to do anything with them but remain proud of myself for having what looks like a bunch of healthy food in my refrigerator.

December 31—7:06 p.m.

I eat some (fifteen) York Peppermint Pattie candies that I have left over from Christmas Eve. Chocolate is a mood booster and after that nap that felt like I entered and was swiftly ripped from a portal to death I need to boost some serotonin. Nobody said that staying home alone had to feel nihilistic. Even though it does—nobody said it *had to*.

December 31—7:15 p.m.

Like a little kid after a Halloween candy binge, I have a stomach-ache. I wonder—could this be just from the candy or am I getting the flu? There was a sick kid at this Christmas party I went to but would it take seven whole days for the virus to have kicked in? Hey, am I the only one who remembers when The Flu just meant throwing up and having a fever? Since when did the definition change and it now refers to a severe head cold? It's just like how I remember that "getting stoned" used to mean getting drunk. Was I just about to beat this intestinal virus but then overloading my body with sugar by eating some (fifteen) York Peppermint Patties ruined my chances? I think about how some people can binge-drink and do drugs like Molly and never seem to get sick but I'm undone by candy. Does this mean that I'm actually so healthy that I can't process sugar anymore, or that I'm destined for an early death and this was the first warning sign? I should call people and tell them that I don't know how long I have to live, but I don't want to ruin their New Year's Eve. If only I knew more like-minded people who didn't make such a big deal out of this fucking date on the calendar, I would be able to call them without guilt and let them know that I may not be around by this time next year.

December 31—7:16 p.m.

I decide to check Instagram. My friend from college is celebrating her one-year wedding anniversary. I didn't even know she was married. I should call her sometime. Then again, on second thought she's the type that gets married on New Year's Eve. That's an annoying character flaw. I'll just Like her photo instead. Another friend has posted a video of her daughter spinning in a circle. A lot of the parents with kids are saying they can't stay up late like everyone else so they're wishing everyone a happy *early* New Year. I want to write defensively, "Some of us without kids can't stay up late either. It's not because you're a selfless, heroic parent—it's because you're forty-one." But I don't. But at least it's written here. In this book.

December 31—7:30 p.m.

I read a text from a friend that says, **I'M IN THE BACK OF A CAR SERVICE. HE ALREADY HAS A TOWEL DOWN FOR DRUNK PEOPLE AND THERE HAVE BEEN THREE CAR ACCIDENTS ALREADY.** I think of how when I was a dumb twentysomething living in NYC I puked in the back of cabs many times and always claimed I had food poisoning. I would always tip twenty bucks. Now that I think about it, I don't think that's enough money after regurgitating a bottle of cheap wine on somebody's floor mats. I just realized that I have no memory of what I did for New Year's Eve in 1998 or 1999 or 2000—I bet it was fun.

December 31—8:00 p.m.

I'm back on Instagram and seeing that a lot of people I know have pets. Mostly it's families who have cats, single women who have dogs, and lesbians who have two dogs.

December 31—8:15 p.m.

I look to my iCal. I have dinner with my friend Tami tomorrow night. I have drinks with my college ex-boyfriend on January second and a birthday party on January third. Those are three quality nights ahead of me. I should not be regretting staying in. Although I don't want to be at a party, I don't exactly want to be stuck on my couch either. What I would really love is to be with a rich, exotic lover who has flown me to Rio or Rome. Oh, fuck it. I don't even care if the private plane never takes off. Just somebody have sex with me on a leather seat.

December 31—8:30 p.m.

I watch some of Anderson Cooper's New Year's Eve special. Footage is rolling of people in India lighting oil lamps, offering flowers, and getting purified in the mighty River Ganges. It looks nice. Way better than a bunch of idiots in Times Square wearing plastic glittery hats in the name of fun instead of a sensible wool cap in the name of not getting fucking pneumonia. *Would I ever go to India?* I wonder. If I got a first-class ticket and had a tour guide and I went to something spectacular like a New Year's Eve celebration, I could probably handle India. I honestly have no desire to go to India, though. But shouldn't I want to go to India if I'm as spiritual as I think? I judged a friend of mine in my head today because she puts such a high value on her career and when it's not going well she takes up smoking cigarettes. One time she yelled at me when I suggested a way for her to relax naturally. She said, "I'm not fucking meditating." How dare I tell someone else what to do when I won't even go to India? But I heard sometimes tourists get so dehydrated that they die at the Delhi airport but you never hear about it—except for the one time I heard about it somewhere and then wrote it down here.

December 31—8:35 p.m.

I am stressed out about the amount of people that are on planet Earth—just mobs and mobs of people. What if we get *so* populated at some point that we're always shoulder to shoulder with someone? I go to Google and start checking in on the Great Pacific Garbage Patch, also known as the Pacific Trash Vortex. This is NOT my fault but I am vowing to use Amazon Prime less.

December 31—8:40 p.m.

Some newswoman is interviewing two young men from Texas who are in Times Square. For people who spent an entire day in the cold to get the prime spot of leaning up against the partition you would think they would have a prepared statement in case they got asked to speak. Instead the two guys just wave into the camera as if they're searching for their own reflection. One of them shouts, "Awesome!" I hope that nobody in India is watching.

December 31—8:59 p.m.

I start to get sleepy again. How many times have I wanted to go to bed at nine o'clock and then didn't? It's also okay to sleep on the couch because I'm too lazy to get up. I shut off the TV and let the glow of my Christmas tree light the room. I smile wondering how many angry homophobes are out there tonight watching Anderson Cooper giggle and talk about his mother, Gloria Vanderbilt, with Kathy Griffin. God bless America. It's 2:00 p.m. the next day in Sydney. I decide that I'm on Australia time and free myself of this stupid holiday.

(Note: I never went on that New Year's Day hike. In fact—the first exercise I did in the New Year wasn't until February.)

16

THE RELATIONSHIP REMODELER

There are two questions a man must ask himself: The first is "Where am I going?" and the second is "Who will go with me?" If you ever get these questions in the wrong order you are in trouble.

—SAM KEEN

Deceiving others. That is what the world calls a romance.

—OSCAR WILDE

In year two of being single again—and not having had an official boyfriend—I met someone. Well, I didn't *meet* someone. I saw someone I already sort of knew in a new light. That's usually how I find men. They have to already exist in my orbit. I like my potential mate and I to have at least one mutual friend so that I can launch a full-scale investigative background check. Does he have a criminal record? (I'll make an exception for a guy who was wrongly accused of a crime and spent his time in jail writing poetry or something deep like that.) What do his ex-girlfriends say about him? (An unacceptable answer: "His ex-girlfriends say that he's great but he would call his mom during sex.") With the exception of my near-dalliance with a British guy I met on a message board, I've never done online dating, never filled out a Match.com questionnaire. Did you know that the Internet is full of *strangers*? I was taught never to talk to strangers and now in order to find love I'm told that it's okay to send them a flattering picture and to arrange to meet them alone in person.

It causes me some worry because I assume that it means that these men are full-on traditionalists and that they want to find a woman who cooks, cleans, wants kids, and loves knitting Christmas sweaters. On the flip side I'm suspicious that if the men *aren't* traditionalists they are perverts who prey on a woman who wants a boyfriend and may be willing to have sex right away if the guy presents himself as trustworthy and nice and wanting to knit Christmas sweaters—but after one hump, she's dumped. The man who I'm really looking to avoid the most is the man who hasn't figured out who he is yet and desperately wants a relationship in order to feel useful and whole—while he continues to halfheartedly follow his career dreams and procrastinates registering his car because he's consumed with finding love. Normally women are stereotyped as being this way—but there are some men like this too. We have to recognize that they're out there or else we will get caught up with these guys because of some myth that tells us we're lucky that someone wants us so much.

So, as a public service to all of you women reading this, here is my cautionary tale of my three-month relationship with the Ab-Master. I call him this because he had six-pack abs plus two visible oblique muscles *and*, much like any exercise equipment designed for home use, our relationship arrived slightly defective but I ignored it at first, in an effort to make it work (out).

I'd known the Ab-Master for a couple of years. He worked as a carpenter. We would run into each other at mutual friends' gatherings. A lot of people dismissed him as gay because he dressed fashionably, had a haircut that took some styling, and occasionally wore a deep V-neck tee. I knew that he was just "artsy" and I like a guy who's in touch with his feminine side. Besides, I've known plenty of closeted alpha males.

At one mutual friend's party I was telling the Ab-Master that I had just moved into a new apartment. He asked if I needed any help unpacking. "Fuck no!" I told him with sass. "I did that all in one day. I can't sleep one night in a new place unless everything is out of the boxes and put away." He offered to help with painting or hanging up pictures, as that was one of his areas of expertise. I immediately dismissed his offer saying, "No. I hired people for that." He asked me what my schedule was like coming up and I lamented, "Awful. I'm just about to go out on a book tour." I had no idea that he was flirting with me or asking me out. But he told me later—after we started dating—that he was trying to ask me out at that party but I was throwing up some major self-defense blocks. I thought we were just two friends chatting. Honestly, I never thought he would be interested in me. I figured he had a bunch of artsy girlfriends. I definitely thought he was gorgeous but I'd never met a man whose idea of putting a move on me was offering to paint my bathroom.

One night while out with The Mutual Friend and friends, I mentioned that I was starting to feel a little bit lonely and when he suggested online dating I went into my speech. I hinted that I would actually like to meet a guy like Ab-Master; artsy-looking, creative, nice, asks lots of questions, seems interested, isn't a gropey pig. The Mutual Friend told me that the Ab-Master was totally interested in me but had given up trying to ask me out because I wasn't getting the cues. That was all I needed to hear. I took matters into my own hands. I sent the Ab-Master a text and said, "Want to meet for a drink? Tonight?" I said, "Peace out," to The Mutual Friend. "No time to waste." And I was out the door and headed down the street to meet my date. Even though I don't know how to use a hammer, I'm a bit of an alpha female. Unlike the Ab-Master, when I ask you out—you know it.

Ab-Master and I had a great talk. He was charming, funny (it's hard to make me laugh), a good listener, a good talker, sexy without being overtly sexual, and he was contemplative. He hit it off so well with the male and female bartenders that they closed the doors and let us stay for one more with the staff. Ab-Master had ease and charm. He knew how to make people feel comfortable. It was a great first non-date. He asked me out for the next night. I happily said yes. We hung out a bunch that week. It felt good to not spend every night going home and working more after I got home from work. It was summer and I had a few months to just work one job before I had to add a comedy tour to my normal forty-hour workweek. I figured that the Ab-Master and I were setting the scene for a great summer fling.

On our third date, he told me a story of how his parents got divorced when he was twenty and he applied to a talk show (something like a local *Ricki Lake* in his home city) to try to get his parents on as guests for reconciliation. His family agreed to it but it didn't work out, which left the Ab-Master devastated. He said that he went into a major depression, gained a hundred pounds, and didn't leave his bedroom (at what was now just his mom's house) for a year. Then he discovered the joy of working out, which he claims brought him back to life, and he concluded that exercise is the key to happiness. I'm all for some good-mood-inducing endorphins after a workout—nobody ever feels worse after going to the gym (unless all you do is get a thousand-calorie smoothie and then hide in the women's locker room sucking it down in the dry sauna).

I've been in therapy for decades and I can break this story down. He never recovered in a real way from his parents' divorce and squat thrusts did not cure his depression but he simply switched behaviors and now he's into having control over his body as a way to control his world. He doesn't have the ability to surrender to the fact that he can't orchestrate how people are going to behave and he doesn't want to feel the feelings.

I started to get a reflex in my stomach—that sense of someone planting a red flag firmly in my solar plexus. There's something to be said for getting to the root of the melancholy. The Ab-Master seemed to gloss over his father leaving and the complete untangling of his family. I asked if maybe he needed to look at that because oddly he seemed to idealize having a girlfriend and getting someone to love him as the one thing that can make life perfect. I know it's codependent of me to notice but he was a classic codependent.

During dessert, the Ab-Master asked me to be his girlfriend. He told me that he was not going to see anyone else and asked me if I felt the same way. I couldn't really believe this was happening at my age. We had hung out three times and the third time wasn't even done yet. I had the feeling that he was just rushing to be involved—and that this had nothing to do with his feeling a true connection with *me*. I told him that I wanted to keep seeing him but that if other people asked us out we should see those people too. If time goes by and no one else diverts us *then* we should become exclusive. I had no plans to meet anyone else but I was certainly not going to just become someone's partner after three dates. That's how relationships started when I was in my early twenties, and on the playground in middle school. It seemed a little childish to just declare someone my boyfriend and then jump in and wait for my emotions to catch up to my decision. I didn't *feel* yet that he was my one true confidant.

We had a semi-annoying, mostly circular conversation and then the Ab-Master, acting like some Paul Rudd look-alike in a ABC Family drama said, "Don't be so afraid to open up again. I know that divorce is traumatic and you're just afraid to open up."

I said, "It wasn't traumatic. It was expensive. I'm very open. I'm opening up now and telling you how I would like to enter a relationship."

He said, "Aw, babe! I see you as becoming set in your ways already."

"Babe"? On the third date? My *ways*? What were *my ways*? My peculiar little way of not wanting to call someone my boyfriend after hanging out with him for what amounted to a total of fifteen (waking) hours?

I wanted to take it slow—not because I was afraid but because I wanted to do things right. We would have to organically spend more time together, let the calendar pages turn. People are like trees. You have to see how they hold up in every season. Right now it was summer and we were both in full bloom, but how would his branches be able to handle the changing leaves of autumn? The heavy, crushing snow in winter? I had a sneaking suspicion that if he *were* a tree he would be a Christmas fir—all too happy to be cut down so that he could go inside and bond with a family, secretly hoping they'll let him stay past the New Year and acting truly surprised when they put him out on the curb with the recycling, lying in a heap on the sidewalk, moaning, "If only that family would take a chance on me they would see that I am good for them year-round!"

I felt another red flag being implanted into my stomach. He was only five years younger than me but he seemed unseasoned in the way he wanted to debate instead of listen. He thought of himself as a

problem solver, compassionate, and ready to help. I didn't need help.
I needed to be heard. If womanhood had a motto, "I Just Want To Be
Heard" would be it—that and "You Have To Tell Me Well In Advance
If A Party Is Going To Be Outside."

Whenever I feel those red flags firmly poking into my gut, I have
a terrible habit of talking myself out of them. I ask myself questions
like, *What am I going to do? Walk away from this guy because I don't
have a good feeling about it?* Um, yes. How about that? That would be
a good place to start. Maybe we were headed for the same freeway
but approaching it from different on-ramps. Maybe referring to the
Ab-Master as my boyfriend wasn't that big of a deal. I wanted to hang
out with him as much as I could and I was attracted to him so what
was my problem? Boyfriend. Why couldn't I just say, "Hey everybody,
meet my boyfriend!" When I'd relay these stories to girlfriends it was
hard to convey the red flag feeling. It's sort of a you-had-to-be-there-
in-my-stomach-when-the-flagpole-carrying-the-red-flag-punctured-
my-liver kind of thing. Most of my female friends just heard the bullet
points.

- A handsome man?
- A handsome man with visible abdominals?
- He wants a relationship and commitment?
- He tried to get his family back together? Aw!
- He offered to help you unpack during a move?

Jen, are you crazy? Why would you hesitate? Marry him! We'll
come to your second wedding. Jen, this guy offered to hang pictures!
Stop thinking someone better will come along! This guy is a magical
unicorn! Ride him through the sky and shit rainbows together! Your
life is solved!

The Ab-Master loved my apartment and often complimented my
décor. I found this to be high praise since he builds furniture for a
living. I took him very seriously when he said that the wooden place
mats on my dining room table didn't fit the rest of my home accessories. I had never been to his place, but then again he had only been
my "boyfriend" for a week. I asked, "Okay. What are your place mats

like? Show me a picture of your place." The Ab-Master pulled out his phone and proudly showed me a picture of his bed, which was covered in wood shavings because he was using a handsaw (inside) working on a piece. When I asked him why he worked on large wood projects in his bedroom he explained that that was the only room in his place. He lived in a smaller than small studio apartment. He oddly delighted in telling me, "It's so crazy it's more like a room than even a studio! The head of my bed is the kitchen sink and right now I'm trying to find a way to live in peace with these cockroaches!"

COCKROACHES. IN THE SINK THAT WAS ALSO HIS BED.

This is why I didn't want to just jump into calling someone my boyfriend only to find out *later* that his ice cube tray doubles as his kitchen counter. I don't need a man to live in a luxury rooftop apartment and have unnecessary decorations like balls of twine in a bowl on an end table but I question how developed a man is who makes things look nice for a living but can't quite do it for himself. I knew Ab-Master as a talented carpenter who often had to create a piece for a cozy living room. Was I remiss in assuming that he had already made a home for himself? He was a woodworker who knew how to make furniture but rather than make himself a bed, he made a pile of wood shavings on his bed.

I told the Ab-Master that if it was okay with him, I would probably never ever under any circumstance come over. I'd already lived through a cockroach phase when I lived in a studio apartment in Hollywood. I woke up with a cockroach on my face and when I screamed, shook it off, and went to the refrigerator to get some water there were over a hundred cockroaches inside of my fridge. It turned out my neighbor was an elderly hoarder who lived in squalor and one night the roaches just rebelled and magically oozed through the walls into my immaculately clean, charming little place. I'd already taken the last copter out of Saigon and I really wasn't looking to get back in one for another tour.

The Ab-Master was hurt. "But, babe, I want to be able to share my home with you, and take care of you when you sleep over." There was no need to "take care" of me during a sleepover, unless we're talking you-know-what. Otherwise, I'm not on dialysis and don't need monitoring throughout the night. A good way to take care of me would be to let me just sleep in my own home—a two-bedroom, two-bathroom condo with a washer/dryer, deck, and central air-conditioning. He and I both had jobs that were within walking distance of my place. And as a woman who is fast approaching "older" status, I have creams—creams for the cellulite on my butt, a morning under-eye cream, an evening under-eye cream, and an oil to apply to my face to get it ready for the cream that's coming. Then there are lotions—lotions for my legs, salves for my elbows (one of the first places to show signs of age), and a leave-in conditioner to put at the ends of my hair. I can't lug a carry-on bag full of creams just to spend the night at a gentleman's . . . *room*. He felt that I was judging him for living in a studio apartment. I said, "I'm not judging that at all. You'll move someday when you can. I'm judging that you want a grown woman to sleep over at the risk of cockroaches getting tangled in her hair extensions."

We were only five years apart but it was our life experience differences that didn't sit well with me. We were just fundamentally different people and I wasn't looking to fix or change him but I felt he was trying to fix and change me. He told me that he had a big talk with his sister about how I didn't want children and that he wasn't sure if he did or not but that the good news was that if he did want kids he could help me change my mind. I told him that I was not going to change my mind. Hello, I wrote a book about it. He said, "Babe, it's not written in stone." It's written on paper, which is good enough for me, and besides, my reproductive system after all these years *is* turning to stone.

Around month three, as summer ended, he seemed to be growing increasingly frustrated. He wanted to know why I hadn't told my family about him. He resented that he had met my friends (over dinner and drinks) but I wasn't willing to meet his by going to an industrial music Goth rave dance club dance in a bad part of town at midnight. He kept insisting, "Jen, you're not letting me show you who I am." I asked him to explain what he needed me to know about him that it was somehow my fault for not knowing.

He said, "Well, you don't even know the most important thing about me."

"Okay. Tell me the most important thing about you."

"Halloween is my favorite holiday!"

"That's the most important thing about you?"

"Yes. Just like you always say, sometimes the smallest thing about someone can shine a light on who they are."

"I meant more psychologically speaking, but . . ."

There's nothing wrong with a guy who loves a good haunted house, but one who says it's the most important part of him? I cringed at a vision of him carving a pumpkin in his room, seeds and guts spilling onto the bed.

I just wanted someone to have some salmon and sex with. Not at the same time. But on a Saturday night I loved the idea of taking a nice hot shower, putting on some makeup, a decent outfit, and having dinner with a man. I just wanted a little bit of companionship. On our last date, the Ab-Master picked me up in his sixteen-year-old car. I hate cars. I don't understand why people want to spend a lot of money on a car, why anyone cares what make or model a car is or how much horsepower it possesses. I see it as a necessary evil that takes me from point A to point B. I don't care if a car is old but I don't care to sit on piles of trash and I don't feel safe sitting in a passenger seat with a dented door. The Ab-Master still hadn't registered his car in California in his three years of residency, claiming, "There are more important things in life to get to every day."

We finally broke up over the phone when I was on the road in Austin, Texas. I didn't mean to break up with him on the call, but when he asked me why I couldn't make a plan with him to meet his mother eight months from then, I sort of snapped. I told him that I would have known by now and it didn't look like I'd be falling in love. He retaliated with, "For someone who has been in therapy for fifteen years, you sure don't know yourself. It hasn't worked at all." *Excuse me?* Anyone who talks about therapy that way or uses it against me, that's where I get all Oprah-in-a-movie-playing-an-angry-mom-yelling-at-her-son's-girlfriend on their ass. "Don't you come around here anymore and tell us our lifestyle is wrong, you trifling bitch!" His final plea of, "What's wrong with my wanting to change you? It means I love you! I want you to change me too!"

The red flags had turned to white. Time to surrender. This. Was. Over. I felt validated that I had been kind of right since the beginning. I wasn't going to let anyone tell me again that I was unwilling to love and just needed the right man. I'm unwilling to love the wrong man just because he's a man. I have nothing to prove. I want to relax with someone—not rebuild him. I'm done with put-it-together-yourself furniture and men. Besides, his favorite holiday is Halloween? That's so immature. Everybody knows that Christmas is the best holiday. It's like, duh, grow *up*.

After my book tour of 2013 finished up, I got an e-mail from my ex-boyfriend Blake, whose cheating escapade was chronicled in *I Can Barely Take Care of Myself*. We had seen each other only one other time since college, ten years earlier. We met up for drinks. Once I sat down, Blake told me that he'd read my book and wanted to clear the air. He said that he had never cheated on me. In his version, he was unhappy in our relationship and was unhappy about being unhappy and once we broke up, then and only then, he took solace in the alleged other woman's arms. I laughed at his explanation—it sounded plausible but it really didn't matter anymore. I only wrote about it in the book to illustrate my past. I wasn't really still holding a grudge. I thought of how my relationship with Blake and all of my relationships from my twenties had seemed so easy, compared to the ones I seemed to be getting into in my late thirties. The Ab-Master wasn't a bad guy. He really would be a great catch for a woman who is maybe in the same place emotionally that he is. Maybe relationships were easy when I was younger because most twenty-year-olds are in the same place and it's not such a glaring red flag when someone has a hot plate as a headboard.

As we finished up Blake gave me the speech—it's a speech I've heard from other exes. I call it the "You Made Me a Better Man" speech, because he started it by saying, "Jen, you made me a better man." Blake told me that I'd challenged him to dare to dream and to achieve his goals. I showed him the meaning of unconditional love by not judging his Friday-night drum circle jams. He said that he understood women better because of me and is proud to call himself a feminist. He said that he could never be the man he now is for his wife and kids if it wasn't for me unknowingly helping in his remodeling. We ended up just laughing and sharing some sentimental tears about how long it's been since we were young. I'm so happy that Blake found that wife and kids he always wanted, and in no way do I want him for myself, but I never meant to fix him up for another woman. I certainly never meant to reupholster him like an old chair so that somebody else could put him in her living room. Although I do sort of hope right now there is a girl out there unknowingly refurbishing some guy and I'll find him in a few years in a thrift store just waiting to be taken home and sat on.

17

AUNT-ARCHY IN THE UK

A subject to which few intellectuals ever give a thought is the right to be a vagrant, the freedom to wander. Yet vagrancy is a deliverance, and life on the open road is the essence of freedom. To have the courage to smash the chains with which modern life has weighted us (under the pretext that it was offering us more liberty), then to take up the symbolic stick and bundle and get out.

—ISABELLE EBERHARDT, EXPLORER

Traveling is the spice of life.

—AUNT JENNY (*THE BRADY BUNCH*)

In September of 2013 I had a six-night "run" at a cabaret space in London—the Soho Theatre on Dean Street in, duh, Soho. I wish I could say I was doing a one-woman version of *Waiting for Godot* or *Liza with a "Z"* but I was just doing my stand-up comedy. Whenever I have opportunities like this that I never imagined I would, I think to myself, *Hey, I'm just this dumb little kid from Needham, Massachusetts, and I was asked to go overseas and tell jokes about my life and my vagina. And this is my job.* That is an honor. For me. Probably not for the audience. But I was looking forward to a completely paid-for, business-class flight and hotel. There's really no better way to experience London—unless you get to stay in Buckingham Palace or with Morrissey.

I'd been to London before back in February of 2008—dolefully remembered by me as "The One Year I Didn't Get A Flu Shot." I boarded an eleven-hour flight with a head cold and exited the plane with some mishmash of pneumonia, swine flu, and death. Thank God (and may He save the Queen) for free clinics. I had a humiliating conversation with the doctor when he tried to prescribe antibiotics about my inability to swallow without panic large, chalky pills, and specifically my phobia of swallowing large, chalky pills in foreign countries. What if the pill gets lodged in my windpipe and I choke? Who is in charge of shipping my body back to America? My parents can't get on a plane and locate a hotel in Sloane Square and carry my body back to my final resting place. My mom has a bunion and my dad has no sense of direction. They wouldn't even make it to the international section of Boston's Logan Airport without getting in a big fight, and my dad missing the flight because he wanted to enjoy a Tiparillo cigar in the one designated smoking area left these days, inconveniently located about two miles away from the airport.

I spent that 2008 trip to London sleeping, waking up every six hours to suffer through swallowing thick liquid antibiotics. When I actually tasted an antibiotic I began questioning everything I'd ever learned about their supposed ability to help fight illness. It seemed like poison. I felt slightly improved on my last day in London. I was able to take about five breaths without coughing, which made me feel like an Olympian. I gorged on fish and chips at a nonauthentic British pub and took one short ride on a double-decker bus. *Oh, there's Big Ben*, I thought to myself as I made grunting noises in an effort to reverse my postnasal drip.

When I got the chance to make a triumphant return to England five years later as a fully flu-shotted woman with a newfound habit of taking probiotics—I was giddy. The Ab-Master and I broke up about seven days before I was to head overseas and I was dismayed at how many friends and acquaintances and just people walking past me on the street said things to me along the lines of, "Are you okay? I always pictured [Name Redacted] going to London with you." *Am I okay?* He was never coming with me. We'd only been dating for a few months and there was no reason for him to come along. After that was cleared up, people's comments veered toward, "Well, maybe you'll meet someone in London! Maybe you're being sent to London 'for a reason'!" Yeah.

The reason was called work. Maybe I would meet someone. Maybe I wouldn't. Maybe I would also exercise caution and not have sex with a stranger who I just met in England. Also, I've heard from some of my more international friends that British men aren't circumcised. I've never seen an uncircumcised penis. But I have a feeling that I would not like the way one looks. So, I guess we can add fear of swallowing an uncircumcised penis in London to my list of oddball phobias.

I am not a member of Led Zeppelin. I know this comes as a shock. But I am not a rock star with a team of security guards who can stand outside or inside of my bedroom suite and make sure that no groupies get out of hand or try to kill me just to have a good story. And unlike Led Zeppelin, any groupies that I might sleep with are men. Men are human beings who are usually more large and strapping than me and my first thought is that it would be unnerving to take one I didn't know back to my hotel room—and although I still have an overdeveloped right arm from scooping ice cream as a teenager at my after-school job at Baskin-Robbins, I can't physically make a man who might be a psychopath leave my room when I start to suspect he's a psychopath. And I really don't want to go to some "bloke's flat"—having no idea where I am and no one outside can hear me scream because at night in London the streets become filled with people fighting one another. My cries for help would blend right in to the darkness.

I have never had a fling on the road with someone who has come to see my show. First of all, I'd like him to remember me how he saw me onstage—funny and in control. I do not want to take a guy back to my hotel and have the fantasy dissipate as he watches me put on my three face creams and take pills for my adult acne before bed. Nor do I want to have to say, "Before we have hot sex, I need to shower because my butt cheeks tend to sweat onstage. And when I am in the bathroom, please don't rifle through my daily affirmation journal."

I was so shell-shocked by how my time with the Ab-Master went from fun to done so quickly that the last thing on my mind was a man. Some people in my life seemed to find my breakup with the Ab-Master and this trip to London a week later tragic timing. "So, Jen, you're really not taking the Ab-Master with you?" "No. We broke up. And I was never planning on taking him to London because I am not his mother and my business trip isn't his playdate." But I was in London for my dream fulfillment and I couldn't believe that only a small handful of people in my life understood that it was not a tragedy that one of my carry-ons wasn't a man. Even the TSA agent who checked my passport looked beside me and said with a frown, "You're traveling to Europe alone today?" Yes. I am traveling to Europe alone today. At least I'm fucking traveling to Europe! She handed back my passport and said, "Well, good for you. You go, girl." (As in the supportive slang "You *go*, girl." She wasn't, like, instructing me to go.) Although I get that she was congratulating me—what was there to be congratulatory *about* exactly? The male comedians in my life never get asked if they're traveling alone. Nobody ever says, "You're not bringing a woman with you? How will you justify your self-worth without a gal by your side? Well, keep your head up. The right princess is out there for you. But in the meantime, it's so strong of you to take this voyage alone. You go, boy."

This attitude started to infect my psyche. As the plane hit its cruising altitude I caught myself thinking, *I'm lonely.*

I started to talk to myself inside my head.

Well, of course you're lonely, Jen. You're sitting alone.

I know.

Besides, do you really want to talk to anyone, Jen?

Fuck no!

I looked around at my immediate surroundings in Premium Economy on Air New Zealand, sitting in a fun little seat pod known as the "Spaceseat." There were so many movies to choose from, including *Caddyshack.* I had four fashion magazines, and an iPod full of music. Most people have to be getting chemotherapy to get this kind of personal downtime.

I don't mean to act like being single and wandering the planet by myself is some fabulous parade all of the goddamn time or that I'm constantly in "You go, girrrl" mode. I think—and again, this is just a thought; I said, "I think" not "I know for a fact"—but I *think* that having a man to travel the world with would be marvelous. I further think that if that man also had a similar type of life and career and our relationship had elements of creative collaboration—that would be miraculously marvelous. I'm okay with no man if I can't have *that* man. And I'm not going to let the fact that I'm minus one man ruin any fun I might be having flying in metal tubes from state to state, country to country, continent to continent.

The most impactful episode of *The Brady Bunch* to me is an underrated gem from season three called "Jan's Aunt Jenny," with Imogene Coca playing Mrs. Brady's eccentric aunt (technically Jan's great-aunt, but let's not get bogged down in the genealogy of a made-up family). In this installment of great American entertainment, middle daughter Jan finds an old picture of Aunt Jenny that's her spitting image, but when she finds a more recent picture of Aunt Jenny Jan is afraid that she will grow up to be as peculiar-looking as her relative. Eccentric Aunt Jenny comes to visit and Jan learns that beauty comes from within and ends up idolizing Jenny.

What stuck with me as a young girl watching "Jan's Aunt Jenny" was not the life lesson that looks don't matter, but that this maxi-skirt-and-purple-turtleneck-wearing woman was unmarried, middle-aged, and had traveled the world alone multiple times and she seemed way cooler than Mrs. Brady despite Carol's badass unique lady-mullet with the flipped-up ends that never caught on in beauty salons in America. Aunt Jenny arrived at the Bradys' house in a limousine and when she exited the exotic-to-me-at-the-time car, she was wearing a giant Russian fur hat.

Aunt Jenny took the Brady family through a traditional Japanese "honorable tea" service in Mike and Carol's living room. (Except for Alice. They kept that ol' bitch slaving away clearing plates. Poor thing. She could have learned a thing or two about independence from AJ.) Aunt Jenny keeps getting phone calls from her secretary on the Bradys' home phone. She's just been invited to a birthday party on "Ari" Onassis's yacht. Her response? "Is he kidding? I'm not canceling my Peace Corps assignment in Bolivia for any birthday party. I'll cable Jackie, though. She's a real trip." She teaches the Brady kids how to eat rice with chopsticks. She tells a story about jamming with the king of Thailand on saxophone in a little nightclub in Bangkok. Another phone call from Aunt Jenny's assistant brings news of a dozen long-stemmed roses delivered to her house with a marriage proposal from a US senator. Aunt Jenny is unfazed. "I get lots of proposals."

"Well, why don't you accept one of them?" asks Jan.

"Oh, I guess I'm too young to settle down yet."

Aunt Jenny ends up cutting the visit short because she forgot that she had to catch a plane to Paris. I'm not sure if it was a calling or just an astute realization of the inevitable, but I remember thinking, *I'm going to grow up to be Aunt Jenny*. Sure, Aunt Jenny might seem lonely compared to the likes of Carol and Mike Brady, who had each other, six kids, a dog, and even a live-in maid, but Aunt Jenny had freedom. She could drop in on that giant family when she wanted to but also get right the hell out, leaving everyone wanting more. Maybe Aunt Jenny just had intimacy issues. Maybe I'm just projecting. Maybe it's Maybelline.

Television people always seemed as legitimate to me as the people in my actual life, and Aunt Jenny was not only a role model to Jan Brady, a fake person, she was a role model to me, a real person. Somewhere in my DNA was the idea that there is nothing sad about exploring on your own—in fact, it's the best way to meet even *more people*. And as Jan said, ending up like Aunt Jenny isn't so bad at all.

It was nice to land in London with only my luggage to look after. After trying to check into the wrong hotel because I had gone by "memory" instead of the $800 computer in my pocket that makes phone calls and keeps information in a calendar, I got settled in my room. I had one night free to do whatever I wanted. My hotel was right smack in the middle of Leicester Square and I was tempted to go see the Liberace biopic *Behind the Candelabra* in the Square's movie theater. In America it was only a made-for-TV movie but our friends in London gave Matt Damon in tighty-whities and gold rings his proper respect by showing it on the big screen.

But I decided to be a sophisticate and take in the West End. I purchased a last-minute ticket to the Ibsen play *A Doll's House*. I remember loving reading this play in high school. I was *that* drama-geek/freak girl. Nobody assigned me that play to read. I read it on my own time, making sure everyone saw that I was reading prose that challenged nineteenth-century marriage norms, sitting deep in thought in a booth at Friendly's. Twenty-plus years later I was at the Duke of York's Theatre with a great aisle seat, happy that champagne was allowed inside of the auditorium. In America, ladies have to chug chardonnay and do white wine spritzer funnels during intermission in some of the lobbies on Broadway. Even though I slept for most of the eleven-hour flight to London, and I guess because of the fact that I took a drug that tells your nervous system that EVERYTHING IS GROOVY EVEN THOUGH THERE IS A LION CHARGING AT YOU and that technically I hadn't been in a bed in twenty-four hours *and* there's this thing called jet lag—I started to nod off. I passed out on the shoulder of the senior citizen woman to my right. The feel of her wool sweater on my bottom lip woke me. She nudged me back to my side right in the middle of Nora's empowering monologue to her husband, Torvald. "I was your little skylark! Your doll!" I flopped not back into my seat but right over the other side of my chair where there was no old lady to catch me—only the aisle. I tumbled face-first into the carpet, my hand still clutching my champagne glass, the champagne spilling on my head. An usher rushed over, shining her penlight in my bloodshot eyes. She escorted me into the lobby to make sure I wasn't injured. I was fine, except for the rug burn to my forehead.

The nice lady running the concession stand said that I could have a refill on my champagne for free, since I had spilled it on my face and all. London wasn't judging. I chatted with the usher while sipping from my newly refilled flute. And then—my seat buddy came bounding through the doors into the lobby and approached my new best friend demanding that she usher me right into a different seat. "That woman is causing a stir, falling into the aisle! She's bringing shame upon herself." I said nothing but thought, *Okay, calm down, lady. 'Bringing shame upon herself' is a tad dramatic.* I wasn't sneaking out of a castle to marry some vagrant from the underclass, I just fell asleep at a play. And might I say that play was *a lot* more humdrum than I remembered it from high school. I guess heavy plays were more engrossing when I was an angst-ridden fourteen-year-old whose only options for things to do were to write in my journal in my bedroom, listen to records in my bedroom, and just basically not leave my bedroom.

Despite that old crow's grousing, I was still allowed to retake my aisle seat after intermission and once those lights went back down my body said, *"Hmmm. Time to go to sleep."* I woke up in the aisle again. At least this time I must have fallen rather quietly—a graceful slide maybe. It went unnoticed by the usher. But I met eyes with my seat neighbor Mrs. Sourpuss Magoo and I knew that I had to leave. Don't anyone remind me how *A Doll's House* ends. Next time I'm in London I'll sneak in during intermission and catch the second half.

I passed a kiosk on St. Martin's Lane and ordered myself up some fish and chips "to take away" as the Brits say instead of "to go." I walked back toward my hotel holding an entire piece of beer-battered cod in my hand, gnawing on it as though sitting at a table and using utensils had been outlawed. As I neared my hotel a fashionably punk rock guy clearly saddled with a heroin addiction told me, "You're a beautiful woman. I'd love to take ya to fish and chips next time." He was probably just attracted to me because my eyes were sleepy and at half mast, but no wonder Amy Winehouse fell into the wrong crowd if these are the only two hang options on a Saturday night in London—snooty old women or charming young drug addicts.

Back in my hotel room, I was still so hungry that I dipped everything I could find in the leftover tartar sauce—even the individually wrapped Q-tips in the bathroom. I was happy when I woke up twelve hours later in my bed even though I had fallen asleep with my shoes on. It beat sleeping on the floor of a theater. And I wasn't sad waking up in a quaint London hotel room without a man. I was just disappointed that I passed out without getting under the covers and who knew what kind of rash I would get from having my face on the outside of the duvet. They never clean those things.

The next day I put on my badass platform-heeled rain boots and fingerless leather gloves. It wasn't raining or cold but I brought these accessories five thousand three hundred and forty-seven miles and goddamn it they were getting worn. I walked up and down the street— here I am, world! An independent woman just strolling through London during the day before the opening night of her cabaret run! I hit Portobello Road and bought myself what I call a "fun coat"—a tradition that I started for myself in Paris the previous year when I bought a giant white faux fur coat that looked like a yeti. I decided that every country I visit my souvenir to myself will be a coat, something out of the ordinary that tells a story. Usually the story is just "I bought this coat," but whatever.

While some Londonites had four o'clock tea, I decided to have four o'clock Cabernet and cheese at a wine bar. Sitting at the bar, I pontificated to no one that drinking at four p.m. with your date is foreplay but drinking alone at four p.m. is kind of just drinking alone . . . *unless* you're talking a lot with the bartender, and then it's called wine tasting.

The most ravishing man took a seat at the bar next to me—sort of a Hugh Grant/Hugh Jackman combo. Double Hugh made me rethink my no uncircumcised penises rule. I could picture myself just staring into his eyes or his hair and never having to see the thing if we were to make British love. He sat down, leaving an empty barstool between us, and coyly whispered, "I'm saving this seat."

"Okay." I decided to pull out a book. The romance was over.

He smiled. "Aren't you going to ask who I'm saving it for?"

Oh? There's more? Romance back on! I pictured us walking hand in hand through gardens in the rain (again, I packed those boots) and making out against brick walls in alleyways.

"Who are you saving it for?"

I shut my book to signal that he had my full attention.

He said, "I'm saving this seat for your fabulous Kate Spade bag. That can't be on the floor."

He's the perfect man and, of course, gay. I didn't think he was gay because he cared about purses but because the next thing he said was, "Don't worry. I'm not hitting on you. I'm gay." I do have a gross habit of just putting my purses on the floors of public places. Nothing I have ever looks like I've owned it less than twenty-four years or like I haven't walked with it through napalm, Pearl Harbor, the beaches of Normandy, Hurricane Katrina, etc. Double Hugh picked up my black shoulder bag, supporting the bottom, and placed it gently on the stool between us.

"That. That beautiful piece of finery needs its own seat," the Two Hugh Look-Alike said. "And I don't care if someone comes in. I'll tell them it's my friend's bag and that my friend will be right back. Are you here alone?" he asked.

"Yes. Yes. Just had a quick hour for some wine and cheese."

"Well, I guess who needs friends with a bag like that, right?"

And on that quip his boyfriend walked in. They embraced and I wanted to tap them on the shoulder and say, "I use my votes to support LGBT rights. I took a gay guy to a prom. I almost exclusively love to hang out with gay men but do you guys ever make exceptions?" But what I actually said was, "Do you know of any straight guys around here that are as stylish as you two who would want to talk to a woman about her handbag?" They laughed. They bought my bag and me another round, and honestly, because my purse is so quiet and demure— it got most of the attention. But technically I met a man in London. I met *two men*. Take that, society. I found a loophole.

The week of shows went great. Even though I didn't have a boyfriend to travel with, I somehow still managed to do my job and not collapse into a heap of self-loathing or find myself in Leicester Square on my knees screaming, "Whyyyy, God?" On my last night in London I had plans to take myself on another fabulous date, hoping that this time I wouldn't fall asleep on myself. I'm a bad date, though. I don't plan ahead. I wander. Wandering is a great thing to do if you're vacationing at a Buddhist retreat in the pines but it's no way to get a table at a trendy restaurant in London. Just like how some women always get caught in a cycle of dating alcoholics—I'm always in a cycle of not noticing a restaurant is shitty until it's too late.

I found myself meandering down Cranbourn Street concerned by how crowded some restaurants already were at six thirty—with lines spilling out onto sidewalks. Even though I'm a vegetarian, I'm a pretty easy-to-please restaurant-goer. I'm happy with bread and cheese. Dining for me is mainly about sitting down, having a glass of wine, and looking at some twinkly white lights that normally only hang at Christmas. This nondiscerning attitude gets me into trouble because I can't tell that a restaurant sucks until it's too late and I've already sat down, ordered a glass of wine, and feel like there's no possible way I can leave—which is exactly what happened to me in . . . some place whose name I don't think I ever knew.

At first the hideaway seemed adorable, with the low ceilings, dark wood, and twinkling white lights on the trees outside. I sat myself, and the only other people inside were an elderly couple. I was handed a menu and before I even looked I said, "Bring me your best glass of pinot grigio." Glancing at the menu I noticed that none of the food made sense. They didn't even bullshit by calling it fusion. It was just *con*fusion. A Greek salad. A hamburger. A sprig of parsley. Falafel. Sushi. Last Thanksgiving's turkey bones. A *Star Wars* action figure. Nothing went together or was from any particular culture.

And then came the final disappointment. My white wine was delivered to me in a stemless wineglass. FUCK STEMLESS WINE-GLASSES. ESPECIALLY FUCK STEMLESS WINEGLASSES WITH WHITE WINE. And don't go telling me that glasses without a stem are European. I mean, sure, I was in Europe, but I should at least have options. As a paying customer I want a stem, or at least a warning. I want the restaurant rating hanging in the window and a sign that says, "We serve wine in glasses that children drink juice out of, thereby sucking ALL of the joy out of being an adult drinking a grown-up drink." The waitress said, "I'll give you some more time to look at the menu." I wish whoever came up with the menu had taken some more time to look at the menu.

Then the elderly couple started to fight. The worst part was that the husband was partially deaf, so he kept telling his wife that he couldn't even hear her nagging. He fell into her trap every time asking, "WHAT?" And she squawked louder, "You're using too many napkins and it's very disgusting!" Normally a woman eating alone watching an elderly couple dine thinks to herself, *That's nice. Those two have someone to grow old with and always have dinner with. I hope I don't die alone tonight*, and not *Jesus Christ. Thank God I'm alone. Imagine being trapped with someone until DEATH do you part and she's harping on you that you're using too many napkins?*

I don't know how I didn't realize that this place wasn't going to be satisfactory. Shouldn't I have realized it when I walked in and they said, "Sit anywhere you like"? Why was I thinking, *Anywhere? Wow. What a little gem I've found on a bustling street filled with otherwise overly full restaurants that people want to go to.* I wanted to be able to say, "I'm sorry. I'm in the mood for something that I don't see on the menu. I should have looked before committing to coming in." But I didn't. I completely spazzed out and threw a twenty-pound note on the table, knocked over my chair putting my coat on, and started to run out. When the waitress asked where I was going and if everything was okay, I shouted, "My boss is paging me! They need me at the theater!" A pager? It was as if I hadn't told a lie since 1998. And what job do I have at a West End theater where twenty minutes before showtime I'm free to have a leisurely dinner and I'm not in any official uniform? It wasn't worth waiting to get my change and having to look her in the eye. I have a fear of confrontation and I even perceive leaving a restaurant that I don't want to eat in as "confrontation." I had a fucked-up fantasy that the owner would come out from the back and get in my face. "Oh, you're not happy with the selections on the menu? That's fine. My husband left me this morning and my mother just died and now you don't want to eat in my restaurant? I came to work today because I had to and I said to myself, maybe *one* person will come in here tonight besides the elderly couple who always take that table and argue and maybe this *one* person will make me feel like I can go on living. But I guess *you're not* that person."

I went back out into the night, bumping into people as I looked at my iPhone trying to find an e-mail from a friend who had recommended the hard-to-get-into Italian restaurant Bocca Di Lupo in Soho. I plugged the address into my iPhone GPS and let the computer lady's voice scream out into the night, "Proceeding to Archer Street. Let's begin." I got a dirty look from a local on the sidewalk and I snapped, "God forbid you see a tourist!"

I was hungry. I get cranky when I'm hungry. I also get cranky when I'm not hungry.

I got to the restaurant and they were booked until the last of the polar ice caps melt—which in one way, yay, that date is actually a lot sooner than it sounds, but it wasn't soon enough to get me a table that night. The bar was first-come, first-served and I was told in a haughty tone that the bar had been full since opening. But I spotted a woman who was using a stool for her purse at the bar. I marched over and asked her if that seat was taken. She scrunched up her face. "Yes. It's taken." She turned around quickly, not able to look in my direction for one more second. I walked back to the hostess area and announced that I would wait for an opening at the bar. She said, "Well, you can't stand in here. You must wait outside." I wasn't about to give up. I saw a burrata appetizer that looked like a small bag of heavenly, oozy cheese—I guess because that's what it is. People should feel bad for people who don't have burrata—not boyfriends.

I stood outside determined to get back in there. I thought about that woman's purse on the stool next to her. That seat wasn't being saved. She was on a date. There was no third party joining them. That seat was for her Marc by Marc Jacobs bag. I marched back in, past the hostess, and went back up to the woman on her date. I tapped her on the shoulder. She turned around with that *what* look. I gathered up the courage for confrontation. I spouted, "I know that this seat is taken but it's taken by a purse. You just don't want to put your purse on the floor. Or you don't want someone next to you but that's not fair. Sure, I've put my purse on a seat in this town but it was at a much less crowded wine bar in the afternoon. What you're doing is squatting and you don't have the right. I am tired and it's my last night in London and I would like to sit down." I would like to say that the restaurant erupted in applause but nobody heard me. This woman barely heard me. She just snatched her purse from the seat, turned her back, and I took my place at the bar. If I hadn't been single I never would have been able to wrangle myself into this restaurant at the last minute. And between you, me, Double Hugh, his boyfriend, and God—her purse wasn't so great that it deserved its own seat.

On my walk back to the hotel I passed two girls sitting outside at a bar. They screamed like they'd just seen a mouse. I kept walking. "Jen Kirkman!" Oh my God. Those screams were for me. I stopped. They squealed and slurred, "We are your biggest fans!!! What are you doing in London?"

I said, "I just did six shows at the theater . . . right there."

"You did? Oh my god! How did we not know?"

After taking selfies with them and letting them squeeze me until my arms were bruised, I left my biggest fans that had no idea that I was performing in London to their blackout drinking and kept walking . . .

I stood alone on the corner of Gerrard and Wardour Streets with lots of other people waiting for the walk signal. A bus pulled up in front of me and a woman banged on the window. She pointed at me and yelled, "WOOOOO!" Could I really be getting recognized again? I looked to the people around me. I hoped that this girl wouldn't start a frenzy of people wanting to get a picture with me. I made eye contact with the woman trying to "woo" me. She screamed, "You're a loser!" She laughed maniacally and continued to shriek, "WOOOOO!" Thank God, I wasn't getting recognized. That was not a specific "Jen Kirkman, you're a loser" but more of a "I'm having the time of my life, unlike you, woman alone on a sidewalk!"

I thought for sure this was a bus that was taking people to a mental institution. The entire bus rocked back and forth with the sounds of the pop song "I Love It" by Icona Pop. It was a Party Bus. I didn't know it was a Party Bus until I asked someone next to me, "What the hell is that?"

"A Party Bus," he said.

"What's a Party Bus?"

He sighed. "It's a bus that has a party." The subtext being, "You fucking idiot."

I guess it *was* pretty self-explanatory. I don't understand why you would want to party on the very type of vehicle that used to take us to and from school and later in life drags our reluctant bodies to and from work. Who wants to listen to dance music while wearing a seat belt? Does the bus escort people to their party destination or is the party actually just on the bus that is always driving around? Can't people sit with their own thoughts anymore? No one can drive about five miles *to* a party without throwing a party? I also thought getting drunk and yelling "WOOOOO!" was something only Americans did. It made me feel better that my country isn't the only one filled with idiots but it made me sad that maybe there's no escape from humans who can't hold their alcohol. I knew one thing: I wasn't a loser because I'd been eating alone and was now walking alone. I was a loser because I got excited about putting my earbuds in and listening to the Cure as I strolled through Soho, hoping that teenaged me—who dreamed of walking around London alone—would appreciate the gesture. I don't care. I love it.

18

PARIS IS ALWAYS A GOOD IDEA

Oh, London is a man's town, there's power in the air; And Paris is a woman's town, with flowers in her hair.

—HENRY VAN DYKE, AUTHOR

Traveling to London was the first time I had traveled alone since my divorce but not the first time I traveled without a man. I'd been to Hawaii with my friend Sarah . . . that somehow flew under everyone's radar. I think because it's socially acceptable for women to drink margaritas by a pool together.

But when I started planning a trip to Paris for a week in the fall of 2012 with my aforementioned good friend Allison, I got some bizarre reactions. My mother asked me, "Jennifah, ah you a lesbian now?"

"No, Mom. I'm not a *lesbian*. I'm just going to Paris with a woman. Okay, admittedly that does sound pretty lesbianish but it's Allison. You know, she was one of my bridesmaids."

"And now she's a lesbian?"

"No. I am not a lesbian now because I'm divorced and Allison is not a lesbian now because I'm divorced."

"Jennifah, I have nothing against you being gay. It's just that it's a hahhd life. Trust me, I would have had it much easier in so many ways if I had lived with my best friend Doreen instead of yah fathah. For example, I bet that Doreen doesn't put clean socks in a dirty clothes hamper. But society isn't nice to gay people and I wouldn't want you to choose being gay because you think it's easier."

"Anything is easier than having this bizarre conversation, but again, I'm not gay. I'm just dying to go back to Paris and Allison and I can both afford it. If we wait for men to take us to Paris we'll probably miss getting to go this coming September, when we both have the same vacation week."

Heading to Paris was something of a do-over for me as well. My husband and I had ventured to Paris and the South of France as a sort of Hail Mary in our marriage—but to the outside world we were celebrating our one-year wedding anniversary. I think we were both feeling *le mort* inside and I know that I picked Paris as a vacation spot because it's pretty much agreed upon to be the most romantic city in the world. If I couldn't feel hopelessly giddy walking along the River Seine with my husband—then maybe it was time to think about *le divorce*. That (surprise!) unromantic trip to Paris still haunted me and I wanted to go back so that my last memories of Paris wouldn't be of a stupid fight we had outside of Dior. (I wanted to go in just to look. My ex-husband was a big believer in not going into stores we couldn't afford just to look. He said it was tacky.) Trust me: traveling with a man doesn't always mean that everything in your life is perfect.

My husband, Matt, and I were walking down the Promenade des Anglais in Nice after a huge dinner in one of those restaurants that has outdoor seating on a cobblestone side street—right underneath the woman who lives on the third floor who looks out disapprovingly as she smokes a cigarette and checks on her drying laundry. It's a scene that if it were a movie, the director would say to the set designer, "Look, you've got the Italian waiters speaking French and flirting with both the husband *and* wife. You've got the moon lighting up the checkered tablecloths and the bottle of house red tucked snug into a wicker holder. You've got the elderly man with the accordion wandering up and down the street playing for no one and everyone. You've got the woman who lives in the building with the pink shutters pursing her cigarette between her lips as she hangs a white sheet on her clothesline. It's too much. Pick ONE European cliché, please, for this dinner scene."

I realized we weren't holding hands as we walked, and three thoughts piled up in my head at once, like cars in a freeway collision.

After the Jaws of Life removed my thoughts from the wreck and un-tangled them—they went like this: *We aren't holding hands. I'm not sure if I want to hold hands. He doesn't seem like he wants to hold hands. People who have been married for almost a year and together for six don't have to hold hands anymore walking down the street. We're not horny teenagers. We're best friends. I sort of want to want to hold hands with someone, though. Jen, grow up. Those days are over. You're a grown woman. No need to display your affection for the world. I wonder if we'll have sex tonight. I'd be okay if we just laid in bed together and listened to the cars drag down the road and the ocean in between them. I'm kind of enjoying this book I am reading. I guess I could enjoy this book after the sex but I might be too tired.*

I turned to Matt and coyly suggested, "Hey. Want to go down to the beach?"

"The beach? For what? It's dark and it's all rocky. We could fall."

"I'm not talking about walking. Let's have sex on the beach."

"Sex on the beach? No way. I don't want anyone seeing me naked."

"Dear God, no. I don't even want YOU to see me naked. I think I saw some cellulite on my knee today. We don't have to get naked. I mean we'll sneak off under the boardwalk and to anyone passing by who happens to see us they'll think we're just snuggling."

"No, Jen. Come on."

"You come on! This is the South of France. I think the people who *aren't* having sex on the beach are the ones that people are staring at."

"What are you even asking me for sex for? To fulfill some kind of exhibitionist fantasy?"

Matt wasn't a cruel, nonspontaneous person but that night I thought he was a dream-killing celibate monster. With perspective I realize that given the thoughts leading up to my request for sex on the beach I'm surprised I didn't just ask, "Can we walk over there and just see if we're still attracted to each other?"

As it turns out, I am the type of woman who wants sex on the beach. I'd just never really shared that with Matt. I don't know why. I'd had sex on the beach once, with my boyfriend Blake back in July of 1996 at Duxbury Beach in Massachusetts at about midnight—not that it left a beautiful memory and made a searing impact or anything. I just remember the way the towel felt, cool on my back on the damp sand; the sight of the moonlight on the water; the steady sound of the waves slapping a few feet away. It was stimulating not because of the danger that at any second we could get caught and arrested by some angry cop who wasn't getting any himself—but because it was so romantic. The climax went beyond a physical orgasm. My heart almost burst as I smelled my boyfriend's patchouli scent and gazed at the unstoppable stars in the sky. That's right. I loved my patchouli-smelling boyfriend. I was young and in love and I take it as a win when a twenty-year-old guy doesn't smell like stale beer.

I thought that maybe if Matt and I had a location cure for what had become sort of a return to a bread-and-butter sex life that perhaps I could really feel in my heart my love for my husband. I knew intellectually that I loved my partner but my heart always remained safely in my rib cage—with no threat of bursting through. We didn't have sex in the South of France but instead watched other people score when we turned on the TV to watch the World Cup.

In stark contrast to that trip with my ex-husband, Allison and I took in every museum, had mimosas with breakfast and sparkling wine with dinner. Allison didn't judge me when I insisted on bumming a cigarette off of someone in a café because she didn't have to kiss my ashtray breath after. (Travel tip: Bumming cigarettes in Paris is a big no-no. The French wish that you would buy your own Gauloises.) Allison and I shopped during the day and even browsed inside Dior. (Of *course* it's not gauche to go in there and not buy anything. Who can afford Dior?) At night over dinner we talked intimately about our fears, our frustrations with our careers, she lamented her single state, I lamented that I was in love with a friend who I couldn't bring myself to be with because I didn't want to have to take care of a man who I felt didn't have his life in order. I cried in my meringue. We stayed in separate rooms. I never understood why traveling is something reserved for lovers only. Who wants to stay with their lover in a small European

hotel where the toilet is next to the bed? It's way too exhausting to be
on vacation and keep having to say, "I'm going to run to the corner and
get us some coffee," just so that you can secretly take a number two
in the hotel lobby bathroom. Besides, have you ever watched the sun
set over the Eiffel Tower and thought, *What I really want right now is
to finish this night off pretending that I don't hear my partner's derriere
having diarrhea in our tiny hotel bathroom?*

19

FLYING BY THE SEAT OF MY SWEATPANTS (LOS ANGELES TO MELBOURNE)

The most difficult thing is the decision to act, the rest is merely tenacity. The fears are paper tigers. You can do anything you decide to do. You can act to change and control your life; and the procedure, the process is its own reward.

—AMELIA EARHART

We don't have any shrinks at Walkabout Creek. No. Back there if you got a problem you tell Wally. And he tells everyone in town, brings it out in the open, no more problem.

—CROCODILE DUNDEE

'm so familiar with in-flight instructions I could train future flight attendants. The most accidentally philosophical instruction being the one regarding using the oxygen mask that falls from the ceiling. Affix the strap to yourself before putting it on your kid's face. People in the midst of a freak-out and full of "I'm a good parent" hormones want to do it the other way around, but if you run out of breath then you and your kid are both screwed. The lesson? You can only help others once you've helped yourself and you've got your oxygen together. As a solo traveler who doesn't have to worry about her kid, or her husband who acts like a kid sometimes, I'm available to help in case of an emergency. (I mean, not like a real emergency like terrorism or anything. Even though I sit in exit rows a lot, I'm lying. I don't think I can push open that fifty-pound door.) Anyway, my point is that instead of pitying me for traveling alone on a sixteen-hour flight from Los Angeles to Melbourne, you should be congratulating me for being there to help someone even worse off than me—a *man* traveling alone, and by alone I mean without Klonopin.

A flight to Australia used to be something I thought I could never do because of my panic disorder. Even with my trusty prescription for Klonopin, my fear was overwhelming in the face of such a long flight. The biggest question that I asked myself over and over and over was, *What if the pill stops working? Then how will I feel?* That's anxiety. Anxiety is a brat. Imagine if your brain was a big boardroom filled with men and women who make decisions every single day. Some committees handle things really smoothly, so well that you don't even realize it—like the committee that handles telling your heart to beat. Every day the board of directors has meetings to decide how our brains are going to behave. Now imagine that the good-for-nothing son of the CEO shows up drunk, unshowered, with puke stains on his shirt from the night before, crusty blood under his nose from a brawl he doesn't remember starting. He sits down full of bravado and arrogance and absolutely no experience and no sense of reality. But he thinks that he belongs. *He* is anxiety. And what makes his presence so awful? For some reason the CEO of the brain—ME—lets him stay at the table while the other committee members must be thinking, *Wait a minute. We have college degrees and years of experience running her brain and this frat boy do-nothing gets the same power to vote, veto, and advise as we do? Why? Why can't the boss see that this guy has no idea what he's talking about? He only causes trouble with his big ideas like 'Let's obsess over a proven medication not working.' Or 'Let's tell Jen's brain she's in danger when she's not.'*

Anxiety is such a strong voice in my head that sometimes it tells me not even to bother with certain experiences. *"Oh, you'll freak out if you do that. Don't do that. That's not for you."* And I used to believe Anxiety! No more. Anxiety is a liar and a lazy little shit. Don't let Anxiety have a seat at the table.

I'd dreamed of going to Australia since seeing the movie *Crocodile Dundee* when I was a kid. But Anxiety told me that on my flight

Down Under, I could have the world's biggest panic attack, not yet documented, the first of its kind, where the panic leads to a heart attack. Anxiety told me that I would have that heart attack on the plane somewhere between Hawaii and Fiji during the "just the ocean" part of the flight and the pilot would not be able to land and get me to a hospital. Because of this one-sided conversation with Anxiety, when I had the opportunity to go on a fully paid working trip to Sydney back in 2009 with the TV show *Chelsea Lately* I almost said no. I'm glad I didn't. I got to fly first-class with a bunch of friends and experience the bliss that is the lie-flat seat. And my medication worked. I did not panic. I loved the flight so much; I went into slight mourning over the fact that we had to get off that fun, intimate laser light tube filled with bars and beds.

The Melbourne International Comedy Festival is a prestigious comedy festival that's an honor—sorry, Australians, *honour*—to be part of, and I was asked to participate in March 2014. I would have to fly the seven thousand nine hundred thirty-two miles alone. Twice. That's sixteen hours each way. In that length of time on the ground you could wake up, hit snooze a few times, shower, go get coffee, work an eight-hour day, hit the treadmill after work, go out to dinner, and drive home from dinner just in time to watch two hours of *The Bachelor*. Think about that next time you're going about your day—that in the length of time it took you to do all that, a bunch of people were thirty thousand feet above you unable to just go open a door for some fresh air. Even on the night flights—designed for us to spend a solid seven hours in a dreamlike state—that still leaves NINE other hours.

And my first thought was, *I can't do that.* This is why Anxiety is such a stupid C student who should be fired from the boardroom of our brains. I'd already had a successful flight to Australia that helped alleviate my fears, but Anxiety told me that was purely circumstantial. It was the friends and the first-class bed that allowed for everything to be okay. Anxiety—who has never been *anywhere*—told me that those thirty combined hours of flying around the world didn't count. But being the occasional, shortsighted CEO of my brain that I sometimes am, I listened to Anxiety while the encouraging and rational words from the other board members remained a low whisper in the back of my mind. I liked what the committee told me about the safety of airplanes, how I'll be asleep for most of it, that the flight attendants are trained to deal with anxiety, that even if God forbid something happened—it, like everything else about flying a plane, and most of life in general—is just plain out of my control.

I managed to stay firm with Anxiety, call the board to a vote (9 to 1 in favor of going to Australia), and say yes to the festival.

(FYI, another trick I use to show Anxiety who's boss is thinking, *What would Madonna do?* Okay, she would have backup dancers, a chiropractor, and a raw food chef traveling with her on a private jet and she would be perfectly made up even while sleeping—her rock-hard arms flexing during her REM cycle. But besides that, she obviously wouldn't be afraid to fly to Australia. She would be afraid to NOT fly to Australia and let Iggy Azalea interrupt her world domination.)

Still, at LAX as I boarded the plane to Melbourne, not even being safe and sound in my cozy sweatpants could stop the familiar rush of adrenaline. The old miswiring in my DNA that tells me that I am in danger. Maybe my DNA was responding to the fact that there was currently a missing plane off the coast of Perth and that it's a vast ocean—there's plenty of room for one more plane. What would Madonna do? I tried to remember her commands from the song "Vogue" and I discreetly tried to "give good face" as I boarded the plane.

I took my seat in Premium Economy by the window. I continued with my inner dialogue. *I'm a grown woman on a trip. I'm Madonna taking the world by storm.* Thank GOD people around me could not hear these thoughts or read my mind. They would have felt such pity for me. "Yeah. See that girl in seat 14A? She's pretending she's Madonna. Madonna wouldn't have to hoist her own suitcase into the bin, though."

I thought, *Other people must be anxious.* I looked around but no one else *seemed* anxious. Travelers were excitedly taking books out of their carry-ons, getting out blankets, ready for the long, cozy haul, confident that the plane wouldn't run out of fuel somewhere off Fiji. And then I spotted someone who had the familiar look of terror: swallowing when there's no saliva left in his throat, a white face—not just a white person, but extra-white skin. He was my seatmate and I could tell that he was having a full-blown panic attack. He put his suitcase in the aisle—forgetting to put it either under the seat in front of him or in the overhead. He sat down and began explaining himself to me as though I had been up late waiting for him and needed to hear a really good excuse.

He breathlessly started, "I hate to bother you. I'm so anxious. I haven't flown in twenty years. I got a tech job in Los Angeles designing videogame software. I was content doing that. I was happy just sitting at my desk, on the ground, not having to go anywhere, until the company became wildly successful in the past year and now part of my job requires me to travel internationally. My friend is on this flight but he's on the other side of the plane and he's already asleep. He can sleep anywhere. So, I'm just here alone with my thoughts. All night."

A flight attendant gently took his suitcase from him to give him more legroom. He grabbed her arm and begged, "Can I please get a drink?" Another flight attendant came down the aisle with a tray of sparkling wine. "Oh my god!" he said. "It's a sign!" I said to him, "It's just a sign that you're in Premium Economy. They always do this." Normally I don't drink on planes—it's too dehydrating—but he pleaded, "Have one with me? As a good-luck thing?" I took one. Who was I to buck the classic good-luck tradition of having sparkling wine out of a plastic cup with a stranger on a flight from Los Angeles to Australia?

Compared to this guy, I was an anxiety expert, a veteran. Having someone who is more frightened than you is the greatest gift to someone who is a little bit frightened. It gives the less frightened person the chance to help soothe someone else—which in turn self-soothes. I get to go into big sister mode, which helps take the focus off of how Madonna and I are feeling.

I know what you're thinking. Could there have been a love connection between my seatmate and me? Nope. First of all, he politely told me that he had a girlfriend and was not trying to pick me up. And he wasn't my type. Trust me, if he'd looked like Brad Pitt circa *Thelma & Louise* I would have tried to get the party started under the blanket once the lights went out, convincing him that his girlfriend sucked and this was obviously our destiny. Although if he were Brad Pitt today, I would respectfully keep my distance for fear of the wrath of Angelina—and I don't want to be a stepmom to *one* kid, forget six.

Jason was my seat buddy's name—or should I say, *is* his name. I'm sure he's still alive somewhere. Jason was overly enthused about the bar on the plane. I explained to him that drinking actually makes one more anxious because of all the sugar.

"But, Jen, if I don't drink I think I'll have a nervous breakdown."

"Okay, well, have a drink then." I would be a terrible sober coach.

Jason and I had different ideas about how to handle takeoff. I wanted to be asleep before it happened. I'm not a fan of the "I can't control anything anymore—we're leaving the ground!" style of coping. I didn't want to be there for that moment. Jason, however, needed to be awake during takeoff so that he could help fly the plane with his mind.

The man I'd known for all of fifteen minutes pleaded with me to stay awake and talk him through this.

"Okay," I said. "But I am not good with takeoff on long flights, so I can't really just talk. I have to do my plan B."

"Let's do it. What's your plan B?"

As the plane started to make insanely loud "I'm a giant machine" noises, and the taxiing began, I explained to Jason that plan B consists of me looking at a fashion magazine because pictures of clothing soothe me.

He was so nervous that he was fine with that.

I opened up the latest issue of *Lucky* magazine.

Jason politely tried to play along and said, "From a graphic design perspective this magazine is laid out really nicely."

"My ex-husband hated when I made him play this game," I said.

"That's because he was your husband. It's much easier to go along with crazy things a woman is saying if you're not dating her."

"Way to put it in perspective, Jason."

Jason's hand started to tremble and he said, "WHAT? ARE PURSES REALLY FOUR THOUSAND DOLLARS? DOES MY GIRLFRIEND SPEND THAT MUCH ON PURSES?"

"No! Jason! Purses are *not* that much money in real life!" I yelled over the sound of the engine roaring into the sky. "That's just the runway price!"

"Oh, so department stores do, like, cheaper knockoff versions?"

"Exactly, Jason."

"So do you think my girlfriend pays, like . . . a hundred dollars for her purse?"

"Probably, Jason. Probably."

"She just has a lot of debt. I mean, some of it is student loans but I want to make sure she's not overspending."

I was starting to panic just from the stress of Jason's girlfriend's debt.

"Jason, we need to focus here. I need to take my mind off of the fact that we're only one minute into this flight. I have to take this game to the next level."

I explained to Jason that the next level is that I find a page with a few outfits and we play the game, "Which Outfit Would I Buy, Which Outfit Would Look Best On Me, and Which Outfit Do I Wish I Could Pull Off?" It's a complex game full of choices and possibilities. I decided that since Jason didn't know me, we would play it with his girlfriend in mind. My ex-husband hated this game. I think mostly he resented that I got to take Klonopin *and* get special treatment—one was supposed to outdo the other. It never dawned on me to ask Matt, "Okay, so what do *you* like to do during takeoff?" Then again, he didn't have a fear of flying. As I thought about Matt, I felt a bubble of what I call "plane emotion." It's the kind of emotion that creeps up, and while it may produce a salient thought—the reaction to it can be extreme. Like . . . crying over the Kate Hudson movie where she falls in love but then dies of colon cancer. (Yes, that's a movie.)

"Jason, I think I was a shitty wife. I'm glad I'm not married anymore but I still wish I could look back on some things and say, 'I was always selfless.' I wasn't."

"Relationships are hard. I mean, that's what everyone says. Mine isn't hard. But maybe it will be and I'm just in the unreality phase."

"But why is the good stuff considered unreal and the bad stuff considered reality?"

"I think things were easier in my grandfather's day."

"I don't. I just found out that my jolly old grandfather was having an affair for most of his life and my grandmother took a job as a waitress just to be passive-aggressive to him about not cooking dinner."

"My grandfather was an alcoholic."

With no sense of irony or self-awareness, Jason then asked the flight attendant when the bar would be open. Drinks could be served anytime but Jason had a fixation with standing at the bar and making himself a cocktail.

We passed the time before he could start shaking martinis by discussing which movies have held up since the nineties. We decided that *Good Will Hunting* was a yes. *Singles* a no. I gave him the extra meat that came with my vegetarian meal (fucking Australians) and he gave me his roll.

At hour three, while Jason finally made himself a cocktail I took to stretching to keep the blood flowing even though I was wearing circulation socks. Jason came back and continued talking about his grandfather. He feared that alcoholism could run in the family and although he doesn't drink daily, he drinks when he's stressed—like on a sixteen-hour flight. I told Jason that I couldn't diagnose him or enable him. I could only listen. But maybe he should find a therapist when he's back in America. I should have charged him by the hour. I would have had a cool two thousand dollars in my pocket upon landing.

I was getting tired. It was time for me to recline my seat three inches and call it a night. Jason decided to stay up a little later to watch a movie—he was feeling more confident about being the only person awake on the plane and not panicking. I told him that he could always wake me up if he needed me. An hour passed and I woke up—the smell of Jason's wine breath was floating out of his open mouth like the humidity off of a sewer grate. I could see the molecules of stale grape floating my way and invading my nose.

"Jason. Wake up. You have to brush your teeth and really gargle with mouthwash."

Within six hours Jason and I had become an old married couple. Now we were both awake and decided to tackle the subject of death. What happens when we die? Jason and I shared the same fear that if we write a Last Will and Testament then we are somehow inviting death into our lives. Besides, since we both believe that when you die it's just lights-out—who cares if your wishes to be cremated were honored? But something deep inside both of us questioned WHAT IF? What if somehow, somewhere, some *way* your dead self knows that it ended up buried in the same small town that its living self worked so hard to get out of? And what if that translated into your legacy becoming just . . . sad trapped energy? We kept asking questions like a couple of three-year-olds. Why do we think aliens come from outer space? What if they come from underneath the ocean? Jason fell asleep in the middle of his thought about how even though going to Australia scares him he thinks he could handle going up in a space shuttle.

I looked out my window at the blackness, and maybe it was the altitude, the Klonopin, or the six rolls I'd had but I felt a small, deep, tranquil joy; a love for humanity that wasn't romantic or sappy. I felt that everyone on this plane was one. And if we were one—then we were one with everyone else. If everyone on earth could take a sixteen-hour flight with a stranger and get to know them, they would actually be able to put themselves in someone else's shoes, or at least put their shoes right next to someone else's shoes underneath someone else's seat. If the purpose of this trip was only to bring me to this realization—it was all worth it. If all of my shows went terribly in Australia or I got bitten by one of their many deadly poisonous spiders, it would still be worth it. People who take ayahuasca are missing out. There's a way to reach this level of enlightenment without the next-day nausea. I vowed from now on that there would no longer be times when I get angry or annoyed at other people for no reason. We are all just love. Even Dick Cheney. Even Dick fucking Cheney is pure love.

When the sun was coming up or coming out or just coming right up to my window, Jason was already up and at 'em—stretching at the bar instead of drinking, just like I taught him. I felt proud of us. Jason's friend, Adam, came over to our seats to visit. We told him all about our successful flight with no panic or anxiety attacks. Jason and I shared a quiet breakfast—just comfortable in our own silence as we read. I kept to myself for the final descent into Melbourne. I looked out the window welling with unnamed emotion as I saw the mass of land come into view. What a miracle that I could be brought around the world, over the ocean for hours, and land safely in this magnificent, mystifying land. The *second* the plane touched down I heard a symphony of beeps and bloops as smartphones were turned back on and the choruses of "Yeah, I just landed" began. As we maneuvered in our seats to gather our belongings and get off the plane, Jason thanked me for helping him and said, "Hey, I didn't even ask you—what's bringing you to Melbourne?"

"Oh, um. Nothing. Just a wedding. And work. A working wedding. Really boring."

I'm a terrible liar but I hate telling people that I'm a comedian. It always invites the worst small talk. People usually assume there's no way I'm a professional comedian since I'm not world-famous. Most people don't know that you can make a living at comedy without being Jerry Seinfeld. The top five things people say to stand-up comics that we can't stand are:

1. You should come to my office. You'll get a lot of material for your skits there.
2. Do you make a living doing that?
3. What's your real job?
4. I always thought I would be good at stand-up.
5. You don't seem funny. Tell me a joke.

After my awkward lie I realized that I could probably trust Jason since we had gotten to know each other so well on the plane, and he would probably be intrigued to know what I was up to. I told him the truth about the festival and that I'm a stand-up comedian.

"And you do this for a living? You didn't tell me one joke on the flight. You don't seem funny at all."

I struggled to get my suitcase to budge from the overhead bin.

"What's your full name?"

"Jen. [*Grunting.*] Kirkman."

"Kirkland?"

"Kirk-man."

"I've never heard of you. And this is your real job?"

"Yes."

"Well, I should try to remember you in case you make it someday!"

[*Grunting.*] [*Struggling with suitcase.*] "There are many definitions of making it, Jason."

"Well, I hope you get into the festival."

[*More grunting.*] [*More struggling with suitcase.*] "I *did* get into the festival. I didn't just fly here to *try* to get into a major festival. They flew me here. Just like your job. This is my job."

The guy in back of me who had to catch a connecting flight grew impatient. He put an end to my overhead bin struggles, grabbed my suitcase for me, and said, "Congratulations. You're a comedian. Who cares if this guy believes it? Just get of off the plane."

And with that I lumbered off of the plane and said good-bye to Jason, probably forever. His last words to me were, "I'll look for your name, Jen Kirkland!"

My compassion for Jason turned immediately to disdain. He WAS an alcoholic, that loser. And I hoped his girlfriend was buying $5,000 purses on his credit card that very minute. I felt claustrophobic in the previous night's realization that we were all one. I didn't want to be Jason. I wanted to be me: a woman dragging her suitcase through Melbourne's airport, heading for the duty-free perfume in lieu of a shower. I spritzed on some Chanel No. 5. "Do you want to buy that?"

"No. I have to run," I lied. "I have to make a connection." Thank God I had no connections to make. Connecting with humanity was exhausting enough and Jen Kirkland just wanted to nap.

20

NO LUCK OF THE IRISH

It's a big con job. We have sold the myth of Dublin as a sexy place incredibly well; because it's a dreary little dump most of the time.

—RODDY DOYLE, IRISH AUTHOR

Even though I'm from Boston and was raised Catholic, I'm not Irish. I'm German/French Canadian/Polish/English. And according to my mother, "You can tell we aren't Irish because we only have three kids in our family—unlike that Irish family down the street who has eight kids and a dog that runs around biting everyone in the neighborhood. God didn't say anything about not using the Pill. As long as you are married anything goes." That was her French Canadian/German take on things, I guess. Church was once a week. No need to go every day—unless you're guilty of something.

Despite my non-Irishness, I got offered a gig to do a comedy festival in Dublin for three days in July of 2014. I'd already flung myself across the globe twice that year to London and Melbourne so what was one more time? It seems insane to go from Los Angeles to Dublin for just seventy-two hours, but if someone is going to pay for the trip and on top of that pay me to perform—why not? It would take me out of Los Angeles for another weekend that I could be getting down to finding another boyfriend to end my many months' streak of utter celibacy, but on the other hand it seemed perfect to enter a Catholic country feeling sexually repressed.

It's important to take in the culture of every audience. Every country reacts to comedy differently. British people don't laugh very loudly. They don't applaud much. But after the show, once the comedian is feeling like he or she should have just stayed home the English will line up to tell you that you were "brilliant." Then they'll proudly tell you that they know that they didn't give you a goddamn sign that they thought you were brilliant but that's just how they are.

I'd heard that the Irish don't admit to much. If a comedian were to ask, "How many people here are in therapy?" it would be met with silence—either they wouldn't ever admit it or they wouldn't ever be therapized in the first place. I like to make direct connections with people in my audience. I'm like if the Statue of Liberty came to life. I seek out the downtrodden, the tired, the childfree, the single, and the divorced. I don't make fun of them, I just ask about what their experience was and then work it into my act. I decided that I would proceed with caution and not bother asking the Dublin audience if any of them were also divorced. I would just get into the material and whoever relates, bonus. The material can stand on its own even if no one in the room is divorced. I wasn't really worried. There haven't been many audiences I haven't been able to win over at least a little bit, even if they only seemed lukewarm to me at first. Or maybe I don't win anyone over. Maybe the two-drink minimum has just finally kicked into their bloodstream.

Before my shows at what I'll call "The Corporate Cell Phone–Sponsored Comedy Festival," I had a day of sightseeing. Dublin reminds me a lot of Boston. It's quaint, steeped in history, with an appreciation for its big thinkers and artists like James Joyce, Thomas Kinsella, Jonathan Swift, Samuel Beckett, George Bernard Shaw, and my favorite, Oscar Wilde. I immediately traipsed to the birthplace of Oscar Wilde just to stand on the front steps and stare at a plaque. I'd already visited his grave in Paris—I was paying my respects out of order.

I sauntered into a dress shop that mixed vintage with brand-new independent designers. I spent an hour trying on dresses, modeling them for the clerk as other women shopping did the same. I settled on a button-down gray dress with small red flowers that had a very

1990s feel—even more so if I were to pair it with Mary Janes or combat boots. Next I went to see a tarot card reader named David who had come highly recommended. He wasn't expecting me. I just showed up at his little storefront. As I shuffled the deck he said, "Divorced?"

"Yeah, how did you know?"

"I'm a little intuitive as well. I can tell you've just put a big obstacle behind you."

Now look, you skeptics. I know. I know that a woman my age, who clearly isn't a local and comes wandering in looking for guidance from a deck of cards without a wedding ring—it's pretty obvious that she's divorced or (*gasp*) worse (*in hushed tone*) *never been married*. I get it. But I think it's magical to believe that someone can see into me and know my past and my future. WHY NOT? It's cheaper than therapy and less work. And, may I add, I wanted to know more about what my life would look like. I wasn't aiming to find out about my love life from a guy resting his arms on a paisley tablecloth. But he seemed to be picking up some information from . . . somewhere, so I let him do his thing. David spread my cards out on the table. I was getting a lot of what he called "kick-ass" cards. I could see for myself that they were pretty kick-ass; lots of women holding big cups and wearing giant hats. In a more modern deck it would be the Hillary Clinton or Oprah card.

"You're very kick-ass. Strong. Independent. There's no man."

He shuffled some more.

"Oh, there is a man. He's over here," he said, motioning under the table.

"He's hiding?"

"He's not ready to come to you yet and that's because you're not ready for a commitment. He's kind of like Clint Eastwood but with the soul of a woman."

The last major event I remember Clint Eastwood from was when he did a bizarre theatrical performance/speech at the Republican National Convention where he yelled at a chair. And he's eighty-five. But the soul of a woman sounds nice. It would be great to be with someone who can beat someone up for me but also understands my fears of early menopause.

"He doesn't mind that you travel. He travels too. But he's not coming for six months."

David the Tarot Card Reader also told me that there's a baby card in my future. When I bristled and said, "I'm about to turn forty. I don't think so," he quickly recovered and said, "Something you do with children is going to make you a lot of money." Either it's that for-profit orphanage I plan to start or maybe my last book, *I Can Barely Take Care of Myself*, will retroactively hit number one, kicking a Bill O'Reilly book off of the top of the charts. I don't think it's going to be an actual baby—seeing as I don't want one. I don't even think I can get pregnant anymore. My current birth control is just to tell someone, "Pull out if you remember, I don't think anything's working."

Overall, the reading was everything I hope my life turns out to be. He predicted that the next seven years will be filled with travel adventure, that I'll live overseas for a short time, and again a badass man with a feminist streak will be joining me. And then the pièce de résistance: David topped off our time together with the ultimate cherry—"You know, Jen, you seem very sensitive and intuitive. I bet you have what it takes to be a psychic too."

I don't know why women feel so complimented by being called psychic but it really is something that lots of us cherish as a virtuous quality. I would rather be called psychic over generous, brave, warm, anything. It's another way of saying, "You're special. You're different. *You're better than most people.*"

Thank you, I am! One time I predicted I was going to stay in bed all day and I did!

With my future clearly laid out before me—and nothing awful to look forward to—later on that day as the sun set, I skipped over to the Iveagh Gardens where the shows were taking place.

I talked to some of the other comics who were hanging out backstage—or rather, outside, behind the makeshift tented theater. Some of the other comedians were Irish but most of them were Canadian or British—all of them with more experience performing in Ireland than me. One girl worked some tough love and gave me heart-to-heart fashion advice that was too late because I had to get onstage in four minutes. "They might not like the leather pants. It comes off as too confident for the audience." Another comic chimed in, "Yeah, they don't really like American performers."

That seemed odd to me because I'd seen a James Dean mural spray-painted on the side of a building with the word "HERO." And there are reruns of *Friends* on at all hours of the night.

"Oh, they like *those* Americans but it takes a while for them to warm up to a comedian. Especially a woman."

I heard my name announced with the introduction, "This next comedian is from America"—that's all it took for some people to start booing. I smiled and tried to get through my set but there were about fifty guys in the back of the room singing some kind of anthem. (I later found out that these guys bought tickets to the show but were having a college fraternity reunion, like they figured out a loophole, that a cheap way to "rent a room with entertainment" was to buy tickets to an already existing event and completely take over.)

After I joked about being divorced, one woman in the front row yelled, "Marriage is sacred. Shoulda made it work!" What, was my Sunday school teacher here heckling me? She yelled out again during a bit I have about sex, "Too much information!" I yelled back, "Honey, I haven't even begun to give information yet. If this is too much you should leave." She left. Another woman in the front shouted, "I can see why your marriage didn't work." I ignored her. I was no longer performing my work. I was just talking on autopilot, counting down til my fifteen minutes of shame was over.

I took a bow and enthusiastically said with a big smile, "Thanks, you've been awful." It was only nine o'clock. I wandered through the otherwise lovely landscape and tried to ignore the sounds of plastic cups being crushed against dudes' heads and burps that sounded like they were coming from the trees. This wasn't an intellectual comedy crowd. Certainly not Dublin's finest. Two guys ran up to me and each grabbed me by an arm, lifting me off of the ground. One said, "You're too pretty to not get teamed." I kicked him in the shin and released myself. "Hey, you rapists! I'll tell a cop." Luckily there was an officer behind me, witnessing the whole thing.

"Oh, they're all right," he said in his plucky accent.

"They're all right?" I said in my Boston accent that I use when I'm trying to sound tough. "They said that they wanted to team me."

The cop laughed it off. "Well, they're not now."

I kept walking, letting my prejudice build. Jesus Christ, Dublin was Paris by day—South Boston by night.

Where were the drunken intellectual poets? I know that James Joyce was often kicked out of bars in Dublin for fighting but at least it was what he did when not writing groundbreaking novels.

I ran into two old friends from America, comedians Neal Brennan and Anthony Jeselnik—both are fiercely hilarious, well respected, and do not put up with any shit. They told me that crowds notoriously suck at The Corporate Cell Phone–Sponsored Comedy Festival. We found a bar to hang out in that was safe from my haters and we started in on the Guinness. Normally I don't have a taste for beer but normally I don't have such distaste coming my way. Guinness was medicine. I told the bartender about the crowd I just performed to. I showed him the reviews on Twitter that were already coming in. Lots of carefully written assessments of my work such as, "You suck." He said, "Oh, man, drunken Irish people are a bunch of cunts. Write that on Twitter."

"I can't say that."

"Yes, you can, love. It will be funny. 'Cunt' is a term of endearment around here. They'll get the joke."

"They'll get the joke" may as well have been said in slow motion, it was such foreshadowing. The expression "famous last words" was invented for this moment. And so I picked up my iPhone and tweeted just as he said, "Drunken Irish people are a bunch of cunts."

At that moment, I saw Ren standing before me. Who is Ren? I didn't know either. He introduced himself and said he was a drummer and his band is well known in Ireland. No, it's not U2. I don't know his band's name so I'll just call them "Not U2." Ren said, "I think you're funny and I loved your set about how you dated a twenty-year-old for one night. I'm twenty-four. Do you have room for one more?"

I see my comedy as a way to share my humiliations so that others can feel less alone. I never see it as a way to solicit men to sleep with. My stories about being single are not cries for help. Or cries for dick. But I was drunk. I was sad and feeling so unfunny I thought that the only cure would be to feel ashamed about something else as soon as possible. So I kissed this kid who was sixteen years my junior from the band Not U2. I felt odd kissing someone in front of people I knew. I hadn't done that since my first kiss in my best friend's basement—oh wait, no, and also at the altar on my wedding day.

We hightailed it downstairs to the bathrooms where just outside the men's and ladies' rooms was a proper chaise lounge/fainting couch perfect for making out with a stranger. We kissed for a while and anyone within a two-inch radius could feel that Ren wanted more. He wanted to go back to my hotel room because he didn't live in Dublin but had to be in Dublin very early the next morning. He said that he didn't want to have to drive back to his mom's house. *His mom's house? Oh, God. No. No. I can't do this. I'm too old.* I said my good-byes to Ren and thanked him for being the only man in Ireland to find me funny.

Hours later, I hit the road and was utterly confused that the sun was rising. Wait. What? My friend Anthony gently explained that we just stayed up all night like a couple of drunken cunts. I had lost all track of time in the bar but I assumed that since I was still in the bar and still being served that it must be somewhere between eleven p.m. and two a.m. I didn't know that bars stayed open until six a.m. in Dublin. Feeling safe because, well, it was morning and people were already out walking their dogs, I walked back to my hotel alone. I stopped in a store to get a doughnut and the shop owner shouted, "We're closed!"

I argued, "But your door is open. So in a way you're open."

"We're not open for *business*," he corrected.

"Okay. I'm a little drunk. And I don't want to be the rude American who thinks she can just get any doughnut she wants in any country at any time but I see a doughnut right there. It's in front of me in a display case. And the display case is open. I have a lot of whiskey to soak up and this glazed doughnut is calling to me like a sponge that wants to help. I have to have this doughnut. I will leave you money and when you officially open for business that's when you can put it in your cash register? Maybe?"

"No! Miss. We are closed. Get. OUT."

"Okay, but this doughnut is leaving with me!"

I rescued the doughnut from its display case like an action-movie hero and I ran out of there . . . probably more like a drunk woman in platform boots. A cop car was parked outside. I decided to turn myself in. I knocked on his window. "Sir. I'm American. I'm drunk and I just stole a doughnut. But I tried to pay I really did."

He smiled, "You have fun, miss."

Man. I know it's a stereotype but of course the cop understood that sometimes you just have to have a doughnut. I strolled down the cobblestone street as the sun warmed church steeples and I thought of something that David the Tarot Card Reader told me. "You'll have one more fling and realize you don't want to keep doing the same thing over and over."

Huh. Maybe he was psychic after all. Then again, who couldn't predict that a woman might have a fling and then want to move beyond chance encounters?

What no one could have predicted was that I would be temporarily and blissfully unaware that I had sent a certain tweet, sleeping off the whiskey while the Internet was catching fire about a tirade from an American comedian about how Irish people are a bunch of cunts. They did not take it as a term of endearment. Imagine that? I had broken my own rule about comedy. Saying awful things as a term of endearment can only be done among the familiar. This is why you can call your best friend a whore but you can't expect a random woman walking down the street to find this greeting fun and kooky. I might be able to call my drunken friend a "cunt" but I had addressed an entire nation and expected them to get a joke that really wasn't there.

I woke up and got on Twitter to let anyone in Dublin following me know that I had one last show that afternoon. That's when I saw this headline on Entertainment.ie: "Jen Kirkman Comedian Calls Dubliners a Bunch of C**ts, Goes on Twitter Tirade."

Whoops. I could declare that I've joined Al Qaeda and no one in America would notice. So allow me to be a little defensive here—this proves there isn't much entertainment going on in Dublin if I'm making news.

I checked the comments in the article. Oof. If they thought me calling them cunts was bad—they should have gone back and reread what they said about *me*. I should die. I'm a whore who should get AIDS. I'm an unfunny waste of space. Someone should murder me while I'm in Dublin. I'm a wretch. (That was a fun one—almost had a seventeenth-century-witch-hunt vibe.)

The worst part of the web is that it's like a virus feeding off of itself. More and more people passed around screen shots of the offensive tweet I had deleted. The more I tweeted to apologize the worse it got. Irish people that weren't even following me on Twitter were finding my feed and just telling me that they've watched my stand-up online and I suck and should kill myself. The only good part about the Internet being like a virus is that it clears up in a few days and everyone forgets how awful it felt.

I had a matinee show that day—which to a hungover person who has been drinking whiskey until six a.m. is like having a show at six thirty-five a.m. that same day. I showed up to the tent completely defeated. I wore one of my vintage dresses—made to look even more vintage with the coffee stains. (Hard to walk on cobblestone in heels and balance a hot coffee). I put on my motorcycle boots so that I could have good arch support in case I had to break into a run from angry mobs. I sat on a stool and said to the audience, "Well, I'm sorry I called your city a bunch of cunts. And I'm so glad that my flight leaves tomorrow morning."

This particular audience seemed to be what we call the Comedy Nerds, and that's not pejorative. It seemed I had some actual fans in Dublin and they were at the afternoon show free from bachelor parties, university reunions, and general alcohol poisoning. And maybe they appreciated that I sat before them with dirty hair, no makeup, a stained dress, and a remorseful soul. I walked out of Iveagh Gardens with a hat pulled down over my face just in case the Internet trolls were out there waiting to give me AIDS or burn me at the stake. I heard, "Jen Kirkman! Jen Kirkman!" I turned around ready to face whatever fate Dublin had for me—which was just a guy who looked like every other twentysomething I've seen in America: plaid shirt, beard, premature gut, and he was drinking an unconcealed beer while walking down the street. He burped. "I'm your biggest fan!"

Not this again. "You're my biggest fan? Did you see the show?"

"You're doing shows here?"

"Yes. About a hundred yards from where we are standing."

"Oh shit. What are you doing in Dublin?"

"Um, that show I just mentioned."

"Cool. Well, come back sometime."

"It's probably going to be a while before I come back but it's nice to know I have a fan . . . who is drinking publicly on the street and didn't come to my show."

I decided to Black Snake Moan myself that night and not go out. I know that nobody knows this reference but it's a movie. A movie I haven't seen but love to reference nonetheless. From what I understand Samuel L. Jackson plays a Mississippi bluesman who finds a troubled and beaten woman (a very thin, very bleached-blond Christina Ricci) on the side of the road and holds her captive in his house (I think by chaining her to a radiator) in an attempt to cure her of nymphomania. Whenever I'm recovering from a big night out I call staying home the next night "Black Snake Moaning" myself. I wasn't chained to a radiator but I was under the covers. I fell into a peaceful sleep—only to be woken up at two in the morning. The drunken "cunts" were getting out of the bars, right underneath my window.

Ironically, a group of Irish men were yelling "Fuck off" at one another and then spontaneously broke into singing "Born in the U.S.A." I was wide-awake. I took listening to this drunken Dublin version of Bruce Springsteen's big hit as my penance. I pondered my contentious relationship with the people of Ireland. Hadn't I also responded to drunks by getting drunk, going on a tirade, kissing a barely postpubescent boy, and stealing a doughnut? Was I any better? I was sure that Oscar Wilde walked these very streets, just as drunk and just as belligerent. But I bet he was dressed in ascots, not backward baseball caps. I really feel that Oscar Wilde would be on my side were he here in my room listening to this new generation say uncreative and unpoetic things like "fuck yourself in your head."

I lay in bed longing to hear the ghost of Oscar Wilde shouting profound things outside my window in his perfect peacoat: "I drink to separate my body from my soul!" I decided that I could not beat these people—and so I would join them, with a little help from ol' Oscar. I googled "drinking quotes Oscar Wilde" and armed myself with a good one. I opened my window (God, I love European hotels—they trust us with fresh air and don't worry about anyone jumping out) and yelled down to the pub-crawlers, "Work is the curse of the drinking classes!" The guys looked up.

"What's that?"

I said, "Work is the curse of the drinking classes!"

They paused. Then cheered. "That's right. That's right," they shouted back.

"Good night, Dublin!" I yelled—taking the bow I felt I finally deserved.

21

GRAY ANATOMY

I am not afraid of aging, but more afraid of people's reactions to my aging.

—BARBARA HERSHEY

It was another perfectly hot summer day in Los Angeles, just weeks before my fortieth birthday, and I was headed to the pool. Not my pool. *The* pool. I pay dues at a local hotel to be part of their summer pool club. I feel the same way about owning my own pool as I do about owning a gun. I just have a feeling that if I purchase either one what I'm really buying is the thing that will eventually accidentally kill me. I slathered SPF 50 all over my white/clear skin, tied my bikini top, and as I pulled my bikini bottoms on, I noticed something. I had a new crop of gray pubic hairs. My gynecologist had already tipped me off to the existence of my first ones a couple of years earlier but I had plucked those. And now they were back. I really thought that the first couple of aging hairs were one-offs, almost like seeing an outdoor bug that shouldn't exist inside your home. "Oh, that must have crawled in from outside because of the rain." But I had to be honest with myself. It wasn't raining outside of my bikini bottoms. These pubes weren't coming in from a storm—belonging somewhere else. They belonged to me. I made a quick decision to not head out into the sunshine. Everything seemed pointless. I knew that this moment of confronting my mortality would pass but I decided to say no way to facing the day. I got into bed for a rare under-the-covers daytime nap—still in my bathing suit. I felt like I was giving even less of a fuck than normal by sleeping in clothes that were specifically meant for outside activity only.

I wasn't quite forty years old yet and I'd been bragging to anyone who would listen and even people who wouldn't that I was going to hit forty without even getting my first fine line or wrinkle. What a stupid thing to boast about. Wrinkles on the face don't necessarily mean that someone is old. A person in his or her twenties can have wrinkles if they have thin skin, smoked cigarettes for half their life, got way too much sun, or even if they've just had a hard life. They can lower their voice like John Wayne and tell you that they've "seen some shit." I wish that my pubic hair changing color meant anything *but* the fact that I'm getting older. It doesn't. I can't say, "Well, my vagina was a chain-smoker in the eighties; of course I have these hairs." I can't say, "Well, I roasted this thing in the sun at least three times without SPF and I aged it." And as much as I would love to be able to say that it's really lived, I cannot honestly say, "My vagina has seen some shit." The only thing that's true is that the machine inside of my body is slowing down. The power plant cannot afford to keep all of its nonessential cosmetic employees anymore. The little elves that lived in my abdomen who paint the pubic hairs black have all been forced to retire.

I wish the pubes were white. I would grow them out luxurious and silky like Kenny Rogers's beard. I would stroke them to look wise while I answered questions. Or I would go the other way and fashion them into a Mohawk, telling everyone that I have a Billy Idol–esque punk rock pussy. But they were gray. Gray is a mean color. Gray is the color of barbed wire that sits atop buildings and sends the message, "Hey. KEEP OUT OF HERE OR I WILL CUT YOU." I'm paranoid that my yoo-hoo is now that house in your neighborhood that you suddenly notice on Halloween is in contrast to all of the nice homes with manicured green grass and white picket fences. People approach that house—usually occupied by an old lady—with a sense of fearful wonder. *Was this house like this last year? I don't remember. But look. There is only dirt where there once was grass. Some strange-colored weeds are popping up on the property where flowers used to grow. Does this house even produce candy anymore or will we only get dry pennies?*

I know that I can remove these hairs. I've been getting Brazilian waxes since before the invention of the iPhone, but they still grow back little by little before it's time for the next ripping. And I know that men don't really care. Men always say things like, "I'm just happy to be down there." That's very sweet, but I feel like I only have a window of a few days a month after I wax to feel sexy while the rest of the time I'll be feeling like someone's nana has moved into my underpants.

And now I'm reading in every women's magazine and hearing from every guy I know that pubic hair is back. The ladies are abandoning their landing strips in favor of letting the brush grow over the runway. Great. Now my hoo-hah is going to be like that old lady who hasn't updated her wardrobe in thirty years. My vagina is the flowered house-coat of body parts.

I've decided that I must accept that my distinguished salt-and-pepper vagina possesses wisdom and will only get more wise as it ages. My lady part is no different from a president who prematurely grays from a tough two terms of decision making. My vagina has had to meet a lot of different men—even when she wasn't feeling that talkative. She's had to endure multiple doctors poking, prodding, and swabbing. She puts up with plucking, waxing, and shaving. She's stayed with me through three hundred and twelve menstrual cycles, and simply grinned and bore it when confronted multiple times a day with tampons. My vagina is one tough bitch and if she doesn't feel like looking young anymore why should I judge her? I was wrong. She *has* seen some shit. I offered her some tea and tried to talk about the possibility of getting her a Life Alert bracelet but she said she feels as young as ever and all I need to do is let her grow old gracefully. She just begged me not to introduce her to any more young men because she would like to meet a penis she can actually talk to and doesn't want to have to keep explaining things like Andy Gibb was *not* one of the Bee Gees.

22

TURNING FORTY AND TAKING STOCK(HOLM) OF MY LIFE

The great thing about getting older is that you don't lose all the other ages you've been.

—MADELEINE L'ENGLE

I told people I was forty years old the entirety of my thirty-ninth year just so that when I turned forty it wasn't a shock. It worked well. My fortieth birthday wasn't a shock, but the fact that I spent it on a blind date in Stockholm, Sweden, ended up being quite the surprise.

My birthdate has always been a bummer for me. August 28. No kid likes the end of the summer—it means that the days are getting shorter, the weather is getting colder, and it's time for back-to-school shopping. Anyone with a birthday right before Labor Day ends up getting Trapper Keepers and pencil boxes for their birthday. Those aren't presents. Those are supplies. Don't even begin to tell me your sob stories, you people who have birthdays right around Christmas. Sure, maybe you get a few less gifts, but the season you were born in is nicknamed "the most wonderful time of the year." People are holly and jolly and enjoying that lazy limbo between December 25 and New Year's Eve where the only thing to do is eat. Everyone wants to go to parties and be social and wear sequins. My birthday is also near a holiday—LABOR Day. I'm in a few unions and so I've benefited from the American Labor movement but the holiday marking said movement is not a *fun* fete. It falls during a time of year that throws everyone into a panic. We have to do everything we can to enjoy these last days of summer! We have to leave town! People are literally *evacuating* in advance of my birthday.

I never got my locker decorated by friends on my birthday because school was not in session. Our first-grade teacher, Mr. Connolly, used to pick up a kid if it was his or her birthday to administer "birthday taps." The class would count in unison, "One! Two! Three! Four! Five! Six! Seven!" as Mr. Connolly gently patted every kid on the bum, spinning them in a circle. I realize now that this guy sounds a little suspect. But at the time, in good old 1981, you could just pick up any kid in a gymnasium and pretend to slap their ass. And even though that's really fucked up, I was always sad to be excluded from the G-rated molestation.

As an adult the tradition of birthday disappointment continues. My friends are never around during my birthday/long weekend. I'm not a fan of those dreaded weeknight birthday parties. "Sorry I'm four hours late, traffic. I had to work. Oh, it's over?"

"No. You're the only one who showed up. You can go. I'm just going to settle up with the bartender for these three drinks I had alone."

Months before the date, friends asked, "What are you doing for your fortieth?" I always retorted, "I don't know. What are *you* doing for my fortieth?" I couldn't believe that nobody was going to throw me a surprise party. Sure, I've never thrown any of *them* a surprise party but they never asked me to.

My two girlfriends I grew up with in Massachusetts had been trying to pin me down for a special fortieth-birthday trip all year. But comedy gigs always come up on short notice for me and I didn't want to make my friends with kids and husbands have to cancel a trip to Italy that we had planned or worse, go on it without the birthday girl. Besides, what if I found a boyfriend before my fortieth? To be perfectly honest, as much as I love traveling with girlfriends and have told you in this very book that no one needs a man to have a good time—if I had a man to be madly in love with in Italy, I hate to say it but I might prefer that right now. And I don't want to be that person on a girls' trip who brings her boyfriend at the last minute. "You guys will love Adam. Feel free to tell him all of your intimate details about your hemorrhoids. He won't mind!"

I just couldn't commit to one idea for my birthday. I could have thrown a party but I already did that for my thirty-ninth birthday. (I feel like that's the year you should really blow it out anyway.) While a couple of my best friends could come, *most* of my close friends were out of town. I had to dip into friends who I see once a year just to make the bar I rented out seem full and lively. When I got the check I thought, *Is this what I want to spend a thousand bucks on? Appetizers and overpriced drinks made by a self-proclaimed mixologist?* I decided that I didn't want to throw myself another party for my fortieth. The expectations of it having to be great, life-changing, and monumental would have made me mental. A lot of my friends who were single the year before were now coupled up. This causes a divide in my circle. One single friend—before I even started to plan this nonexistent party—said, "I can't go to a party where it's all couples. I'm just too depressed about it. I know you're single too but you're the birthday girl so it doesn't count."

My coupled-up friends preannounced that they couldn't make it to this, again, nonexistent party because they were going away for a three-day weekend, but they promised to have me come over so they could make me dinner some night. (Attention, couples! No one but other couples wants to come over to your house for dinner. That's fine and dandy that you love cooking. Cook your face off. But I'm not in the marriage with you so I find it snug—but not in the good "as a bug in a rug" way. When single people sit at your dining room table with you and your spouse we feel like your kid—the one you're secretly disappointed in for still living at home at age forty.)

So when I got an offer to perform at a comedy festival in Lund, Sweden, the week of my fortieth birthday—I knew that was the answer. Yes. I'm going to get straight OUTTA here and go overseas alone . . . again. I was the only American asked to fly in for the festival and I felt it was quite an honor. What isn't an honor is flying on

Norwegian airlines. Their tagline should be, "You want a blanket on this overnight flight? Fuck you. We don't have any." Performing in the festival was a comedy utopia. Some acts performed in Swedish, some acts performed in English. The perfectly bilingual audience didn't miss a beat on English slang or expressions. The last night of my thirties was spent performing for this once-in-a-blue-moon crowd. People came up to me later to tell me that although they loved my jokes about how divorced people are treated weirdly, they couldn't personally relate. Divorce, sexuality, and marriage equality have been normalized in Sweden and mostly they were laughing at American attitudes toward these subjects. I thought, *Wow. I could really love living here for . . . a few weeks, then I would have to move.* Their winters are too brutal and everyone is too good-looking. I like living in America because I need to lay eyes on terminally ugly people every once in a while just to feel better about myself.

At the after-party, I told the festival coordinators my plan to take the train in the morning (my fortieth birthday) to Stockholm—just for a little twenty-four-hour getaway. They were concerned and flustered. It was my birthday the next day and I was going to go to Stockholm alone? And do what? And see whom? If I had only told them that it was my birthday they would have had a cake and tried to make it special. I assured them that I don't like birthday cake. I really don't. I would rather eat a bag of candy corn or black licorice than a piece of cake. See? I'm a sociopath.

I made a few new friends that night, and when the bartender in the hotel's restaurant refused to sell us a bottle of champagne at five minutes to midnight, they lowered their voices and in Swedish said . . . something. Within minutes we had two bottles of champagne and four birthday candles. There wasn't a cake so we just lit and held the candles while I blew them out. Greg, one of my new friends, an American expat who moved to Sweden for love and marriage, told me that he could hook me up with his friend in Stockholm for my birthday. Greg was very concerned that I would regret not making a solid plan for my birthday. I did have a solid plan. I was going to wander until I found an Italian restaurant. It's a Classic Kirkman travel move; a table for one,

some ravioli, and red wine. Greg insisted that I give him my number
so that he could pass it on to his buddy—a divorced forty-year-old
American guy living in Stockholm. I said, "Fine. Give him my number
but I may not text back."

"It's up to you, Jen. But you'll like him. He's my only friend who
isn't a total loser." What a ringing endorsement.

I sat on the train to Stockholm smiling. My birthday still makes
me happy. I just thought to myself, *It's my special day*. I checked
into my hotel in Stockholm and was told by the front desk that a
friend of mine from America had tried to send me a bottle of wine.
He apologized that the bottle of wine *did* make it to the front desk
but they weren't allowed to sign for alcohol unless I was there so it's
gone now. I said, "Can the guy with the wine come back?" The con-
cierge explained, "Yes, but we don't know what time he can come
back and you would have to sit here all evening." I figured that
would be a pretty stupid way to spend my birthday so I got dressed
and headed out into the night. I found an Italian restaurant, a table
for one, and I got busy enjoying good food and a good book (well, a
good Kindle). Just as I was finishing up I started to get tired. I felt
content.

And then a text popped up from Greg's friend Max. I really wanted
to just go back to my room but I had that nagging feeling. I found myself thinking, *What if this is why you were supposed to go to Stockholm
on your birthday, Jen? Maybe you'll hit it off with this guy. You're always
saying you would date an age-appropriate divorcé—well, one is texting
you right now!* I don't know if I'm a true romantic or just an idiot with
an ample imagination or if there's even a difference.

Max told me where to meet him and I got a little lost on the way
there. I had to stop in a pastry shop to ask directions. The cashier
tried to help me by showing me a map. I had to explain to him that
I really don't know how to comprehend maps. I know that's not an
acceptable attribute. I'm working on it. Actually I'm not working on it
but it's on my list of things to figure out how to do—right after "figure
out the meaning of life." Once I was properly armed with a list of lefts
and rights to take, a female customer said to me, "You may not have

direction but you have style. Your outfit is fantastic. And I hate people and talking to people so for me to even say this—you know you've got it going on." Those kinds of interactions always make me think that if women ran the world there could be world peace.

Max and I met up at the Gondolen restaurant and bar, which lies like a bridge across the street and offers views of the city out of its floor-to-ceiling picture windows. That is probably the nicest thing I can say about that evening. I'm not someone who warms up to anyone slowly. If I'm attracted to you, I know within the first second. It doesn't mean I'll sleep with you, date you, or move in with you—it just means anything is possible and I'm sticking around to find out. Max and I had no initial spark. He made a joke about my lateness due to my bad sense of direction, which I tried to defend by saying, "Well, I've only been here about three hours and I don't have my glasses on."

"Why don't you have your glasses on?"

"I mostly refuse to accept that I have to wear glasses."

"Why don't you get contacts, four-eyes?"

Okay. No one should call anyone four-eyes after age eight. In fact no one should call anyone four-eyes if it isn't 1965. I told him the story of the woman in the pastry shop who complimented my style and he said, "That didn't happen. You're just making up stories about people who weren't actually there, now aren't ya? Is that what you do with your time? Talk to imaginary friends?"

A little romantic tête-à-tête is fine. I can spar, but this guy was already full-on busting my balls. I could have said, "How long have you been divorced, and did all of your hairs leave your head when she did because they can't stand you either?" But I didn't. I kept the faith that Greg had said this was his least worst friend.

I figured I would give him a minute to relax—maybe he just didn't know that you don't have to try to be funny to hang out with a comedian. We ordered some drinks and he told me about his life. He was vague about what he did for a living. He had just left a job in some kind of finance financing of something to do with financials but he said that he would rather be camping now or surfing. Whenever someone tells me that they surf it always stops me in my tracks. *Ohhhh, that's cool. I should give him a chance. It would be fun to date a surfer and have someone to hit the waves with.* Then I remind myself, *Jen, you don't surf.**

----

* Quick story: I tried to surf. I took a lesson once. I can't swim without holding my nose. I'm petrified going under water and I've never actually swum in the ocean. I've only stood in the ocean. I figured my first surfing lesson would cover the basics of swimming and that maybe we would take a boat out to the waves where I would be placed on my board and lowered into the water somehow. I was dismayed when my instructor asked me to paddle out into the waves. The problem is that the waves that seem so tiny when you're standing on the shore seem gargantuan when you're on your stomach paddling head-on toward them. It's the same kind of bait and switch that a baby pulls when she reaches her tiny little hand toward your hair and when she yanks it she's got the strength of an MMA fighter. I couldn't quite get the hang of jumping up on the board, relaxing while jumping, tuning in while zoning out, or keeping my balance long enough while standing up to ride out a wave. Halfway through the lesson, I was convinced that a jellyfish had stung me in the chest through my wetsuit. It was just an asthma attack brought on by actually having to breathe heavier than I do during my only other workout—mild power-walking. I did my version of "swimming" back to shore to grab my inhaler. I tried to end the lesson early on account of this mild asthma attack and the fact that I no longer had any interest in risking my life by trying to conquer the sea with a board. My instructor looked me in the eye and said, "You can try to stop the lesson but you'll never stop surfing. Surfing is life, whether you're on a board in the ocean or not."

"Cool. So I think I'll do that one. The one where I surf without the board and the ocean."

"You don't respect the ocean by avoiding the ocean. You respect the ocean by joining the ocean. Join in the knowledge that the ocean is controlled by the moon and you have no control over either."

"Right. But I do have control over taking off this wetsuit, paying you in full, and going back to my car."

Anyway, back in Sweden I started to figure out that Max might just be bad at holding down a job. Upon further questioning it turns out that he had never actually camped or surfed—it's just what he would *want* to do. Just like me, he doesn't want kids and isn't sure if he would marry again but he enjoys Stockholm, where he moved for his now ex-wife. (Sidebar: Is this where all the men are going? I felt like performing a raid all over Stockholm, knocking on doors asking, "Is there an American man in there? I need him to give *me* a shot first before he settles down with this blond beauty.")

Our conversation certainly flowed but after an hour I noticed that Max never asked me one question about myself. It's okay, though, I can have a good time with anyone because I just pretend I've replaced Barbara Walters and I'm doing an interview special in my head. "Max, what do you say to people who say that you're just a dreamer who is never going to go camping? It's okay to cry, Max."

I tried to ask for the check but Max insisted that we have one more drink. He said he couldn't let me go home at eleven on my birthday—it would make him feel sad. It seemed like staying on a blind date that I didn't want to be on was way more sad than climbing into luxurious hotel bedding and reading *InStyle* magazine. After some back-and-forth I won the battle. We would close out after only one

---

My instructor did some weird thing with his hand and put it between my eyes. "Jen, you can't stop the waves, but you can learn to surf."

Either he had successfully hypnotized me or inspired me to try just one more time, because I found myself back in the ocean with a board twice my height and weight strapped to my ankle. After catching a mouthful of salt water, I finally caught a small wave for three seconds before I freaked out and jumped off of the board. Later, I posted pictures of my surfboard and me on Facebook with my newfound spiritual philosophy that we can't stop the waves of life. My friend Heather McDonald pointed out, "You're acting really newly divorced right now." Ugh. She was right. I wasn't a surfer. The only ocean I can really get into is Billy Ocean and even then I only like one of his songs.*

* "Get Outta My Dreams, Get into My Car."

round. The bartender handed me the check. Okay, listen, I'm glad that Sweden is so progressive and feminist and all but it was my birthday. I let the check sit there, giving Max plenty of time to reach for his wallet, but he just said, "Are you ready?" I could have stood up but I feared he would lead us out without paying. So I plunked down my cash. He didn't say thanks. He didn't even offer to pay half. I spent my birthday buying a stranger drinks. What a bunch of *skitsnack*.

Max sent me a text later asking if I got back to my hotel safely. (If I hadn't, he was about an hour too late in asking.) He said that he had fun and that if I'm ever back in Stockholm we should get together again. If I'm back in Stockholm it will be because I married a hot blond Swedish woman just to keep her from stealing any more available American men.

As I brushed my teeth before bed I felt like my left leg had just completely given up. I had a major cramp in my calf. Jesus. I couldn't even have one day as a forty-year-old without *feeling* forty? I diagnosed myself as having a blood clot from too much traveling. I called my doctor back in Los Angeles. (Thank God for the nine-hour time difference. It makes it possible to have a hypochondriac moment in the middle of the night and still reach someone.) She told me to immediately go buy full-strength aspirin. I spent the last minutes of my birthday at a 7-Eleven hunting for Bayer to thin my blood and begging God to spare my life. I promised Him/Her that if He/She let me live through this blood clot I would never again think my life wasn't meaningful unless I found another divorcé to share it with and that I would just enjoy life itself. I would no longer be impatient that I don't have all of life's answers. I would just enjoy the questions. After an hour the "blood clot" went away. (It was later officially diagnosed as a recurring charley horse from walking in heels.) I stayed up way past midnight in my hotel room reading Internet message boards where people like me were asking if their charley horses could be blood clots. These people's lives were a mess. They didn't even use periods at the end of their run-on sentences about how they know that they shouldn't smoke cigarettes while on the Pill. Reading their stories was life-affirming. I don't have a blood clot. I don't have a lot of extraneous drama in my life and I am smart enough to know that "charley" in "charley horse" isn't spelled "Charlie."

There's no reason to stress out about what to do for your fortieth or whatever-ith birthday. It's not about doing something one night to make memories for the rest of your life—it's about looking at the rest of your life and saying, "Am I going where I want to go? Am I who I want to be? Am I defining my personal success based on other people's morals or goals? Can I only achieve happiness with outside validation or would I be truly happy just sitting in a pile of wood chips, being me? How can this year not be a repeat of last year's mistakes and patterns?"

I saw my fortieth year as a calling to be awesome. The number isn't scary but it's a challenge. Forty means no more fucking around. Do what you've always said you've wanted to do. And remember, you can't stop the waves but you can learn to surf, and you don't need to almost drown in a surfing class to learn that.

23

EVERYBODY'S WORKING FOR THE WEEKEND (EXCEPT FOR ME. I WORK *ON* THE WEEKENDS.)

Diamonds are nothing more than chunks of coal that stuck to their jobs.

—MALCOLM FORBES

Back in 2002, I was waitressing by day at a fancy Beverly Hills country club (that only started letting Jewish and black people in in 1982). I waited on important humans like astronaut Buzz Aldrin and former secretary of defense under Ronald Reagan, Caspar Weinberger. One time, while waiting on his table at a wedding, Buzz slapped my hand as I tried to refill his water glass. He snapped, "How much hydration do you think I need?" I wanted to say, "A lot, you dried up old moon rock." But I didn't. I needed that 15 percent tip.

I was often the victim of unsolicited consolation by the affluent, WASPy members who were distressed at seeing a nice white girl waiting tables. One time, a woman with too much sambuca on her breath pulled me aside in tears and said, "Honey, why are you a waitress? That's fine for the Korean women that work here, but you? You could at least be a catalog model or something, can't you?"

I was technically a stand-up comedian back then too. I just didn't get paid for it. But I got to perform at comedy clubs in Los Angeles for five minutes here and there. Those unpaid showcase spots are how every comedian has to start out. But back in those days when people asked what I did for a living, in order to honor the tenets of *The Secret*,

I considered every answer a "manifestation" and always said, "I am a stand-up comedian," instead of "I am a waitress who performs comedy for free as a side 'job.'"

Folks would usually follow up with, "Oh? Do you travel the country? Where do you perform? Do you make a living at that?" And I'd reply with shame, "No. Right now I'm serving multiple glasses of chardonnay an hour to unhappy old-money women who pretend to enjoy the sport of golf. But I do pursue stand-up a few nights a week." Usually that comeback was not good enough for whoever asked and they would look at me with pity and say, "Well, good luck for however much longer you pursue this. At least you can say you tried, right?"

Comedy seems to be the one job where people don't seem to understand just how many hours on the job comedians have to put in before getting their first paid gigs. It's not just massage therapists that have to practice on people before they move up from chair masseuse at an airport to someone in command of pricey essential oils and nude bodies at a fancy spa.

"Career" is often written about as some kind of albatross around a woman's neck. It's the thing that keeps her from fully committing to her family, or it stops her from having a family altogether. It allegedly intimidates male partners or gets in the way of her having time to spend with that special someone. Women who are career-focused are often seen as missing out on "life"—but I never wanted the kind of career where I drive home from work and then forget about what I did all day. I know I'm not Picasso, but I see myself as an artist. I'm writing, traveling, thinking of material, performing, tweaking, and dreaming. I somehow turned this into a job, and a life that includes travel that I don't have to pay for. (And if you're an aspiring comedian, please don't offer to take me to lunch and ask me how I got here. I'll save you the cost of two Cobb salads and iced teas: it just happened . . . over nearly two decades of sacrifice and putting in my ten thousand hours, as Malcolm Gladwell theorizes about in his book *Outliers*. But don't go read one of his books right now. Stick with me.)

Because I do stand-up shows on weekends, *my* weekend is Monday through Wednesday. I love it. I can go to the pharmacy and no one else is in line to hear me pick up my prescription for yeast infection medication. But that doesn't mean that what I do is easy. The twenty-three hours a day that I'm not performing aren't always totally "free" time. There is a huge administrative side to being a traveling comedian, and if you ever wonder why someone has an entourage it's not just because she's an egomaniac who has to surround herself with yesmen, but because sometimes there are so many details to keep track of eventually a performer gets to the point where she is too goddamn overwhelmed to hold her own sunglasses.

Anyway, the other day I was sitting in my orthodontist's chair letting my mind wander. Mindfulness meditation teachers encourage the labeling of thoughts that won't stop running through our minds—such as "worrying," "planning," and "judging"—and then letting them pass; almost like tagging a bag at the airport. Place the sticker on the suitcase, put it on the conveyer belt, and let it roll off somewhere else. If you absolutely need that thought you can always retrieve it later. My mind was working its way down the conveyer belt.

I think I left my iPhone at home. (Worrying)

I haven't seen it all morning. In the future I'm going to double-check to make sure I have that phone before I leave home. (Planning)

I realize this is a lot less important or traumatic than a parent realizing that they haven't seen their kid all morning, but then again, your kid doesn't keep your entire calendar and contacts in his overalls. (Judging)

I hope it's somewhere at the bottom of my purse next to a penny, some broken sunglasses, and probably an open tube of lipstick. I need two assistants to keep my life together. (Grossly exaggerating)

Then I started thinking about how even after correcting my teeth with Invisalign and then getting a few porcelain veneers, I still had to wear a retainer at night. Of course I wasn't actually wearing my retainer every night and of course I was lying about it and *of course* my orthodontist knew that I was lying and knew that I knew he knew I was lying. "Jennifer (he's one of the only people who doesn't call me Jen—even though he's ten years younger than me), I have to make a whole new retainer for your bottom teeth. Your teeth moved again and this one just doesn't fit." At least my incisors, bicuspids, and molars are consistent with my personality. My teeth are as restless as me.

They can't stay in one place. They love to move about freely and it's hard to contain them.

My orthodontist and I tried to find a mutually agreeable date that I could come back to try on my new mold. My schedule was erratic and every day that he was going to be in the office I would be on the road anywhere from Oklahoma City to Stockholm. He said, "So, this comedy thing is really what you do for a living? And you have to travel?"

"Yup!" I said with a perfectly veneered smile. I took a moment to feel proud of myself. Finally a conversation about what I do for a living that didn't leave me feeling ashamed.

After we failed to come up with a date in the near future when I could come back and make sure my chompers hadn't moved, my orthodontist shook his head as he labeled the mold of my teeth. Then he sighed.

"I don't know about all of this travel, Jennifer. Be careful."

He had the somber tone of someone who was about to warn me about airport shoe-bombers or Malaysia Airlines flights that go missing.

"Careful?"

"Well, you might want to have a real life someday."

I bristled. "Am I not in real life right now? Did you just give me some trippy laughing gas or something? Am I high?"

"You can joke," he said, "but I've seen this happen to women that I'm close to. They *thought* they wanted to abandon the norm in order to live free but after a while they realized their life just wasn't a real one."

There was that word "real" again! "Maybe this is why none of my retainers work out," I said to him. "Maybe I'm a hologram! Are you trying to tell me that you're the only person who can see me but that I don't actually exist?"

"I'm just saying that when you want to finally start a family, it might be too late."

"Oh. I don't need to start a family. I was born with one. And they're quite enough for me. Also, I'm forty. I picture my ovaries like sweaters in those compression bags—just flattened and being stored under my bed somewhere."

He said, "Well, what about marriage? Do you think a man would want to marry someone who was never home?"

"Well, I *was* married, so at least I checked that one off of society's to-do list. Also, I know what I want. I waited a long time to get what I want and I'm happy."

Then Dr. Doogie Howser proceeded to tell me a story about his cousin. He said, "She was a career woman. She was a power lawyer. She kept telling everyone that she didn't need a man, that she was happy. She said she was married to her work. Well, once she turned forty and saw all of her sisters having kids she felt really left out and lonely. She lives in a beautiful high-rise in Chicago but she gave up being a lawyer and now she's totally lost. She can't find any man who wants to date someone her age."

I said, "Well, that's certainly a beautiful story and I'm sure your cousin would appreciate you telling your patients the excruciatingly disappointing parts of her life. But first of all, I'm not your cousin. We may handle things differently. Secondly, something tells me that she probably never wanted to be a lawyer in the first place. She just became one because it's probably the type of thing that we think we're 'supposed' to do. I'm sorry that nobody in the family sat her down ten years ago and said, 'It's okay if you don't want to get married yet and you also don't have to be a power lawyer either. Women have more choices now than just Super Mom and Super Bitch.'"

My young orthodontist sat on his wheely stool and his shoulders slumped. He quietly stammered, "What's so great about travel anyway? Isn't it nice to build a home and stay grounded?" I was the only other person in the room so it was obvious he was asking me this question, but it also seemed like he was talking to a deeper part of himself.

How could I answer his question? I personally don't mind even what are seen by most people as the hassles of travel. I go into a Zen mode taking my shoes off at airport security and like to give a knowing smile to the TSA agent who has to answer some dumb-dumb when they ask, "So, I can't bring my water through the X-ray machine?" I find it a moral challenge to see how little I can pack in a suitcase, proving to myself that we don't really need too many things in life—just the important stuff like my shampoo and conditioner laced with caviar. (Sorry, PETA.)

I don't make fun of my orthodontist's life. I never asked him, "Hey, don't you get sick of going to Costco every weekend to buy ingredients for your spinach dip that you'll serve on a tray on your leather living room ottoman during the Big Game on Sunday?"

Dr. Teeth prodded, "So, you don't think you'll get sick of it and want to rest?"

"Sure. I get sick of it all the time. I come home from trips with a tweaked back from having to pull my fifty-pound suitcase off of the baggage claim at an odd angle because some woman is standing in my way texting, leaving me no room to properly bend from the knee. I get dehydrated from flying. Sometimes I'm so jet-lagged, I won't even care that I'm somewhere exotic like Australia and I'll stay in bed for a day and just tell people that I went to the zoo. It really produces the same effect on them and everyone's happy. I don't have to hear, 'What do you mean you didn't see any kangaroos?' Just tell someone that you saw a kangaroo once and it will make his or her fucking day."

"Well, I just hope that you're up-front with any man you meet about the fact that you don't know when this travel schedule is going to slow down."

This is when I said, "We're not actually talking about me, are we?"

He paced the office and finally confessed, "My girlfriend just dumped me last night after a year and a half. I thought things were going fine. She says she doesn't think she wants to have kids and that she thinks she wants to travel the world instead of settle down right now. What does she mean she *thinks*? I mean, why didn't she tell me that at the beginning?"

"It sounds like she didn't know. She's in her twenties. She'll probably think she wants a lot of different things and will try them out before deciding on one path."

"But I was ready to marry her. I don't even know if she knows how to buy a plane ticket!"

"You wanted to spend the rest of your life with someone who doesn't know how to buy a plane ticket?"

"I don't care where she wants to go. I don't believe it. I think it's a phase."

"People aren't teeth. You can't put a clamp on them and correct them."

"Should I call her?"

"No! The answer is always no to the question 'Should I call him/her?' Nobody should call anybody."

He said, "I just don't believe she'll actually travel."

"Well, maybe you can drive by her house sometimes and see if her lights are on."

I was hoping that because I had listened to his relationship struggles I wouldn't have to dish out twenty bucks for my co-pay. I should be charging him. I ended up no longer being annoyed with my seemingly judgmental orthodontist and instead felt sympathy for him. I told him that I was sure there was a woman out there who wants a guy who wants to stay home together on weekends. I promised him that he'll find this woman and eventually he'll even not be able to remember why he wanted a woman around the house all the time. "Enjoy being able to leave your dirty socks on the kitchen table for now."

I also reminded him that since he thinks there are a bunch of fortysomething women out there who have fulfilling jobs but empty, regretful wombs and hearts, they may want a nice thirty-year-old doctor to date. I suggested that if he wants to find love maybe he could start hanging out in front of a Botox clinic or a strip mall Zumba class.

24

THE BRIDGE OF BRISBANE COUNTY

"Things change. They always do, it's one of the things of nature. Most people are afraid of change, but if you look at it as something you can always count on, then it can be a comfort."

—ROBERT KINCAID (PLAYED BY CLINT EASTWOOD)
IN THE BRIDGES OF MADISON COUNTY

While I was touring this past year, I went back to Australia—this time with a lot less nerves and no enmeshed relationship with my seatmate. But I did meet a man on tour in Australia and we fell for each other. We had an impetuous one-week affair and he ended up coming to America for three months to be with me. Monogamy. Meeting my friends. Traveling America together on planes, trains, and automobiles. We dove head first into a quasi-relationship. (We're in the beginning of his last month here before his visa expires or as I call it, "Month Number . . . Fuuuuck, We Didn't Think This Through.")

But don't worry, you distressed single people who were almost at the end of this book hoping to find solace in the fact that my life, like yours, remains a shit show—by the time this book is in your hands, I'm sure my romance will be over. It's going to end. We don't live in the same hemisphere. He's a performer. He can't just leave the career he's building there and I can't leave the one I'm building here. Sure, we *could* do a long-distance thing rather than a double suicide, that's one ridiculous option on the table. But Melbourne, Australia, is *so* stupidly distant it makes my friend's New York-to-Los Angeles romance seem almost convenient. "My God. You guys are just a six-hour flight away at any given moment? You're practically on top of each other! How do you get any space? What if you have to poop?" I'm in Los Angeles and my guy lives . . . in *tomorrow.*

But back to my decidedly fated breakup that looms. I'm just being realistic. *All* my romantic relationships have ended. Were those relationships not successes? Is success in a relationship only determined by it *never* ending? That's like saying that someone's life was a failure because . . . well, death. Think about it this way. Who are the most successful guests at a party? The ones who are committed to seeing the whole night through, raiding the fridge, and drinking the host's secret stash? Or the guest who arrives on time, charms the pants off strangers, washes the mozzarella-encrusted nacho dish that she brought, and leaves before anyone can slowly grow to resent her?

My relationships ended for the right reasons and exactly when they were supposed to. (Even if at the time during a few breakups I thought that God, Jesus, Buddha, and former president Bill Clinton were very cruel people who *weren't helping me at all* by not forcing some of my ex-boyfriends to change their minds.) But on the bright side, if all my relationships hadn't ended a bunch of men would be reading this right now thinking, *What do you mean you* met someone? *Well, Jen, after reading this book I have to say that this information is seriously going to impact our future together!*

I guess I should tell you his name. It's David. He hasn't pissed me off yet for him to earn a derogatory nickname in this book, like Stupid Dickhead Who Had a Crazy Idea to Have an Intercontinental Affair. Lots of people just call him "Dave." I'm one of those assholes who calls a man by his full name. I'm not trying to sound like I own him and I'm sure I just sound like I'm his uptight kindergarten teacher. I just like the sound of his name and it's the closest I'll get to being with David Bowie.

We were sitting on my deck in Los Angeles (okay, the Valley) one night when David asked, "Am I in your book?"

"No. It's already written and it's really just about how no matter what I try to plan, or who I intend to be, it feels like I so rarely get life 'right.'"

Then I realized. *Shit. I absolutely have to write about David in this book. It's messy and magnificent and exactly what life looks like.*

If you'll recall, in Chapter 17 of this very book, well before I met David, I wrote:

> I don't mean to act like being single and wandering the planet by myself is some fabulous parade all the goddamn time or that I'm constantly in "You go, girrrl" mode. I think—and again this is just a thought; I said, "I think" not "I know for a fact"—but I *think* that having a man to travel the world with would be marvelous. I further think that if that man also had a similar type of life and career and our relationship had elements of creative collaboration—that would be miraculously marvelous.

First of all, I don't know if anyone has ever had the audacity to quote themselves from earlier in their own book. Second of all, I am not trying to just pull a cheater move toward fulfilling my contractual word count. And third (of all?), sometimes when we dream about what we'd like, when we order right off the menu and find out it is possible to get what we think we want, life acts like a half-witted waiter who brings us a slightly not right version of what we requested. "Oh, you wanted the dressing on the side? We're out of ramekins so I took the liberty of drenching your lettuce in oil." And we have to adjust. "That's fine. I'll just have to deal with the fact that the situation on my plate is wilted."

So, a year and a half after my orthodontist lay into me for traveling too much to find a man, and ten months after a psychic said a feminist yet Clint Eastwood–type dude was coming into my life I met David in the lobby of a hotel in Brisbane. We were on a tour together. I saw his name on the advance itinerary and googled him. "He's cute. He's so my type," I caught myself saying. "*But* I'm not doing one-night stands anymore." Besides, I already had a new comedian tour friend, Gay Nath. He became a surrogate little brother and even came along with me to the Great Barrier Reef despite his contentious relationship with the sun. He couldn't stand seeing me take all these "Single

Woman Sees Australia Alone" day trips. It was pathetic enough I had gone on a crocodile tour and gleefully shrieked in a boat by myself while the families in other boats bonded over seeing these great reptiles lunge out of the water to snatch a chicken in their jaws. On my own, I hopped alongside wallabies at an animal sanctuary—much to their dismay that a loud American human was up in their business. I'd jumped aboard a scenic railway and took a subsequent Skyrail cable car down the side of the Kuranda rain forest by myself. Had any one of the many poisonous spiders that exist in those tropics bitten me, no one would have known, including me. I'd be dead as fuck.

I'd had a really *single* year. It seemed like once I decided I was ready for a relationship, all the available men disappeared. Were they Raptured? I would go to Target and notice that only female employees were working. "Yes, ma'am. All the men called in sick today. It seems they all got a sense that there's a woman out there who wants more than a fling." I started slinging bullshit like, "I'm just going to take some time for me." (Yeah, because no one wants to spend time with you.) "You can't love someone until you love yourself." (What? It's so fun to love someone when you don't love yourself. What a quick way—without doughnuts—to fill the ol' heart hole!)

I'd been tangled up with so many emotionally unavailable men. Men who will freely take your call but would be totally fine to never call you in the first place. They weren't bad guys. They weren't cheating or lying. They were just Ambivalent Guys. Unfortunately, Ambivalent Guys are oftentimes drawn to Aggressive Women. AWs are magnetizing at first but eventually their forthrightness becomes misinterpreted by the AG as needy. Then the AW has to aggressively set the record straight. "Look, mister. I'm not *obsessed* with *you*. I'm hung up on finding distraction and I don't have the balls to try heroin."

Back to Brisbane.

I remember asking myself as I ran a curling iron through my hair, "Why am I getting dolled up to go down to the lobby before a show? I usually just bring my gear backstage." The aforementioned Google confirmed that cute David would be on this leg of the tour with us, therefore in the lobby to get in the van to the theater. I had spent so many months alone in Oz; I really got to know myself.

"Jen, you're doing your hair for a guy. A guy you haven't met. You have no idea if he's single or even interested. Also, he could be a Nazi."

"So?"

"So, Jen, you leave Australia in five days. What could possibly happen? And you don't want to do one-night stands so who cares if your hair has a fun bend?"

"Can't I flirt? GOD!"

"Nothing wrong on paper with flirting, Jen. But you've never been able to just flirt. You dive headfirst before checking if there's water in the pool."

When David and I met I was glad I did my hair. By the way, I know that guys have no idea how to differentiate between when a woman's hair is "done" or when it's lice-ridden. But it made me feel like my light was on, blinking AVAILABLE FOR FLIRTING, advertising the current vacancy in my soul. I hip-checked Gay Nath so that I could sit next to David in the van. We talked nonstop. He's a Ramones fan, like me. I told him if he were ever in Los Angeles I'd take him to Johnny Ramone's grave. (Three months later we were doing just that. It was like some punk rock version of *The Secret*.)

Cue montage of stolen looks, laughs laughed, drinks drunk, finding reasons to touch ("Oh my god, you guys, let's get a picture! No. I'll stand *here*." *Elbows everyone else out of the way.*). End montage with us in my room overlooking the Story Bridge over the Brisbane River, a half a bottle of wine, and iTunes open as we each pick songs to play, switching on and off to provide the soundtrack to this scene we will call, Two People Pretending Like They Always Stay Up Late Together Drinking Near a Bed.

The Story Bridge was lit up with stark red lightbulbs—like hundreds of red-nosed reindeers outlining its shape. A subtle sign from the Universe? STOP! DO NOT GO! DO NOT START THIS! We ignored it. At three in the morning he announced he was going to bed. He stated confidently but without a hint of perv, "And I would like that bed to be yours." I joined him. ONLY SLEEP. It wasn't so much a test for him as a sober moment for me. Absolutely. No. One. Night. Stands. At. My. Age. I woke up to the feel of being snuggled. I'm irritated by snuggling. I'm not trying to say a traditionally masculine thing in a misguided effort to sound chill. I really find snuggling impossible—especially with a neck that's prone to go out just from sleeping on a pillow, never mind sleeping in the crook of an arm. But something about this cuddle fit. And it was then I decided that although a *one-night stand* is not an option—an *affair* was most definitely okay. Unlike a one-night stand, which implies, "I want instant gratification with zero feeling—except in my junk," an affair has an air of respectability. Except for affairs involving a politician with good hair and his love-struck videographer during his wife's struggle with cancer.

I had made a promise to myself to get organized during the last five days of my stay in Australia. I had tons of e-mails to return, a calendar to update, and Brisbane was experiencing flash floods on ac-count of relentless rainstorms. There would be nothing else to do. After our first morning together, I assumed maybe David and I would fling regularly every night but I didn't expect we would be inseparable for five days. We drank coffee every morning and wine every evening. We went dancing at a gay club. We sent texts back and forth during the half hour a day we weren't together. I didn't open my laptop once. I let myself be unorganized. No affair story ever started with, "Well, first I paid some online bills, emptied my spam folder, and *only after all that was done* did I fall into the arms of a guy who was the first person in a long time who made me feel like there was something special at first sight going on. Oh! AND I ran a thorough backup on a second hard drive!! It was such a whirlwind."

Despite the fact that passionate dalliances usually involve lots of sex—that wasn't what was intoxicating to me. One afternoon when it seemed like the rain was going to wash our hotel right down a hill, David and I sat lazily entwined on his couch reading books and magazines, stopping to read things aloud to each other. This was the intimacy I had been craving. It's conventional wisdom that for the sleep-deprived, a marathon night of deep REM can't make up for lost sleep but according to my research, I felt like the lack inside me from a year without intimacy was being filled instantly by an afternoon on a couch. Normally, it would undo me to be happy with someone know-ing that a plane is waiting to take me seven thousand one hundred and eighty-two miles away but I felt this incredible sense of calm. I had a quiet knowing that everything would be okay. That sounds stupid. Of course we would be okay. We weren't refugees from a war-torn country. We were two white people who got up to some kissing at the risk of getting a little heartache. Big deal, right?

On our last day together—the first day the sun returned—we walked across the Story Bridge. Only halfway. I couldn't make it all the way to the other side without my fear of heights kicking in, which would probably result in a massive panic attack. The symbolism of not being able to "finish the story" in Australia is not lost on me. (It probably wasn't lost on you either but I'm a codependent author and I really felt I needed to point it out.)

During our five days together, David and I talked in an abstract way about who we were, who we've been, who we wanted to be. When he said he might be in America soon, I told him, "Great, if you come to Los Angeles, we can have coffee!" I was ready to go back home and continue to be with myself—unless someone came along who made me want to try a relationship again. Someone like David. But obviously *not David because he wasn't coming home with me.* This affair would have to end in Brisbane. I wasn't going to allow myself to be on the receiving end of dick pics (not that he's the type to send them) and I wasn't going to be just another girl in his Rolodex. (I explained what a Rolodex is . . .) There was no teary good-bye, although some jokes were made about jumping off the bridge together. Thank God for that fear of heights keeping me alive.

I told David I have this issue with not feeling my feelings in the moment. My therapist says my feelings tend to send me a postcard about a week after a big incident in my life, letting me know where they are and that they'll be back soon. I knew that being back in America, back in the day-to-day of life, actually having to return e-mails, no bridges to hold hands on, that I would start to long for him. But I also knew enough not to long for someone who I still didn't know that well. I would not allow any interruptions to my sanity. I asked him if we could just not keep in touch right for the time being, just in case my heart caught up to my brain and realized, "Wait! Where is that guy we liked? He's really not here anymore?"

David didn't listen. He contacted me every day. I have to admit it felt good to be pursued. And I didn't feel gutted because he was so expressive—leaving me voice mails with sentiments like, "I don't know where you came from but I knew the minute I saw you I wanted you in my life . . ." I made every effort to not text, call, or Skype back. After a month of talking every day—I got that postcard from my feelings. I was falling in love. (And fuck people who take love too seriously and think that it can only be between two people who have two point five kids and are practically sick of each other.) I wanted to see him again. His trip to America to visit friends turned into a specific trip to Los Angeles to visit me—talk of visiting for one month turned into a booked stay of three months. And here we are. Even though he eats about eleven bananas a day and keeps them in an unsightly paper bag on my deck so that they ripen— I actually don't mind someone living in my home right now. I know we wouldn't live together under normal circumstances. But for now, for what this is—an affair turned into a circumstantially challenged relationship—I like having someone here who does the weirdest things—like take all my clothes out of my energy-efficient dryer in the middle of the night and spread them out to dry on my dining room table to "save even more energy."

A week before David arrived, I was driving through Iowa on tour. I kept seeing signs alerting me to the fact that if I turned off the road I could see THE BRIDGE from *The Bridges of Madison County*. A few days later I came down with exhaustion and after canceling a gig (sorry Pittsburgh) I took to bed (I'm really good at that by the way) and decided, "Hey, I'll watch *Bridges of Madison County*." I never saw the movie about Francesca Johnson (Meryl Streep) and Robert Kincaid (Clint Eastwood) having a four-day affair centered on their time spent NEAR A BRIDGE. This was sounding vaguely familiar. The conversations Francesca and Robert have sounded eerily similar to ones between David and me. Then I remembered the psychic's prediction that I would meet a man in my travels with a CLINT EASTWOOD quality. This character was also a traveling man, just passing through, who finds himself wanting more than an affair. Fuck. Maybe I should have been like Meryl Streep's character and resisted this intensity going more than five days. Unlike her character, I have no resolve. I'm all in. I want this relationship to last even if the Universe has deemed it not meant to be.

I WANNA CONTROL THE UNIVERSE!

And I'm not sure that I can. Clinical research trials on whether my will can bend the cosmos are still being conducted.

As I write this I've found out I will work on a project that will keep me from traveling for a year. I'm sad. I'm pissed. Australia? I meet a super feminist guy who unlike most male comedians LIKES the fact that he's dating another comedian. He's smart. Passionate. Funny. Politically motivated. Dresses cool. Even voluntarily talked to my mom on the phone . . . and he lives all the way at the bottom of the earth? And yes, he would love to live in America. But things like that take time to figure out and in the meantime I'm not free to return the gesture of a massive visit to his country. I don't want a relationship that comes with ten months of long distance. And no, I'm not going to marry him so he can get a green card as one married person I know suggested. (Have you met me? Get MARRIED? Ahem, AGAIN?) Some of my coupled-up friends are giving me advice. "If you love someone set them free and if it's meant to be you'll find each other again." Really? That's how you see the world, Jane and Josh?*

I feel a little changed. I know now that I can function in a relationship and still feel like ME—not some neutered version of myself. Maybe David is the guy I was supposed to meet who gets me ready for *the next guy who actually lives in America*? Maybe life isn't that linear and signposts aren't that vague? Maybe it just IS. I met someone really amazing and we have limited time together. Goddamn it. We would have had a good long run together before continental drift.

There is no right answer. There is no right way to have a happy ending. Is there? Why do we care so much about endings anyway?

---

* Made-up names. I notice when you guys started dating you guys didn't move to the opposite ends of the world for a year to "see what happens." In fact, you two went to the Cheesecake Factory together every night.

Nobody ever talks about happy beginnings or happy middles. The last minute of a massage when the overworked woman jerks off some creep is known as the "happy" part but what about the fifty-nine minutes before that where it was all delightful rubbing, loosening of muscles, and sighs of relaxation?

At least unlike Francesca Johnson, I don't have a husband and kids who are about to pull into the driveway once my Robert Kincaid leaves. I'm free to walk across any bridge I find—alone or with whomever I want. And if I don't cross the entire thing—it's still a happy ending because I'm alive.

25

WOMEN AREN'T FUNNY. THEY'RE HILARIOUS.

I would not want to live if I could not perform. It's in my will. I am not to be revived unless I can do an hour of stand-up.

—JOAN RIVERS

Joan Rivers has been a hero to me since I started my journey in stand-up comedy back in 1997. I'm sorry to say "journey." I don't mean to sound like I'm a guest who's overly proud of herself on an episode of *Oprah's Master Class*. But stand-up is an actual journey because it can take you places—literally places that exist on maps and figuratively places in your head that make you wonder, *Why the hell am I doing this? Am I even funny? Why aren't things going better for me? I'm funnier than him/her/it/everyone. Maybe I should quit. Why doesn't everyone else quit and make room for me?* If you're smart you'll also journey to therapy. Neurosis can always be mined for laughs as long as the audience is confident that the performer is not currently having a nervous breakdown on stage.

Joan's first memoir, *Enter Talking*, was my bible. I carried it around with me in my purse when I was a lowly temp pounding the pavement in New York City. (That isn't an expression—I used to wear very heavy John Fluevog brand Mary Jane heels.) Joan became a stand-up in her twenties and by her midthirties she still hadn't found the big break that her peers Woody Allen and Bill Cosby had. She also hadn't married her stepdaughter or allegedly drugged and raped countless women—which illustrates my theory that if you're going to be jealous of people, you have to be willing to trade places with the ENTIRETY of who they are, their whole life, and not just their success. Joan may not have been making millions as America's favorite TV dad but she also wasn't an (alleged) rapist, so life wasn't all bad. She taught me to never compare and despair and to never fucking stop doing what you love. At the very least you'll drop dead having done what fulfilled you.

Joan's big break came on her first appearance on Johnny Carson in 1965—an appearance that was hard fought. She had been rejected by the show many times—not by Johnny directly but by the gatekeepers, the talent bookers on *The Tonight Show*. That's another lesson I learned from Joan. There will always be people in life who tell you no and sometimes it's because they have nothing else to do that day except exert their power, and if you let their no stop you, you've just validated their opinion of you as worth more than your own.

I admired Joan for being one of the only stand-up comedians who also happened to be a woman at a time when women weren't supposed to be doing men's jobs, least of all comedy. Women weren't supposed to be funny. Women weren't supposed to speak their truth about how hard it is to be pregnant and feel sexy. Women weren't supposed to talk about abortion, being single, sex with their husbands—not even in private, let alone on television. Also, I say "stand-up who also happened to be a woman" because I don't believe in saying "female comedian." A comedian is a comedian is a comedian. "Female" is not a type of comedy. You can say that someone is a one-liner comic, a storyteller, a prop comic, or a shitty comic, but when you write "female" it's implied that male is what a comic really is and a female comic is a lesser version. It also implies that females only talk about "one thing"—being female, and that men, just regular old comedians, discuss more important, universal things. You know, like their dicks.

I held Joan's story in my heart when I saw many of my peers and even men who started comedy after I did get their own TV shows or start selling out comedy shows on the road while I still struggled to get noticed. Joan was funny, wildly original, indefatigable, and she couldn't get noticed for over a decade? Maybe, just maybe, Joan's story was my story too. It gave me hope. And hope is what you live on when you're young and broke. That and free ketchup packets.

On a particularly down day when I was working as a temp at

DKNY I got reprimanded by my fabulous gay boss for what he called a "fashion sin"—I was wearing ankle socks with Capri pants and flats. "Honey, no socks. Ever. I don't care if it's negative ten degrees. Socks make people here sad."

I worried about the people working at the DKNY corporate office if ankle socks were affecting their serotonin levels. Did they read the newspapers? (Page Six doesn't count.)

I took my socked feet on a walk during my lunch hour. I had also been told that bringing my own lunch every day made everyone sad (someone please get some Zoloft over to DKNY headquarters in Midtown stat). So that I didn't accidentally spark chain-reaction suicides in the office, I walked up and down Fifth Avenue eating my peanut butter and jelly sandwich. Coming toward me—on what was normally a bustling sidewalk but at this moment seemed to be occupied only by us two—was Joan Rivers. I stared at her, letting her pass. She had no idea she had just brushed by a young comedian who idolized her and had a copy of *Enter Talking* in her purse—a purse that probably made everyone at DKNY utterly despondent. I wanted to stop Joan and ask her for advice. But I already knew—there is no advice. She can't give me some fast-track option. That doesn't exist. The advice? The advice is stop asking for advice and just keep fucking doing it, open mic after open mic, and then when you get better at it—Indian casino after Indian casino.

Fifteen years later I'm sitting with Joan Rivers and our mutual agent at lunch somewhere on Fifth Avenue. We've had two glasses of wine and she's holding my hand as I tell her the story of walking by her—the lowly temp eating a peanut butter and jelly sandwich—and now I'm eating chopped salad with her as she willingly gives me advice on how to continue in this business and in life as a divorced woman. We both got misty-eyed about how much our work means to us. She joked, "You were right not to stop me that day fifteen years ago, bitch. Those socks sound awful."

We talked about men. I told Joan that I have a hard time "getting it up" for guys who don't do something similar to what I do, but that a lot of men who do what I do would rather a wife who isn't also coming home on a Sunday night from the road, too tired to rub his feet or cook. "If this is what you want," Joan said, "you'll do it no matter what and you might not have a man. You might not meet someone again who can handle what you do until you're sixty. But what's the alternative? Be in a relationship but be miserable in life?"

She knew that our lifestyle is a quiet sacrifice. This isn't something to boast about or brag about or feel superior about. No one wants to *not* have everything they want in life but sometimes what you really want has to outweigh what would also "be nice to have." I'm not in it for fame or fortune. It's the other "F" word: Freedom. I don't want a boss. I don't want to work for a major corporation. I don't want to sit at a desk.

Joan told me to keep my options open. That there may be men in my life who aren't in my business who are still funny and will embrace my lifestyle. She warned against falling for comedians. "Expand your horizons. Most comedians I know want a woman who eats salad with her mouth open and just stares into their eyes."

Joan and I met through a combination of good luck, good timing, and fifteen years of preparation in my mind of how I would behave if I were ever in her presence. After a guest dropped out at the last minute, I had the chance to appear on her YouTube series *In Bed With Joan*. When I arrived at the infamous bed Joan warned me that she only talked on camera and had some things to do before the shoot. But she overheard me joking around with the crew. I wish I could remember what I said but whatever it was, the crew laughed and Joan turned around and pointed at me, making eye contact. "You're funny," she said. That's all I had ever wanted: validation from Joan.

The next thing I knew, she broke her rule of not talking before she was on camera and we sat and chatted. One of my favorite stories in Joan Rivers's book is that when her peers had risen to fame and out of the small Greenwich Village scene and she was at her lowest point and agents weren't able to book her on gigs, Lenny Bruce was around. He came to see one of her shows and afterward gave her a note that said, "You're right. They're wrong."

When I asked her about that story she said to me, "Oh my God, years later I was talking to George Carlin and he said that he got that same note. Oh well." And that's the epitome of being a comic—sometimes a story is inspirational and sometimes it ends up being a great opportunity to say something self-deprecating. But both of us knew that note still meant something to her.

Back in 2005, a little under ten years into my stand-up "career," my parents started to get very frustrated. They had lent me money to move to Los Angeles and they thought—naively, as I did—that my seven-minute spot on a TV show taped in Hollywood called *Late Friday* would bring me to the next level. There would be fame, fortune, and food not bought from 7-Eleven. But performing a quick stand-up set on NBC in their 1:30 a.m. slot isn't really going to do much for anyone—not the person who performed it and not the people who watched it with one eye open on their way to sleep.

When I needed a sudden root canal but my credit wasn't good enough to apply for a payment plan at the dentist's office, I called my loan officers, Mr. and Mrs. Kirkman. They were frightened—would I keep asking for money? Did I not realize they weren't rich? Today it's a root canal but what will tomorrow bring? A toe amputation? We had a huge fight. Our relationship felt strained despite the fact that they lent me the money and I paid them back five dollars a week until it was paid off.

Years later I read a self-help book that suggested we have to parent ourselves—otherwise known as self-soothing. One exercise in the book was to picture in your mind two parents that completely understood things about you that your biological parents don't and just talk to them in your head. I picked Joan Rivers and Howard Stern. For years I talked to Joan and Howard in my head when I had money problems due to having career problems and the problem was that I didn't have a career. This relieved the stress of having to tell my real parents that I thought I made a huge mistake in following my dreams. Calling your parents for money is sometimes really calling them for validation, and you're not going to get that in a conversation that's wrapped up in trying to figure out how they can get eight hundred dollars across the country to your dentist before the novocaine wears off. Although your parents may believe in you and root for you, they still worry. They don't always realize that you feel like a five-year-old when you talk to them about YOUR worries and that what you're really saying when you say "Okay, we can work out a payment plan" is "OH MY GOD, I AM SO SCARED I AM OUT IN THE WORLD ALONE—CAN I JUST MOVE BACK HOME AND WATCH GAME SHOWS ON THE COUCH? I GIVE UP! I NEED SOME COMFORT!"

Just a year before her death, my parents went to see Joan perform and she took care of them. She arranged for them to have great seats and they had a private meeting after the show. Joan told them that she believed in me and she hoped that they realized my talent. (She knows the right thing to say to people's parents because her parents tried to push her to be a doctor.) By that point my mom and dad were no longer worried about me since I was gainfully employed and my teeth weren't falling out. I would have loved Joan and my parents to have had this discussion during the year of the root canal but I'm sure back then they would have been thinking, *Why is Joan Rivers telling us what to think?* I felt like my whole life had come together when my mom told me the story of her and my dad meeting Joan and how she made them feel special by announcing, "Everyone out of my dressing room, please, the Kirkmans are here!" The mom in my head had met my real mom and they all agreed—I'm just such a goddamn delight.

The last time I saw Joan we were performing together at a theater called Largo in Los Angeles in the summer of 2014. She was kind enough to agree to share a bill with me and let me keep all of the money. I bought brand-new wineglasses and a bottle of Cakebread chardonnay for us to toast with backstage and to thank her. She rehearsed her opening with the pianist. She made notes backstage up until she went out there to perform. When the lights dimmed and the crowd roared, ready to greet her fabulousness, she said to me, "Well, you know what Ethel Merman said, 'If they could do what we do they'd be backstage ready to go on and we would be in the seats.'" I said, "That's great. Is that your mantra now?" She said, "No, that's Ethel's mantra. I'm always nervous and insecure before I go on." And she took her gum out of her mouth, stuck it to the wall, and walked toward the stage in her sequined jacket. She giggled to herself, shook her head a little, and said, "It's time."

At Joan's funeral I watched Howard Stern make a speech that started with "Joan Rivers had the driest vagina" and ended with him choking back tears. I thought of my "parents in my head" and even though I don't know Howard and the funeral would have gone on just fine if I weren't there—I felt like my life had come full circle. I thought about how Joan never stopped, until life had to forcibly stop her. I thought of her coming up in the repressed 1960s with only Lenny Bruce and gay audiences on her side. She had it a lot harder than I do when the only thing that truly annoys me is people asking, "So what's it like being a woman in comedy?" (My answer? "I don't know, I've never been a man in comedy.") Hey, at least people are asking questions, trying to understand why it's so hard for some people to accept women as funny. But I don't feel like teaching. I just want to make jokes. And I learned from Joan that making jokes is the best way to teach and to heal.

It would be acceptable for a dentist in 1965 to maybe question his female patient for not wanting a traditional life, but enough is enough. It's 2014. Well, it's 2014 when I'm writing this so hopefully the world is even more progressive by the time this book is in your hands. (Has Artificial Intelligence outsmarted humanity yet?) I don't have to convince anyone that my decisions are okay—I only have to laugh it off and then secretly make fun of them behind their back.

I always think about what Joan said to me when I told her that my orthodontist had intimated that my life isn't "real." She said, "Your life is a gift and you know better than to waste it with your fingers inside of people's mouths."

ACKNOWLEDGMENTS

Thank you once again to Sarah Knight at Simon & Schuster for giving me another opportunity to a write book and for pushing when I needed to go the extra mile for a better joke or a more honest sentiment. And for encouraging me to let myself be a very flawed non-advice-giving role model for other "Jen Kirkman types" out there.

Thanks to my manager, Kara Baker, at Avalon for being patient with me while I finished this book and not pushing me to do more "showbiz" things instead—like host a TV show where contestants see who can eat wood chips the loudest.

Thanks to my agent Simon Green, who lets me whine over e-mail how hard it is to write a book sometimes and never points out how easy it is for me to write a whiney e-mail. Thanks to all my agents at CAA for never ending their e-mails with #teamjen.

Thanks to my friend Sarah Colonna for reading an early rough draft and telling me this is why she loves me.

Thanks to Jake. Whenever I am feeling low and critical of myself, I think of what you told me. That I am not as I picture myself, destructive like Godzilla, stomping through cities, ruining lives. That I am "the Rockefeller Center Christmas Tree—big and bright and full of warmth."

Thanks to the planet we live on. I hope to see more of you.